Still Right Here

Still Right Here

A TRUE STORY OF
HEALING AND HOPE

Suzanne Giesemann

Cover design by Rob Johnson, www.toprotype.com

ISBN-13: 9780983853947
ISBN-10: 0983853940

Printed in the United States of America First Edition

Published by One Mind Books

Praise for *Still Right Here*

"An incredible account of connection to another world. Inspiring and sensational—a must read for anyone interested in what lies beyond." Raymond Moody, MD, PhD, author of *Life After Life*

"*Still Right Here* is a touching story of healing and awakening. Suzanne presents compelling evidence of the continuance of the soul after life in this physical realm. The book should be on the reading list for those who want to understand what happens after we make the final transition. I see it as mandatory reading for anyone who has lost a loved one." Bob Frank, President, IANDS (International Association of Near Death Studies)

"It's hard not to be changed as we experience the deep love and hope revealed in this inspiring book." Gary E. Schwartz, PhD, Professor of Psychology, Medicine, Neurology, Psychiatry, and Surgery at the University of Arizona and author of *The Afterlife Experiments* and *Super Synchronicity*

"Whether you are grieving or simply curious if your loved ones in spirit are around you, I highly recommend *Still Right Here*. Filled with insights, the book shares many accounts of creative, amazing, and even surprising ways that our loved ones who are no longer in bodies let us know they are with us. *Still Right Here* is an uplifting book that helps us learn to keep our hearts open, receive signs from spirit, and know the truth: that no one we love is ever really 'lost.'" Susanne Wilson, evidential medium-teacher, Director of Mediumship for the Afterlife Research and Education Institute, and author of *Soul Smart: What the Dead Teach Us About Spirit Communication*

"How do you recover from the death of a loved one? How does a parent go on living after losing their child? Evidential medium Suzanne Giesemann writes vividly and beautifully the true stories of how eight parents discover that their loved ones are never lost in death but are in fact still here. This is a book that will bring comfort and healing for those whose hearts have been broken." Dr. Connie Mariano, White House Physician (1992 – 2001) and author of *The White House Doctor: My Patients were Presidents: A Memoir*

"Suzanne navigates the waters of grief and loss while giving hope and insight to all." Gloria Horsley, PhD, President and founder of *Open to Hope*

"*Still Right Here* feels like being on a grand adventure with eight new friends who have experienced the physical death of their children. During their journey they discover the magical evidence of how alive their children really are and that they are still an important part of their daily lives. You will feel comforted that death is an illusion and that living your life to the fullest is why you are still here." Sandra Champlain, author of *We Don't Die - A Skeptic's Discovery of Life After Death* and host of "We Don't Die Radio Show"

"What do you do when the world gets you down?
You realize that this is not the only world,
and that awareness
makes all the difference in the world."

SANAYA

Contents

Acknowledgments

THE WORDS "THANK YOU" ARE inadequate to express my gratitude for those who played a vital role in getting this book into your hands. In my work as a medium I often communicate wordlessly with those in the spirit world, simply by tuning in to the heart—a method I find so much more efficient and meaningful. May the beautiful souls mentioned here feel the gratitude that flows from my heart to yours. . . .

Susan, Morgan, Chelsea, Devon, Carly, Brandon, Andy, Kyle, and Kiara, our Shining Lights. Your constant inspiration and ever-present love smoothed the way time and time again from across the veil.

Cyril and Elizabeth Boisson, Lynn and Jeff Hollahan, and Irene and Tony Vouvalides. Do you know how special you are to Ty and me? Thank you for sharing your challenges, your transformation, and your beautiful children with all of us.

LeAnn Hull. You are so courageous. Thank you for showing the world through your family's journey that "You matter!"

Elizabeth Boisson and Mark Ireland, co-founders of Helping Parents Heal. Your vision and efforts continue to help "bereaved parents" become "Shining Light Parents"[1].

---

[1] If you don't yet know what a Shining Light Parent is, you will understand by the time you reach the end of this book!

Debbie Hansen. You expertly transcribed hours of interviews with pictures of our kids taped to your computer screen. You are a member of The Club by proxy, and we love you.

Zoe and Ted Kharpertian. Thanks to you and Kiara for your expert editing. These words shine as brightly as you do. Zoe, you are far more than a wordsmith. I consider you my dear friend. Your love radiates across the miles.

Acclaimed medium James Van Praagh, who blazed a trail for mediumship. You honor all of us with your beautiful foreword. Thank you for using your exceptional abilities and love to bring awareness to the masses that love never dies.

Patty Loftus Jones and Harry Jones. Our work has just begun, and Harry knew what he was doing when he roped you in!

And finally, our captain, my Ty, the man who makes my heart sing and brightens my world beyond measure. You married a naval officer, not a medium. You didn't knowingly sign up for this aspect of our journey together, yet no woman could ask for a more perfect husband and life partner.

Foreword

§

THE MOST UNIMAGINABLE HEARTBREAK ANY human can experience is the death of their own child. No parent expects to bury a child—it goes against the natural order of things. Over three decades working as a spiritual medium, I've counseled thousands of grieving parents as they struggle with overwhelming despair, denial, and disbelief. They have anticipated watching their child experience the milestones of growing up, getting married, and having children of their own, only to have those dreams snatched away. All I can do is try my best to prove to them that death, as they perceive it, is an illusion.

It's difficult for any mortal to provide comfort to bereaved parents after such a devastating loss. I believe Suzanne's light-filled message that their beloved children are *Still Right Here* will help parents, grandparents, and anyone touched by the death of a child to take the first steps out of the darkness.

The first time I caught a glimpse of Suzanne's mediumship was on YouTube. I've watched countless mediums at work, but something about Suzanne grabbed my attention. I liked her strong energy, sincerity, and no-nonsense, almost analytical approach to mediumship. I remember thinking, "She's just the person I'd want around if I had lost someone." As I clicked through her videos on my computer screen, I had a powerful feeling that our paths would cross, and naturally, a few months later, we met at a spiritual expo in California where we were both hosting programs.

We arranged to have dinner after the expo, where Suzanne shared how her own spiritual journey began when she and her husband learned of the sudden death of their daughter Susan—tragically struck by lightning while pregnant with her first child. Suzanne took me through her transformation from pragmatic Navy Commander to grieving stepmother, and explained how she came to realize that while Susan had left her physical body, her soul was still very much present. The signs that Susan sent from the afterlife brought her parents hope, and with some help from Spirit, brought them in contact with the nonprofit organization, Helping Parents Heal.

I often say that the dead never go without leaving a gift behind. In Suzanne's case she received the gift of mediumship and was able to fulfill her destiny—bringing hope and healing to those struck down by tragic loss.

I believe that everyone comes to this earth with a soul plan, a contract agreed upon in the Spirit realm. This plan maps out the soul's purpose for this portion of its journey—bringing it closer to its goal of pure soul enlightenment—the embodiment of unconditional love. Just as some children are here for just enough time to fulfill their purpose on earth, some adults are destined to experience difficult lessons in order to achieve a deeper understanding and to fulfill their purpose of spreading love and light.

As you turn the pages of *Still Right Here*, I think you'll notice two things. First, how the beautiful souls in this book signal their loved ones in so many ways, proving that they are always there and that love never dies; and secondly, how life after loss can itself bring unexpected gifts. I hope you'll let the beauty and light of the spirit messages permeate your soul, and share that light with those around you—bringing us closer to a heaven here on earth.

James Van Praagh

Preface

§

THIRTEEN SOULS ON A 48-FOOT sailboat for seven days might seem a bit crowded, but in this case, it wasn't. The crew consisted of eight parents and our five beautiful children. Our kids needed no staterooms. They no longer inhabit their earthly bodies, but they were with us just the same. In fact, it was they who had brought us together and planned this sailing adventure after their deaths.

Sound crazy?

I am an evidential medium, and I can tell you with full faith and certainty that our loved ones who have passed are not forever lost to us. I *guarantee* it. Having communicated with thousands of souls, I know that life goes on, that spirits remain well and active after they leave their physical bodies. If I'm wrong about my "still right here" assertion, let me know when we meet up on the other side.

Those in spirit have much to tell us. In my readings, they tell me how they died, what kind of work they did, what they enjoyed doing here on earth, validating their presence with facts I couldn't possibly know. Best of all, they let me know that they remain part of their families' lives, popping in often to check up on things.

Death is by no means the end. Our physical life, as stated beautifully by mystic Joel Goldsmith, is but *a parenthesis in eternity.* But too often we view our loved one's "angelversary" as a day to dread, reliving the difficult details of their passing over and over, instead of celebrating the special moments we shared. Pleasant memories become only painful reminders of our loss.

Recently I had the honor of dining with my esteemed fellow medium James Van Praagh. He shared a poignant message that a child in spirit had delivered to his parents:

"I died once," said the child. *"Don't make me die every day."*

Puts things in perspective, doesn't it?

Grief is understandable, reinforced by our references to death, which often invoke a sense of finality—"I lost a child." But those who have passed try hard to let us know they're not lost at all. Adjusting to the absence of their physical bodies can be incredibly challenging for us, but I can assure you beyond a doubt that the vibrant spirits we know and love are still very much around.

When my husband Ty and I received the news that no parent wants to hear—that our beautiful daughter Susan was "gone"—our lives were changed forever. At the time of Susan's passing, I had no idea that death is not the end. I had not yet begun my spiritual journey and certainly had no idea that I would one day serve as a medium. Susan's death sent me looking for answers. Happily, I found them. The evidence that Susan sent and continues to send us of her continued existence has transformed our lives. She has taken us beyond hope to full knowledge that she remains an active part of our family.

It's my honor to share Susan's story with you, and to introduce you to three remarkable couples whose children inhabit the spirit world. It's my hope and belief that you will come to know and love them as much as Ty and I do.

All eight of the parents featured in this story are associated in various ways with the nonprofit organization, Helping Parents Heal. This extraordinary group supports parents and families who have a child on the other side of the veil by providing resources and inspirational meetings to aid in the healing process. Helping Parents Heal goes a step beyond similar groups by allowing the open discussion of spiritual experiences and evidence of the afterlife. This critical step helps not only those who grieve, but our kids on the other side as well. I deeply respect and appreciate this openminded and positive approach.

Back to our sailing adventure—despite the self-imposed togetherness of relative strangers, no tempers flared, and no sparks flew—other than those from the barbecue grill! There was not a single raised voice, not a hint of judgment or semblance of dissonance. Instead, we enjoyed seven days of communal living, full of laughter and love. Along with the sun and fun, we deepened the bond that comes from having suffered profound grief and emerged the stronger.

Those of us who embarked on this trip—Elizabeth, Cyril, Lynn, Jeff, Irene, Tony, Ty, and I—know what you are going through. We're all in the same boat. It's called *Earth School*. We've encountered some of the most challenging lessons in the curriculum, and we've survived. By sharing our pain and ultimately our joy, we hope to show that healing is possible for you too, whether you are suffering the loss of a spouse, parent, sibling, or anyone you hold dear.

Our children passed as the result of illness, accident, and "acts of nature." Recognizing that some readers must deal with a death due to suicide or overdose, I've included an addendum addressing these far-too-common tragedies. The deep and healing insights in this section come from LeAnn, a mother whose beloved son Andy chose to end his earthly life. Faced with irrefutable evidence that Andy is surrounded by love on the other side and still very much a part of his family's life here, LeAnn has been able to put her fundamentalist beliefs aside and find joy and peace.

This book evolved from an article I felt inspired to write even before our trip was over. I knew I had struck the right tone when a reader sent me this feedback: "I tried to find inspirational books to help me along my new journey. Unfortunately, they're all so depressing that I couldn't read them. One of my dearest friends sent me a link to your article a few days ago, and I cried with joy to find there are others who grieve, but celebrate in the light of their children."

While my aim is to make our story as uplifting as possible, I know that parts may be difficult to read, in particular the details of our children's transitions. I offer these highly emotional stories in order to strengthen our shared connection. You may feel that no one could possibly hurt the way you do right now. You may not be able to see even a glimmer of light in the midst of the darkness that envelops you. When you read how similarly devastated Irene was after her daughter Carly passed, it's my hope that you'll be able to appreciate and take comfort from her phoenix-like rise from the ashes.

"To have come from such a place of darkness to where I am now is miraculous," Irene told me shortly after our sailing adventure. "For many, many months I thought of nothing but leaving and being with my daughter. I just wanted to die, and look at me now! My heart is so open today, I'm not quite sure what I'm supposed to do with all this love. I feel as if I've been blown open."

This kind of transformation is what your departed loved ones want most for you. They are *still right here*, and they will pull off the most amazing feats to let us know that truth. There is no end to the creativity and imagination those in spirit will use to prove they are safe and well on the other side and that they continue to play a part in our lives.

Those who are deeply grieving may have trouble relating to our optimism. We understand. Grief is isolating, often characterized by anger and hostility towards others. But I encourage you to keep reading. Let our stories and lessons soften the pain of your experiences on this journey you never planned to take. When you're ready, you may choose to return to these pages and discover a renewed sense of healing in the stories we've shared.

In my experience, the more we consciously seek out accounts of others' interaction with a higher consciousness, the more likely we are to experience life-changing episodes of our own. I can't wait to share these "magical moments" with you. Wait until you read about the balloon incident—and the "prima donna" story—and the blackbirds! Oh, my! At times, these narratives may seem like pure fiction, but on my honor, I haven't fabricated or exaggerated a single detail. There's no need to elaborate when the signs from our loved ones in spirit are so stunningly sensational.

All the evidence in this book from readings with mediums is verbatim and validated. The details come from live, real-time interaction with those on the other side. How is this possible? Because they're not gone. They're not lost. They're *still right here*.

May these lessons of what we have gained through our understanding of what lies beyond the limits of physical loss heal and inspire you. May the magical moments motivate you to get out and live your life to the fullest. This is what your loved ones want most for you, and it's why *you're* "still here."

Part I

CHAPTER 1

Totem

§

THERE'S NO OTHER NOISE LIKE it. I hadn't been paying attention to my surroundings as I traipsed blithely along the dusty path from our coach to the campground bath house. Suddenly I was brought up short by what sounded like an angry pair of maracas.

I froze, fully focused now on the five-foot rattlesnake coiled less than four feet away. If I'd been wearing headphones and not heard the rattle, I'd have stepped right on him. My mind raced, determining the best course of action.

I am a retired US Navy Commander. I served as a commanding officer and as aide to the Chairman of the Joint Chiefs of Staff. I'm trained to be calm and cool in challenging situations. Standing face to face with a rattler reared and ready to strike, I did what came naturally: I screamed like a madwoman.

I took my eyes off the snake only long enough to see who might have heard me. Not a soul emerged from the nearby trailers, including our bus, only 25 yards away. The snake held his upright position, clearly unimpressed by my hysterical outburst. Had I known that rattlers are not generally aggressive, I might have reacted differently. Instead, I took three slow steps backwards, shrieking rhythmically like a car alarm with each footfall. But with our air conditioner running full-blast in the Arizona heat, my husband remained unaware of my distress.

When I had backed up far enough, the snake lowered his upper half to the ground. I bolted for the bus. I can only imagine how I must have appeared to Ty when I burst through the door. He looked up from the kitchen table, surprised and concerned to see me back so soon.

"What is it? Are you okay?"

I shook my head and tried to speak. No words emerged between my gasping breaths, so I resorted to charades. I grabbed my chest with one arm and made a slithering motion with the other.

"A snake? Outside?" he asked. "What kind of snake?"

The realization that I had survived my brush with death slowly brought my brain back online. I rasped out the word "rattlesnake!"

Ty's eyes widened, and I began to let down my guard. Surely now my husband would understand my distress and move to comfort me. I dropped my arms in anticipation of a reassuring hug as he rushed towards me.

"A rattler?" he said. "Where's my camera?"

I gaped as he yanked open a cabinet and pulled out his Nikon.

"What about me?" I asked petulantly.

"Is it a big one?" he asked, rushing past me with nary a pat on the head. "This is going to make a great blog entry!"

I didn't know whether to laugh or cry. The frightened little girl in me wanted sympathy and coddling. Ty was normally the most attentive partner a woman could ask for, but clearly I was on my own for this one. As he shot out the door, I comforted myself and invited my inner grown-up to step back in. Ty was right. We looked forward to the unusual encounters with wildlife that our travels afforded us, and if I stood there and sulked, I was going to miss one heck of a cool experience.

"Do you want me to phone the ranger station?" I called.

"Yes!" he shouted back without turning.

I found the ranger's phone number on a campground map and called to alert him about the unwanted visitor. After hanging up, I stood on the metal steps outside the bus door. By now the snake had slithered into the shade of a nearby tree. Ty hunkered down no more than ten feet away and snapped one photo after another. The snake flicked his tongue angrily at my husband.

4

That made two of us. "Ty! Are you crazy?" I hissed.

He seemed to have gone suddenly deaf.

A couple in their seventies approached from the other direction, carrying a white plastic bucket. "We're the campground hosts," the man announced. "Someone seen a snake, we heard."

I left the safety of the bus and stepped tentatively behind Ty. I pointed toward the base of the tree. "It's not going to fit in that bucket."

The couple's eyes widened. "Oh, he's a big one," exclaimed the woman. "Most of them are about a foot long."

"And he's aggressive," the man added. "Better get the ranger."

"I told them it was big when I called," I said. I pictured the rangers rolling their eyes: *We've got another flatlander tourist.*

"Never seen one this big," the woman said.

"Must be my lucky day," I replied as Ty continued snapping photos.

The picture I posted on Facebook later that day was National Geographic quality. The video showed the ranger holding a writhing snake as long as the pole he used to grab it. My post garnered plenty of sympathetic remarks from those who follow our travels. One comment in particular snagged my attention:

"Snake is good medicine," wrote the Facebook friend. "He teaches us about transformation and shedding those old skins. Glad that you are okay after being 'rattled'!"

This comment was followed by a few others who reminded me that everything significant that happens to us, every remarkable encounter with another human being or with any of God's creatures, holds a special meaning. When I Googled "snake as totem," I found the following description on several sites:

"If snake enters your world, expect swift changes to sweep through your life. These changes denote death of the old and a birth into untapped psychic energy, creative power, and wisdom. Snake medicine is the energy of wholeness, cosmic consciousness, and the ability to experience anything willingly and without resistance."

I perked up when I read this. Did the rattlesnake foretell a gift? Since becoming aware of my abilities as a medium, I'd devoted my life to increasing my psychic energy and wisdom. If the snake as a totem—a sacred symbol—had crossed my path for a reason, perhaps I was meant to welcome him instead of running away screaming. If swift changes were on their way, I would be open to them, "without resistance."

The visit to Arizona marked our fifth summer of traveling the US and Canada to share the messages of hope I glean from across the veil. When not giving workshops or presentations, Ty and I frequently hike and ride our mountain bikes, enjoying being out in nature as much as possible. Until that day in the campground, we had not come across a single snake during our travels.

My meeting with that granddaddy of all rattlesnakes marked the beginning of a remarkable string of up-close-and-personal snake encounters over the next two months. Our tally went from zero in five years to a remarkable seven sightings in as many weeks.

"The snake's medicine is not to be treated lightly. If you are ready to shed your own skin, snake is ready and waiting to guide you through the spiral path of transformation."

These words echoed in my mind on a quick trip I made to our home base in Florida during that surprising period. Having been gone from the house for a while, I ventured into our front yard to do a little weeding. There, in the wood chips next to a bush, I came across an entire snakeskin, shed by some slithery visitor who left his meaningful message not five feet from my doorstep.

Was the Universe trying to get my attention? There could be no doubt. I prayed to Spirit: *Guide me, lead me, show me what I need to learn from this.* In response to my prayers, and with gratitude to the snakes, I discovered deep-seated fears going back to my childhood. Once revealed, I could release them. As promised by the totem, the result was nothing short of transformational in my work. Free of long-held blockages, I experienced a noticeable increase in the clarity of my connection with the other side.

The day before we departed the park, Ty, ever the jokester, presented me with a gift from the visitors' center: a frighteningly realistic ceramic rattlesnake.

What a guy.

At first I could barely look at it, even though I knew it wasn't real. Then I realized that this was just one more fear I needed to come to terms with. We would be spending several more weeks in rattlesnake territory, and I had no plans to pass them walking about on high alert.

I talked to the rangers and learned that rattlesnakes rarely attack, using their rattles only to make their presence known. Armed with this new awareness, I determined to use my conscious thought to overcome the automatic survival response of my own reptilian brain. Any future hysteria I might experience in the presence of these desert dwellers was only due to my old B.S.—my subconscious Belief System.

The fake snake and I had a little chat, and we came to an understanding. As strange as it sounds, I now keep him by my bathroom sink as a daily reminder of the lessons his visit and those of his six friends taught me.

I stand ready to shed my skin at any moment if it means revealing more of the Light within. And while I greatly appreciate the growth the snake encounters engendered within me, those changes can't compare with an earlier transformation: a bolt out of the blue that altered our family's lives forever. The snake totem's most striking reference echoed in my mind as we left the Tucson area, heading north:

"On the deepest level Snake's skin shedding symbolizes death and rebirth. Snake signifies manipulation of lightning, transmutation, exploration of the mysteries of life."

My life has become an ongoing exploration of a greater reality as the result of a most unexpected death: that of Ty's daughter, my beautiful stepdaughter, Susan. At the age of 27, six months pregnant with her first child, Susan was struck by lightning. Despite working on her for seven hours, her doctors were unable to save either Susan or her baby.

Susan's passing ultimately led me to discover my abilities as a medium. It is the reason I am so dedicated to this work. As the snake's visit highlighted, and the snake reference to lightning in the passage above underscores, my life today represents a complete rebirth from my previous life as a naval officer. I have been transformed from a woman who once saw the world in black and white, who believed a thing was real only if I could perceive it with my physical senses, to one who now understands that reality has many faces. I have learned that love is all that matters, and in that regard, Susan is my role model.

As a result of Susan's death, my life and that of her father have taken on new meaning, and new purpose. In his seminal book, *Man's Search for Meaning*, holocaust survivor Viktor Frankl writes, "What matters is to make the best of any given situation. . . . When we are no longer able to change a situation (such as the death of a loved one), we are challenged to change ourselves." By grace, I and many others have transmuted devastating tragedy into the gift of service to others.

I was able to do this thanks to the unmistakable signs Susan sent to let us know she is still very much a part of our lives. I should not have been surprised. She always did enjoy a bit of drama.

CHAPTER 2
Susan

§

"I'M THINKING OF ENLISTING," SUSAN announced to us one day. I held my breath, aware of Ty's thoughts. She'd been offered a full Reserve Officer Training Corps scholarship at a big-name university, but this was not her cup of tea. Always independent and feisty, she left after one semester to find her own way.

Her father had served for 26 years as a surface warfare officer in the Navy, retiring as a captain. I was still on active duty when she dropped this bombshell. We both knew of the discrepancies in the treatment of service members between the officer and enlisted ranks. I gave her some unsolicited, motherly advice, born of my years' experience as a woman in the military.

I described the Army, Navy, Air Force, and Marine Corps, and what a twenty-year-old enlisted woman might expect in terms of types of jobs available, the amount of respect she was likely to garner from fellow service-members, and the lifestyle associated with each branch. I ranked the four services according to my personal observations from most to least desirable. Things have improved in recent years, but at the time of our discussion, I told Susan in no uncertain terms, "Whatever you do, *don't join the Marines*."

Susan listened to my advice, weighed it carefully, and promptly enlisted in the Marine Corps.

I had known Susan since she was thirteen. She changed roles and costumes as deftly in real life as in the school dramas she so enjoyed participating in. She played the girly-girl in skimpy shorts and camisole tops with equal finesse as the cocky, give-me-what-you've-got contender on the boy's wrestling team. Smart, sassy, funny, and a friend to everyone, her leading role was as Daddy's girl—a part which required no acting.

Once she set her mind to something, she would excel. She survived boot camp at Parris Island with little difficulty and thrived at the School of Infantry that followed. The Marines sent her to aviation training, where she qualified as a helicopter airframes mechanic. Far braver than I could ever hope to be, she earned her aircrew wings, an accomplishment that required several challenging physical and mental tests.

To qualify as an aircrewman, she was strapped blindfolded into the fuselage of a mock helicopter which was then submersed in a swimming pool and flipped upside down. She failed in her first attempt to find the exit underwater in the dark and had to be rescued. At that point, I would have said, "You can keep those wings," but Susan's response was, "Put me back in there!" On her second attempt she succeeded and went on to graduate third in the demanding Sergeants' Course.

Susan made two deployments to Okinawa. When her squadron asked for volunteers to deploy to Iraq, she raised her hand without hesitation. Her husband Warren, a sergeant assigned to the same squadron, felt that the Middle East assignment was too dangerous for his new wife, and Susan agreed to stay behind in North Carolina. It's hard not to wonder how things might have turned out had she gone to the combat zone.

§

On September 11, 2001, I wasn't aware that those who die remain with us; that they are *still right here*. I had no inkling that death was not the end. When word came through about the attacks in New

York City and Washington, I felt the same emotions as most others did. I was on my way to Europe, where my boss, the Chairman of the Joint Chiefs of Staff, was to be knighted by Queen Elizabeth. When we were notified of the attacks on the World Trade Center, the general ordered me to have the pilot return us to Washington. I issued a sharp, "Aye, aye, Sir!" and headed for the cockpit.

Our flight path took us directly over Manhattan. I peered down at the billowing cloud rising from the towers, wondering what awaited us back in Washington. Moments before, I'd been speaking through a headset with a colonel back in our Pentagon office when he announced, "Something just happened here. I think it was a bomb."

On landing at Andrews Air Force Base we discovered that what the colonel thought was an explosion was actually the impact of a jet filled with passengers. A parade of motorcycle police escorted us across the bridge leading to the Pentagon. Smoke billowed from the roof, and I tried to reconcile the scene with the way things had looked when we'd left there just hours earlier.

We could have been inside the Pentagon when it was hit. Why were some people in the wrong place at the wrong time? I wondered.

We were met by the general's terrorism expert, who gave us a quick briefing. Then we headed to check out the impact site. Noxious smoke filled my nose as we strode through the darkened hallways. When it became clear that it was too dangerous to proceed, we changed course. Out on the lawn, I stepped gingerly over pieces of a jet engine as we made our way toward the gaping hole where emergency personnel were working frantically, trying to find survivors.

I wanted to rewind the clock, to go back to a safer time and place that I wasn't sure would ever exist again. Unable to shut out the images before me, I did as I'd been trained to do, and "sucked it up."

In the days and weeks following the attacks on our country, I tried to come to terms with death, but I didn't do a very good job of it. The lives of over three thousand people had come to a sudden and shocking end—at least, according to my beliefs at the time. I couldn't bear to think of the grief their families were going through.

I spent a lot of time questioning the meaning of life and our role in it. Raised with no religious tradition or training, I stopped by a few churches and gathered their bulletins and booklets in search of answers but found nothing that spoke to my heart.

The television and newspapers kept up a steady barrage of frightening news, replaying scenes I could no longer bear to watch. I read about young Americans joining the military to fight the new war on terror. I admired their patriotism, but felt I had little to add to the cause. My boss was due to retire, and the new chairman would choose his own aide. My career path led only to paper-pushing personnel jobs which held no interest for me, no matter how many stripes or stars I might eventually add to my sleeves.

9/11 showed me that life is too short not to live your dreams while you can. Ty and I had long shared the dream of selling our house and cars and sailing into the sunset on our boat. With the sights and sounds of September 11 forever seared in my mind, I submitted my retirement papers, and we bought a seaworthy sloop. On the day that I was eligible to leave Washington, we sailed down the Potomac and left the Pentagon in our wake.

Some who knew me couldn't understand how I could "give it all up" to go sailing. Yes, it was a great adventure, but secretly, it was my escape. I turned away from the memorial boards in the hallways where I worked, showing the smiling faces of those who had perished in the attacks. Temporary duty as an escort to the bereaved families of the victims left me in an even darker place. Death was just too painful to deal with.

Ty was in his glory at sea, more at home on the water than ashore. For me, the sailing life allowed me to live in a bubble—one that demanded constant vigilance for our personal safety and that of the boat. It proved to be an idyllic lifestyle, living fully in the "now" without constant reminders of the painful past we'd left behind.

Free from news and worldly distractions, we sailed north to Newfoundland and then south to the Bahamas. After two years of coastal cruising, we decided to sail east, fulfilling a long-held goal of crossing the Atlantic Ocean. Our departure port of Beaufort, North Carolina, was just down the road from our daughter Susan's duty station at Marine Corps Air Station Cherry Point.

We enjoyed a week with Susan and Warren, her new beau. Knowing that we would be out of the country for an indefinite period, we cherished our time together. Susan loaned us her car to pick up provisions for the ocean crossing. The 1973 Chevy Nova garnered strange looks from the Marine at the base gate when Ty drove up and presented his retired captain's I.D. card. The rumbly car was five years older than Susan and prone to frequent breakdowns, but she loved it.

Once we left the United States, communications were few and far between. After 27 days at sea, we arrived in Portugal and checked in with our families. My parents and both of Ty's daughters, Susan and Elisabeth, were doing well. On we sailed through the Mediterranean, staying in touch by email and sporadic phone calls when ashore.

We flew home in November for the memorable occasion of Susan's wedding to Warren. It was clear that they adored each other, a fact that endeared him to us even more. We returned to the boat and three months later received the welcome news that Susan was pregnant. She and Warren already had Zoso the cat and their two dogs, Thor and Loki, but they had wasted no time starting a family.

We sent Susan emails as we sailed through the Mediterranean, but she didn't answer every one. We understood that she was wrapped up in her new life as a wife and mother-to-be, and we felt her love across the miles. One night, while anchored off a deserted island along the coast of Croatia, I awoke from a vivid dream. The details were so clear that I shared them with Ty the next morning.

"Susan walked right up to me at a party," I told him. "She was smiling, and she looked right at me and said, 'We're fine. The baby and I are very happy.'"

"It's been a while since we heard from her," Ty said. "Maybe we should send her an email." He sat down at the navigation desk and composed a brief message to send via our single-side-band radio. It was a cumbersome system, but better than nothing while at sea.

We checked the system for messages the following morning. There was one incoming email, not from Susan, but from her sister, Elisabeth. The message was short: "Phone home. It's important."

We felt no apprehension. Elisabeth and Ty had recently been corresponding about her finances, and we figured she wanted to continue the conversation in real time. The nearest town was an island away. We sailed all day to get there and went ashore in our dinghy. When we finally located a payphone, Ty called Susan and Warren's house, knowing that Elisabeth had been visiting them for the past week.

I pressed against his side to listen in as the phone rang. When we heard Warren's voice on the other end, Ty said, "How's it going, Warren?"

His reply was somber. "It's not going well."

I felt Ty stiffen. My mind instantly raced through a flurry of possibilities. Was it the baby? Had Susan had a miscarriage?

No airplane slamming into the World Trade Center or the Pentagon could have impacted me with the force of the words that followed.

"Susan is gone," Warren informed us, and our world came crashing down.

§

I retired from the Navy to go to sea, running away from the grief and despair 9/11 engendered. Now it was our family who was in mourning, and there was nowhere to run. Upon receiving the news that no parent ever wants to hear, I watched my rock of a husband drop like a stone. I thought my heart would break to see him huddled on the ground, sobbing his heart out. I had never seen him cry. But that night was only the first of several body blows to come.

The Marine officers who met us at the airport in Charlotte could not have been more compassionate or caring. They took us, at our request, to the spot where Susan and her unborn baby, Liam Tyler, had been struck by a bolt of lightning from a storm over ten miles away. I leaned down and touched the tarmac while her commanding officer described the heroic efforts of her fellow Marines to perform CPR before the ambulance arrived. He described how Warren had come running from the hangar but had been held back by his squadron-mates.

I stared up at the clouds, tears streaming down my cheeks. I had no real belief in the afterlife, no evidence that life goes on. I looked upwards because that's what people did. They talked about heaven as some place where people went, but how could you prove it? My grandparents had all died, and as far as I was concerned, I would never see them again. But the thought of never seeing Susan again was unbearable.

Until we arrived at her house, Susan's death remained surreal, an ungraspable concept. There we met up with Warren, Elisabeth, and Susan's biological mother Angie. I kept expecting Susan to emerge from the bedroom and give us one of her bubbly hugs. Instead, we saw in their eyes an emptiness that mirrored our own.

Together we all followed Susan's executive officer to the funeral home in New Bern. He introduced us to a well-practiced mortician, who greeted us with a perfect mix of sympathy and professional-ism. I couldn't fathom how anyone could spend their days dealing with grieving families for a living. The whole atmosphere inside the funeral home made my skin crawl.

I waited while Ty and Angie went together into the viewing room where Susan's body lay clothed in her Marine Corps dress blues. I tried to ignore Angie's quiet sobs, lest they trigger my carefully controlled emotions.

When my turn came, I approached the coffin, unsure of how I would react. The next moments would change my life forever.

My eyes traveled up the familiar blue wool jacket, past her ribbons and the coveted gold wings to her face. I stared, shocked, looking at a stranger.

That's not Susan! I thought. Then I spoke the words aloud, several times. "That's not Susan!"

Anyone who has seen a deceased person will know what I'm talking about. The body before me was so drastically different from the young woman I had known and loved that it suddenly became crystal clear to me what I had heard others say: The body is merely a vessel for the soul.

Susan had been so vibrant, so alive, that I knew then and there her spirit could not have been killed. The part of Susan that gave her life was clearly absent, and without it, the body in the coffin was unrecognizable.

My mind flashed back to my dream on the boat when Susan visited me. I struggled to put the timelines together. When did I dream of her, in relation to her passing? I realized with a start that it was shortly before she was killed. How was that possible, I pondered? If the soul is what animates the body, did Susan's soul somehow know in advance what was about to happen? Did she use my dream state to give me a heads-up? Her message that she and the baby were fine seemed more relevant now than ever. Had she chosen me to be her messenger for the rest of the family?

As we flew to Susan's home in Havelock, my mind whirled. If her spirit still existed, where was it? I couldn't imagine her sitting on a cloud playing a harp, so what *could* I believe? I determined to investigate theories of the afterlife at my first opportunity.

Back at the house we were joined by the Marine Casualty Assistance Officer, who reviewed with us the order of events for the funeral scheduled the next morning. When he asked if Ty would deliver the eulogy, I tensed. Hadn't he been through enough? How could a father say goodbye to his daughter, let alone do so publicly?

But of course he said yes.

At three in the morning, I sat by Ty's side in the officers' quarters and held him as he typed. I found it increasingly hard to breathe as he repeatedly stopped, breaking into sobs. It was all I could do not to join him, but I felt I had to be strong for this man I love with all my heart.

With that most unenviable of tasks completed, we crawled into bed to try and get a few hours' sleep. We lay silently side by side, not touching. I could tell that Ty, too, was wide awake. In the darkness with nothing to distract my thoughts, my emotions welled up like lava in a volcano about to erupt.

I threw back the covers, grabbed a pair of jeans and a shirt, and told him I would be back in a bit. Ty began to protest; he did not want me going outside alone. I told him I needed time to myself and grabbed the keys to our rental car. "I'll just be sitting in the parking lot."

Shielded by the car's soundproofed shell, I had a complete meltdown. Agonized wails, held in for too long, erupted from my throat. I pounded the steering wheel with my fists. I cursed and railed at the unfairness of life, but I had no one to yell at. Susan's death had been called "an act of God." With no real concept of God, I wanted nothing to do with anyone or anything that could cause such distress to so many people.

I don't know how long I stayed in the car. When I finally crawled back to bed, I was spent. Ty reached out to squeeze my arm.

"Are you okay?"

"Yes," I answered, far from okay. "Are you?"

"Yep," he replied. I knew he was lying.

The memorial service proceeded with full military honors in an auditorium filled with somber Marines, Susan's civilian friends, and our family. My sister Janice had driven in from Pennsylvania.

"You're going to be totally focused on Ty," she said when she arrived, "but someone needs to take care of you." I didn't believe in angels, but she sure looked like one to me that morning.

When the time came for Ty to deliver the eulogy, I held my breath. His voice cracked, but he spoke at length with the utmost of dignity, delivering the most difficult speech of his life. He addressed his words directly to Susan:

"We admired your spirit of adventure, your love of the wilderness, the mountains, and the forests. I remember the times we spent hiking the Appalachian Trail; we would often stop, not talking, just listening to the wind in the trees and the songs of the birds. We admired your ability to balance your roles as a tough Marine sergeant, a soft and feminine woman, a beautiful, loving wife, and a mother-to-be.

"We will always remember and cherish your impish grin and sometimes goofy expressions. You never took yourself too seriously, and you made sure I didn't take myself too seriously, either. Fathers hope to teach their daughters things, but you taught me a lot, especially to be more tolerant and understanding. We know that you are watching and listening now, and that one day we will be together again in a better place."

Did he really believe that, I wondered? Or were those just the words that everyone recites after a death? Ty and I had never discussed our views of the afterlife, and I assumed that, like me, he hadn't given much credence to the survival of consciousness. What happened as we left the memorial service let me know that he was more open-minded than I thought.

As our family left the auditorium, a strong wind whipped up, in striking contrast to the stillness moments before. The branches on nearby trees rocked back and forth in an unfamiliar swaying motion. Dead leaves swirled up from the ground and danced around us in joyous whirlpools. Ty, who had not smiled in days, looked up in wonder.

"That's Susan," he said, and I felt the slightest stirring that we might actually survive this.

A second natural wonder followed shortly thereafter. The passion flower was Susan's favorite—an appropriate choice, considering her passion for life. The day after she died, Warren and Elisabeth purchased a passion flower plant in her memory. The vine had many blossoms, but none had yet opened.

As we left Susan and Warren's house for the memorial service, the plant stood forlornly in the front yard, its blossoms hanging limply. When we returned, two had bloomed fully and one had opened halfway, as if to symbolize Susan, Warren, and baby Liam. By the next day, the blooms had closed, and no more opened that week.

After a reception hosted by the Marine Corps League, Ty and I joined Warren at the kitchen table. We made small talk, speaking softly as if someone might overhear us, though there was no one else in the kitchen. When we ran out of words, Warren rested his head on his arms.

I looked across to Susan's place at the table, thinking of the meals we had enjoyed together. The empty chair reminded me of the seat set at formal military dinners for those who have made the ultimate sacrifice for their country.

Susan, was that you who made the leaves dance? I asked silently. *Did you make the passion flowers bloom? Did you somehow know you were going to die, and are you trying to let us know you're still here?*

I heard nothing in response, but just then Susan's cat strolled behind me, letting her tail brush from left to right across the small of my back. I turned to pet her. To my surprise, Zoso was nowhere in sight. I leaned down and peered under the table, then glanced behind me a second time. No cat. I ran my hand over my back where I'd felt her tail. My shirt was tucked neatly into my slacks. But I had felt the distinctive sensation of fur against my bare skin. How could that be so?

I was about to share what I'd experienced when Warren slowly sat up. "I feel Susan's arms around my neck."

His tone was emotionless, though the words were stunning. He might as well have said, "The plumber's coming tomorrow to fix the drain."

I stared hard at the space around him. Was Susan there? I could see nothing different. Still, his offhand remark directly followed my own sense of being caressed by the cat's tail.

"Do you mean you *imagine* her arms around you," I asked, "or do you actually feel them physically?"

"I feel them around my neck," he said, again with no emotion, no surprise, as if this were the most normal thing in the world. His grief was so profound that I understood then how nothing short of Susan walking into the room would have roused him.

I turned to Ty. "Do you feel anything?"

He shook his head. "Nothing."

"Well, just before Warren spoke up, I thought for sure that Zoso had brushed against my skin, but she's nowhere in sight."

Ty cocked his head.

I realized my story sounded crazy. In defense, I asked, "Did you see me looking under the table a moment ago?"

He nodded.

"I felt a very clear touch. All the way across the skin of my back, even though it's covered by my shirt. And just a moment later, Warren felt Susan's arms around his neck."

Warren stared blankly ahead. "I still feel them."

"She's here," I said to Ty. "Susan is here."

Ty inhaled slowly. "I wish I could feel her."

"I do, too," I said, but not with the grief that had lately consumed me. Something within me had shifted.

When we first heard the news that Susan was "gone," that's how it felt: that—like those who had perished on 9/11—she was gone forever. The sense of finality that accompanied that thought filled me with a helplessness l had never previously experienced.

But my sudden insight at the viewing, that our Susan and her body were two distinct entities, opened a door to the possibility that she wasn't really gone—at least not the part of her we cherished.

The dancing leaves after her funeral caught my attention, to be sure. The three blossoms on the passion flower plant seemed a timely sign, as did the lucid dream. Still, my military mind could explain those occurrences away as mere coincidence.

I had no explanation, however, for the tactile sensation against my back, followed by Warren's description of a tangible hug. What I did have was something that until that moment of grace had been sorely missing: I now had hope.

CHAPTER 3

Mariposas

§

With our Honda CRV in tow behind the bus, we departed Catalina State Park. "Remind me where we're staying this week," I asked Ty, opening my iPad and pulling up Google maps. I only knew that we were headed for Phoenix, with speaking engagements booked in the coming days. Ty handled the logistics of our travels, allowing me to focus on my work.

"Check northeast of Phoenix for the town of Cave Creek," Ty replied as he pulled onto Oracle Road. "We have a spot at Cave Creek Regional Park."

I located the park and set our GPS, then opened my calendar to review my upcoming events. A reminder caught my eye: "Call Elizabeth Boisson."

I'd first heard of Elizabeth from Anne Puryear, a wonderful psychic and minister whose son is on the other side. She mentioned that Elizabeth had started a support group called Helping Parents Heal for bereaved parents that allows for the open discussion of the afterlife. Anne painted a picture of Elizabeth as an angel in human form.

Several years later, Elizabeth's name came up again, in a conversation with my friend Irene Vouvalides. Irene and I met by phone when I connected her with the spirit of her daughter Carly. The connection was nearly as good as the one Irene herself and I enjoyed. When we met later in person at a conference, we clicked immediately.

That weekend we shared a profound experience with Carly and subsequently developed a close friendship.

I knew how greatly Carly's death had affected Irene. Her transformation from massive grief to a life filled with hope inevitably led to her desire to "pay it forward" and help other grieving parents. She confided to me that she was thinking of starting a chapter of Helping Parents Heal in her hometown of Hilton Head, South Carolina. I encouraged her to do so. She connected with Elizabeth Boisson, and the two spent hours on the phone planning the new chapter.

When Irene heard that Ty and I would be in Phoenix, she reminded me that Elizabeth lived in the area. "You have to get together with her," Irene said. "She is such a wonderful person. I just know you'll love her." She paused. "I'm going to be extremely jealous," she confessed, "that you get to meet her in person before I do! But please give her a big hug from me until I can deliver one myself."

Prompted by the note on my calendar, I scrolled through Irene's old emails looking for Elizabeth's number. As I did, my cell phone rang, from a number I didn't recognize.

"Hello?" I asked warily, expecting to hear a telemarketer.

"Suzanne?" said a soprano voice. "This is Elizabeth Boisson."

I let out a delighted laugh, drawing a glance from Ty in the driver's seat. "You're not going to believe this," I said, "but I was just going to call you."

"Perfect," Elizabeth replied. "Irene sent me the information about your events in Arizona for our group's newsletter. I've been so looking forward to meeting you." She spoke with a delightful, singsong lilt that reminded me of a bird flitting from branch to branch.

"Me, too," I said. "I'm so impressed with the work you're doing. Ty and I would love to have dinner with you and your husband while we're here."

"How wonderful!" exclaimed Elizabeth. She paused. "But what day is this? You'll have to forgive me. Cyril and I just flew in last night from Hong Kong, and I'm a bit fuzzy headed."

I checked my calendar. "Today is Friday, April fifteenth. I have an official dinner Sunday in Mesa, and a special event at Unity Church of Phoenix on Tuesday—"

"I already have my ticket for the Unity event," Elizabeth said, surprising me.

"You're going to be there? That's great. I'm free after that until my workshop the following Saturday. But how about dinner tomorrow?"

"Oh, I'm so sorry, we're not available tomorrow," said Elizabeth, with a note of genuine disappointment. "We're holding a special ceremony to dedicate benches in memory of our son Morgan and our friends Nita and Glenn Erickson's son Kyle." Her tone brightened. "You and Ty are more than welcome to come, if you'd like. In fact, we'd love to have you join us."

An introvert by nature, I would normally have politely declined the invitation to join a group of complete strangers, but picturing such a unique gathering, I reacted with unexpected interest. My intuition was confirmed when Elizabeth added, "We'll be joined by about forty parents from Helping Parents Heal. And all of our kids on the other side will be there, too."

I smiled at Elizabeth's matter-of-fact acknowledgement of the role our departed loved ones continue to play in our lives. Her words carried such infectious excitement that I was filled with anticipation.

"Let me check with Ty." I held the phone away from my ear, repeating the invitation to my husband. He nodded enthusiastically.

"We'll be there," I reported happily. "When and where do we meet?"

"We're gathering at five o'clock. The benches are in a beautiful spot in the Spur Cross Recreation Area," Elizabeth said. "We'll meet in the parking lot at the trailhead and hike up to the area. It's an easy trail, not much of an incline."

"That's no problem. We love hiking," I assured her. A momentary flashback made me add, "I have to ask you one thing, though—do you see many snakes up there?"

"I had one follow me down the trail once," she admitted. "It paralleled me the whole way. It was kind of freaky, but I don't think you have to worry. There will be about sixty of us, so any snakes will keep their distance."

I reminded myself that the snake was now my friend and asked how to find the trailhead.

"Where will you be coming from?"

"We're staying at a park near Cave Creek."

"Oh, my goodness!" Elizabeth exclaimed. "That's where we live—in the town of Cave Creek! And Spur Cross is just over the hill from the park. Seriously, you could almost walk there."

I smiled. "This feels like a setup from Spirit."

"I think it must be," she confirmed. "Everything about this dedication has come together so magically. Nita and I have wanted to put a memorial for our sons in Spur Cross for a long time. It's a beautiful, sacred place."

She went on to explain how she and Cyril had spent a day checking out the available sites for the benches, but none of them felt right. On their way home from the exploratory excursion, the ranger called to inform them a potential site had just opened up. They hiked back immediately, fell in love with the spot, and called Nita and Glenn to share the news.

Arriving home, they were met by a dozen deer lined up across their driveway. The animals stood like statues, their gaze fixed on Cyril and Elizabeth. Over the years, Elizabeth had often photographed deer in their yard, but lately none had appeared. Never had so many assembled in one spot, motionless and alert, as if to deliver an important message.

"I told Nita the deer were a sign from Morgan and Kyle," Elizabeth said.

"How great is that," I replied, knowing how our loved ones in spirit often blend their consciousness with that of animals, birds, and insects in an act of mutual cooperation to get our attention.

"But the whole thing is even more perfect than you think," she said. "I knew I'd be seeing you at Unity, so I just finished reading your book, *Messages of Hope*."

"That's great! I hope you enjoyed it."

"Oh, my goodness, yes! Especially when I read about the butterflies that Susan sent you after she passed. The spot for the benches that suddenly became available is at the top of Mariposa Hill."

"No way!" I exclaimed in delight, knowing that "mariposa" means "butterfly" in Spanish.

I so appreciated these special winks from Spirit, and I loved that Elizabeth appreciated them as well. If Susan had not managed to send us irrefutable signs of her continued presence in our lives after she passed, Elizabeth and I would not have connected. In fact, I would not be working as a medium, traveling around the country speaking about the afterlife, were it not for Susan and the butterflies.

§

We're often told that we're never given more than we can handle. One way Spirit helps us through our trials is by putting people in our path to help us in challenging times. The kindness shown by strangers in crises has the power to pull us out of our grief and remind us that we are all part of a loving universe. So it was for Ty and me in the wake of Susan's passing.

We had been sailing toward Venice, Italy, when we got the call about Susan. We left the boat in Croatia to return for her funeral. As we prepared to fly back to Europe, we both agreed that the wind had been taken out of our sails. No matter how enticing the destination, we had no desire to sail farther north.

When I went online to arrange our trip back to the boat, I found it ironic that our flight would land in Venice, followed by a train through Slovenia to Croatia. We had no interest in playing tourist, but after the emotional upheaval of the past week, we decided to spend a few days in the city before we transitioned back to life afloat.

Ty usually handled logistics like hotel arrangements, but he was in no shape to think about such mundane things. The thought occurred to me that there was a US Air Force base in the town of Aviano, just outside Venice. I knew from serving overseas and from working as a protocol officer in several of my Navy assignments that foreigners in host countries often provide discounts for US service members abroad.

I sent an email to the protocol officer at Aviano Air Force Base. I explained that we were two military retirees on our way back to Croatia after our Marine Corps daughter's funeral and were looking for a quiet place to stay for a couple of nights. I asked if there might be a discounted hotel where we could decompress.

A reply came within hours. The protocol officer offered her condolences and informed me that she had discussed our situation with one of their "Friends of Aviano" who managed a Venetian hotel. He kindly offered us a room at his hotel for two nights at no charge. We were not to worry about a thing: we would be met at the airport and all our needs taken care of.

Tears came easily that week. They flowed down my cheeks immediately upon hearing this news. I marveled at the generosity of these strangers. The final paragraph of the email provided the name of our host and the hotel he managed. I typed the hotel's name into Google, picturing one of the small, cozy, three-star guesthouses so prevalent throughout Europe.

When the search results came up, I did a double take. Rated five stars, the prestigious inn was listed as the number-one celebrity hotel in Venice, having welcomed such guests as Elizabeth Taylor, Elton John, Angelina Jolie, and Madonna. The minimum daily price for a room was over a thousand dollars.

The beautiful photos revealed a location set apart from the hubbub and crowds of the tourist areas, the last thing our battered souls could handle. Instead, we would be treated to the peace and privacy of jasmine-shaded gardens in an ideal location across the lagoon from St. Mark's square.

Grief has an anesthetizing effect. Normally, we would be thrilled at the prospect of such deluxe accommodations. Instead, when I shared the news with Ty, we merely nodded in appreciation. While our gratitude at the generosity of this gift was genuine, we remained painfully aware of the reason it was being offered.

As promised, we were met at the airport in Venice—not by a chauffeur, but by the hotel manager himself. Such compassion he showed us, such understanding as he led us to the hotel's private launch—a pristinely restored classic Chris-Craft—for the ride across the lagoon to our refuge. We forced a half-smile in gratitude, but even speaking was difficult. Our broken hearts were incapable of feeling the normal joy and excitement that would usually accompany such an exotic adventure.

I doubted the hotel was pet-friendly, but the manager displayed no concern about our pup Rudy as we crossed the elegant lobby. He showed us to our exquisitely appointed room and again offered his condolences, along with the services of the launch if we wanted to venture into the city.

We did spend a few hours the next day exploring the famed canals and bridges, palaces and piazzas, but it was with relief that we returned to the sanctuary of our room. We could not have asked for a more perfect place to begin to heal. We each chose a book and retreated to the quiet balcony to read.

On our way to the airport in North Carolina we had stopped at a Books a Million store. There I bought three books on the afterlife. The one I chose to read on the balcony in Venice was a collection of accounts by medium George Anderson, gathered from his client sessions. I found the stories fascinating, if not a bit fanciful to my military mind. But the sheer quantity of factual evidence he provided allowed a stirring of hope in my heart that life after death might be real. My greatest desire was to connect with Susan's spirit.

As I came to the end of a page, loud voices broke the silence around us. They seemed quite close. I glanced beyond our balcony, but saw no one in the gardens below. Oddly, the commotion seemed to be coming from our room. I set my book on the chair and got up to investigate. To my surprise, I found the room empty, save for two newscasters conversing on the television screen. We had not turned the TV on since our arrival. The remote control sat untouched beside it.

Puzzled, I returned to the balcony and reported the mystery to Ty. Absorbed in his book and his thoughts, he simply shrugged. I sat down and continued reading where I had left off. The next paragraph left me gaping at the page. With impeccable timing, George Anderson explained that spirits often try to make us aware of their presence by manipulating lights, electrical appliances, and electronic equipment.

I shared what seemed to be far more than a coincidence with Ty. I had no explanation for the fact that the television came on by itself, and did so precisely as I was about to read an explanation of such a phenomenon. Could this have something to do with Susan, I wondered?

I did not know then what I have come to understand clearly today: Those we love who have passed are still very much a part of our lives. They are keenly aware of our activities and drop in from time to time to check up on us.

Our Susan—perhaps with the help of more experienced spirits— knew that I was reading a book about the afterlife, about to learn how spirits manipulate electronic appliances to get our attention. She must have enjoyed waiting until just the right moment to switch on the television set.

As if to prove this point about the spirit world's impeccable timing, Susan pulled the same trick one week later. By then, Ty and

I had returned to the boat and were sailing south on the Adriatic Sea. Our world seemed to have come to a complete halt, but our nomadic lifestyle compelled us to keep moving. It was just as well; we wanted to get away from Croatia and our traumatic memories there as quickly as possible.

With Ty at the helm, I filled my off-watch hours by immersing myself in my new books. I finished George Anderson's first book and moved on to a second volume of his spirit stories.

"Hey, Suzanne," Ty said, interrupting my reading. "Have you noticed the yellow butterfly that's been following us the past two days?"

I laid my book in my lap and followed his gaze. I had seen the butterfly flitting in our wake but until now not given it much thought.

"I did," I replied. "Now that you mention it, I don't think I've ever seen a butterfly this far out."

"It's as if it's following us."

This time it was my turn to shrug. I went back to my book. The very next paragraph brought me up short, just as it had on the hotel balcony.

"Ty!" I said, incredulous, "Listen to this. George Anderson says that 'Signs from the Infinite Light can often be right under our noses . . . as subtle as a tiny butterfly in December.'"

Ty blinked, looked aft, and added, "Or on the Adriatic Sea. . . . "

At precisely that moment, our butterfly caught up to us in the cockpit and flew directly between us before heading back to shore.

Was this yet another coincidence? A fluke of nature? I stared at the disappearing fleck of yellow in amazement and wonder.

Hours later, on our arrival at the island of Mljet, we were met with another odd encounter. No fewer than twenty yellow butterflies hovered around our boat as we adjusted the dock lines. Six other boats lined the sea wall around us, yet only ours was surrounded by butterflies that lingered for a good half hour. I had no way of explaining these experiences, but I still couldn't quite fully credit them to Susan.

The next morning, rather than getting underway first thing, Ty and I set out on a hike. A winding path led through thick woods to the island's highest point. Still dazed and numb, we trod along in silence. The stories from Anderson's book swirled in my head. Many described wispy figures that appeared to those who were grieving. As we trudged upward, I willed Susan to make her presence known to me in similar fashion.

Higher and higher we climbed, but I saw nothing out of the ordinary. I grew more despondent with each footstep. Why couldn't I see her? *Susan*, I prayed, *please give me some kind of sign that you're around. We so desperately need to know you're not gone forever.*

I can just picture Susan at that moment. I'm sure she was shaking her head at me, chuckling and saying, *Haven't you noticed the butterflies I've been sending?*

We reached the summit and turned to retrace our steps. Ty walked on ahead, a good fifty yards down the trail. A flicker of motion to my left caught my attention. Turning, I spied a yellow butterfly with a red dot on its back flying directly towards me. I stopped and stared, transfixed, as it arrived at my side, flew a complete circle around me, then tapped my chest at the level of my heart. The butterfly then flew in a straight line down the trail toward Ty.

Incredulous, I called out his name. The shock in my voice made him stop and turn. By now the butterfly had reached him. As if by remote control, it flew a complete circle around him, just as it had done with me, and gave him a similar love-tap at heart level before flying off into the woods.

I stood rooted in place, awestruck. The unusual events of the past week flashed through my mind. So far we'd experienced a self-starting television set, a butterfly that accompanied us for two days at sea, a special swarm around our boat, and now a butterfly that flew a specific and meaningful path between me and my husband.

I may have been new at noticing signs, but I finally got it. I couldn't see or sense Susan's spirit, but I was now convinced that she was trying to get our attention.

Over the next few months I read everything I could find in books and online about the spirit world. I learned as much as I could about mediums and became convinced that at least some of those who purported to be able to connect with deceased loved ones possessed a legitimate gift.

Ty decided that he needed to return to work to give himself something to focus on other than Susan's passing. We left our boat in Turkey and flew back to northern Virginia, where we owned a townhouse. It was there that I found a medium who might be able to help us connect with Susan. She is no longer practicing, so I will simply call her "Penny" for privacy's sake.

The skeptic in me knew that information about Susan was readily available in a special tribute I had posted on our sailing website. When I called Penny to set up an appointment, I deliberately left out all details about our loss and did not provide our last name.

The reading with Penny went far beyond my expectations. It didn't just give me pause; it turned my worldview upside down.

Penny had no way of knowing that Susan had been killed by lightning, yet moments before sensing the presence of spirit, she complained of a tingly electrical feeling up and down her arms. She then reported the presence of a young woman in her twenties who appeared to have died rather suddenly. She told us this woman was dressed in a brown uniform and stood in front of Ty saying, "Daddy, Daddy."

I had to hold back my sobs. Ty was visibly shaken. This was the answer to my prayers: verifiable details about our daughter that Penny could not have known. The thought that Susan was standing there with us even though we couldn't see her was beyond belief, yet undeniable.

In the middle of the reading, a leafy fern in a heavy clay pot on a table beside us suddenly crashed to the floor, completely of its own accord. Absorbed in her link with Susan's spirit, Penny ignored the broken bits of clay and dirt scattered at our feet. Susan must have been a bit frustrated that no one commented on her trick.

Later, when Ty and I compared notes about the reading, we could find no earthly way to explain how such a heavy object could move on its own. I had seen the movie "Ghost," where the spirit of Patrick Swayze's character toys with a penny, moving it up and down a wall to get his bereaved girlfriend's attention. I had dismissed such antics as the product of some Hollywood screenwriter's wild imagination.

Having failed to get our attention with the potted plant, Susan then played her trump card. This became evident when Penny stated matter-of-factly, "And now there's a second person with this spirit, a child. It's somebody from the other side that she's taking care of and she wants to present this child to you. She says *they're fine.*" Unwittingly, Penny delivered the same message Susan had given me in my still-vivid dream right before she passed. "She wants you to know she's very happy."

Penny had no way of knowing that Susan was pregnant with a boy when she died. The statement that Susan wanted to introduce her baby to us left me breathless.

"She wants to sit on your lap," Penny said, addressing Ty, "and to wrap her arms around your neck."

By now Ty and I were both crying. How many times had we seen Susan do exactly as Penny described when it came time to say good-bye? Tough Marine Corps sergeant or not, Susan was still Daddy's girl.

Until that reading, I had hope in an afterlife, but I wasn't sure that it existed. Yes, we'd experienced some amazing signs and synchronicities, but my skeptic's mind wasn't completely convinced. The evidence we received in our short meeting with Penny removed all doubt. For days I walked around in a daze, processing the experience. The belief system that had served me my whole life had proved faulty. The world was no longer flat.

That stunning session set into motion a series of life changes that I could never have foreseen.[2] Thanks to the healing that ensued from that evidence-filled reading, I went on to write several books about mediumship. I felt that if through my writing I could bring to others the hope and healing that our reading with a medium had brought to us, I was all-in. In the process of writing those books, I discovered my own latent ability to connect with those in spirit. Mediumship became more than a fascination; with time I realized it as my calling.

Ty went with me to that initial reading because I asked him to. Only later did I learn that he had no real understanding of a medium's work. The irony of our situation isn't lost on either of us: when I took him to see Penny, he didn't know what a medium was. Today, he is married to one.

What has allowed a former destroyer captain to fully embrace my work and support my efforts 100 percent? Beyond our deep love for each other, beyond the overwhelming evidence I have received through connecting with thousands of souls across the veil, Ty has his own reasons.

For him, it's the two fingers pressed firmly against his arm on a trail in Virginia that he and Susan used to hike together. His personal experience of his daughter's presence occurred as memories of her filtered through his mind. He turned to see who had touched his arm, but there was no one there. So startled was he by the physical sensation of those fingers that he had to sit down on a nearby tree stump to regain his composure.

He and Susan had planned to hike the Appalachian Trail together one day. Since her passing, Ty has backpacked several segments of that epic trail with Susan in spirit. Today we treasure the photo of a twenty-something woman he encountered as he trekked across Georgia on one of those hikes. With her dark, wavy, shoulder-length

---

[2] For the full story, please enjoy my memoir, *Messages of Hope.*

hair and deep brown Bette Davis eyes, the girl bore an uncanny resemblance to our Susan.

Moments after Ty snapped her photo, capturing the same over-the-shoulder pose as Susan holds in one of our favorite pictures, the young girl asked a simple question, with no idea that she was serving as Susan's messenger from heaven: "Did you see the yellow butterfly that just flew past?"

By this point, Ty was on daily alert for butterflies, yet in four days of hiking the trail, he had not seen a single one.

We each recognized Susan's hand at work in these encounters, just as Elizabeth Boisson recognized the deer in her driveway as a sign from her son. And I loved that Elizabeth acknowledged Kyle and Morgan's assistance in locating the perfect spot for their memorial benches. We laughed with delight that this sacred place of honor was named Mariposa Hill, but we had come to expect such gifts from our kids.

Our arrangements for the bench celebration the following day confirmed, I hung up the phone and smiled, savoring Elizabeth's lingering energy. I knew that our mutual friend Irene was right about one thing: I would come to love this woman.

CHAPTER 4

Morgan

§

IF I LEARNED ANYTHING IN my Navy career, it's that a group leader sets the tone for its members. The moment Ty and I met Elizabeth and Cyril Boisson, we understood why those gathered for the bench dedication appeared so uplifted by their presence. The pair are as beautiful on the inside as they are in person.

I had seen photos of Elizabeth on the Helping Parents Heal website, so I recognized her immediately. I knew to look for a tall, thin, blonde woman, but the black t-shirt with "Morgan" spelled out in rhinestones across the front gave her away. From thirty yards away, I cocked my head in wonder. At a willowy six feet tall, the subtle tilt of her chin and her flowing walk told me she was no stranger to a fashion show runway.

She must have recognized us, too; when Ty and I approached, she gathered us in a warm embrace as if reuniting with long-lost friends.

"Oh, my goodness! It's so nice to meet you!" she exclaimed. "And Susanne Wilson is here, too, so this is just wonderful!"

I smiled at this unexpected treat. I knew of Susanne, an evidence-based medium, from our mutual friend Dr. Gary Schwartz, an afterlife researcher and professor at the University of Arizona. Like me, Susanne focuses on bringing credibility to mediumship. We had spoken at the same conference a year earlier, but our schedules hadn't allowed us to meet.

As I glanced around to see if I could spot Susanne, a teddy bear of a man bearing a large bouquet of dove-shaped balloons walked toward us. His thick white hair matched the doves that floated above his head. With a nod and a smile at Ty and me, he rattled off something in French to Elizabeth.

"Oui, oui, je sais. Ils sont là-bas," she responded, pointing to a group standing nearby.

Despite their last name, I was startled to hear perfect French being spoken in Arizona. I hadn't realized that Cyril Boisson was a native Frenchman. I learned later that Elizabeth studied and taught the language in France, and they raised their three children to be bilingual.

Elizabeth introduced us to her husband, continuing to speak to him in French. When he greeted us in English, his words had a charming accent.

"You will join us for the party afterwards, no?" he asked. We nodded as he hurried off with his flock of balloons. I looked forward to trying out my rusty skills over a drink with the Boissons, and then laughed at my unintended mental pun. Having studied French myself, I knew that "Boisson," pronounced "bwah-sohn," means "drink" in French.

Had anyone crossed paths with the group that struck out along the Spur Creek Trail that late April afternoon, they might have thought they'd encountered a Volksmarch. Such was the vibrant energy emanating from the hikers as they marched purposefully uphill, chatting animatedly as they went. The atmosphere was far from the somber tone one might expect at a memorial service for departed children.

True to Elizabeth's promise, the half-hour hike to Mariposa Hill proved easy and scenic. Tall saguaro cacti dotted the Sonoran Desert, standing sentinel with their brethren prickly pear, teddy bear, and cholla. As we approached our destination, I could see why the families had chosen the spot. It overlooked the winding riverbed of Cave Creek, with impressive Skull Mesa standing to the northeast and Elephant Butte providing a balance to the southwest.

Two new benches had been placed at a slight angle, forming a wide "V," facing west. I envied future hikers who would enjoy the majestic views from this sacred place, and I couldn't help but smile at the irony when I thought of the benches as a "resting place." For the hikers, yes, the benches would provide a welcome rest, but I had come to know that, contrary to traditional human belief, not all those in the spirit world are "resting." Most continue to work in ways that serve those on both sides of the veil.

Ty and I approached the benches and leaned in to read the shiny brass plaques. The one on the right read:

In loving memory and tribute to our son & beloved brother to Ethan
KYLE ADEN ERICKSON
Forever Loved, Forever Missed, Forever Our "Freebird"

We hadn't yet formally met Kyle's parents, but I could tell by the deference given to one couple that they must be Glenn and Nita. Glenn wore a military-style desert camouflage hat, and I made a mental note to ask if he or Kyle had served in the Army.

We stepped to the left to read Morgan's plaque. I was stunned to find the names of two children engraved there:

In loving memory of
Morgan James Pierre Boisson 11/23/88 - 10/20/09
& Baby Chelsea 1/21/91

I recalled Irene Vouvalides telling me that the Boissons' first child had passed as a newborn. Seeing the single date for Chelsea, I was struck by what a short time Elizabeth and Cyril had had to enjoy their daughter's physical presence.

The words that followed read:

Il est allé au sommet du monde pour être plus près du ciel
Nous vous embrassons tendrement, Papa, Maman, Alix & Kiki

I translated the first line for Ty: *"He went to the top of the world to be closer to heaven."*

Just then, Elizabeth stepped up and joined us. "Cyril's father wrote those words for Morgan's funeral."

"They're beautiful," Ty said quietly, and I nodded.

Elizabeth said, "There's a Buddhist belief that if you pass on Mt. Everest, you go directly to Paradise, which is Nirvana, so ..."

"He passed on Mount Everest?" Ty asked, surprised. At that point we knew only that Morgan had died from altitude sickness, but none of the details.

"At Base Camp," Elizabeth confirmed.

Her gaze rested on the mesa in the distance. "I consider this Paradise, but Morgan was about as close as you can get when he crossed."

Turning back to us, she shrugged. A soft smile played across her lips. "Either way, I know from what I felt at the moment he transitioned that he's right here with me. . . . "

§

"The big brother to everyone." That's how people knew Morgan Boisson. Always ready to help those in need, he came to the rescue more than once during a summer exchange program in France. If his friends enjoyed a bit too much French wine, he would be the one to pick them up and carry them home. Back home at his alma mater, the University of Arizona, his sturdy, six-foot-six frame made him the perfect base for the cheerleading squad's pyramid.

Morgan's choice of major as an undergraduate was East Asian studies. After receiving his degree, he planned to attend graduate school at the prestigious Thunderbird University. As a sophomore, he had completed a program at Nanjing Normal University in China, and during his senior year he decided to participate in an exchange program there to focus on Chinese and International Studies.

Elizabeth helped him pack for his semester abroad. As they worked together, trying to figure out how to fit everything he needed into one suitcase, Morgan turned to his mother and said, "I don't think I'm coming home from China this time."

"If that's true," she replied, taken aback, "then you shouldn't go. You don't need the credits."

He gave her a reassuring smile. "Don't worry, Mom. It will be fine."

He seemed so excited about going that Elizabeth dismissed her fears, not wanting to dampen his enthusiasm, even though she would have loved him to spend his senior year close to the family.

Already proficient in Chinese after his first semester in China, Morgan thrived in Nanjing. As he had done throughout his life, he quickly found ways to be of service to others, coaching local Chinese high school students in basketball and playing with them several times a week. In addition, he began studying sign language in order to communicate with a group of deaf and mute students he had met.

A few months into the semester, he called home to discuss a possible side trip to Hong Kong. Elizabeth and Cyril advised him against going, concerned that he might have a problem with his visa when he tried to return to China. An opportunity then arose for a school trip to Tibet. His visa would not be an issue there, and he jumped at the chance.

It would prove to be a fatal decision.

Morgan and his fellow exchange students had been studying Tibet, but what interested them more than politics and economics was the chance to visit the famous Mt. Everest Base Camp. Two professors were slated to accompany the group, but at the last minute, plans changed. The students traveled directly from Nanjing to Chengdu and flew from there to Lhasa.

Had they traveled through Nepal, the trained guides there would have limited their ascent to no more than 2000 feet per day, mindful that their bodies must be allowed to acclimate to the higher altitudes. Their Chinese guide was not so careful. They traveled directly from Nanjing to Chengdu and flew from there to Lhasa, then immediately boarded a bus the next morning. Onward and upward they rode, the air growing thinner with each kilometer. Instead of allowing the prescribed nine days to ascend from sea level to an altitude of nearly 19,000 feet, they covered the distance from Nanjing to their final destination in a mere two and a half days.

Symptoms of altitude sickness include headache, difficulty sleeping, dizziness, and nausea. When his fellow students began to display these telltale signs, it was Morgan who helped them off the bus and, in full big-brother mode, held their heads as they vomited. Nobody noticed that he, too, was increasingly affected by the lack of oxygen in his lungs and brain.

Once they arrived at Base Camp, those who still possessed an appetite ate dinner. Morgan downed a beer with his food. Seeking relief from a massive migraine, he took the only medication he had with him: Nyquil. He had no idea that, like alcohol, the medication was contraindicated for altitude sickness.

That night the fourteen students slept together in a large round tent known as a yurt. Several times during the night Morgan got up and wandered aimlessly through the room. Although struggling with their own confusion, many noticed that he called them by the wrong name.

By morning, Morgan's body was in extremis. When he failed to rise, his friends saw foam at the corners of his mouth, the result of pulmonary edema. Panicking, they shook his shoulders and called his name but could not rouse him.

Back in Arizona, Elizabeth was feeling a growing sense of concern. Normally she talked with Morgan at least twice a day, either by cell phone or Skype. It wasn't that she was a meddling mother; the two simply enjoyed an enviable closeness. Most often, it was Morgan who initiated the calls.

Since the group had arrived in Lhasa, she had heard nothing. Morgan, she knew, was with a large group. Surely if something were wrong, someone would have called her. Still, she couldn't help remembering his strange premonition about not returning from China.

At Base Camp, the students were in shock. One of the boys called the program director back in Nanjing. Another placed a call to his mother, a physician in the United States. When he described the situation, she commanded, "Get him to lower altitude as quickly as possible."

It took several young men to pick up Morgan's 280-pound frame and carry him onto the bus. As they started down the mountain, their worst fears were realized: Morgan stopped breathing.

Frightened and sick themselves, the students hoisted him off the bus and laid him on the ground. Another bus on its way up the mountain stopped to help. One of the passengers initiated CPR.

When the phone rang at their Cave Creek home, Elizabeth jumped. She knew something was terribly wrong when the Nanjing program director introduced himself and informed her that he was in cell phone communication with a member of the group in Tibet.

"I'm sorry to tell you that Morgan is very sick," he said. "They're trying to bring him down the mountain. I have the phone number of one of the students in the program, if you'd like to try and reach him."

"Please give it to me," Elizabeth replied, hastily copying down the number. With Cyril at her side, she dialed the phone. The young man who answered was Morgan's roommate, Colin.

"Mrs. Boisson," he said, "I don't have good news." He repeated what the program director had already told her: "Morgan is very sick."

Colin's next words made Elizabeth's heart skip a beat. "They're doing CPR on him right now, but I don't think he's going to make it."

Elizabeth responded instinctively. "Listen," she said calmly. "Please put the phone up to his ear."

She paused a moment to allow Colin to do as she requested. Then she spoke directly to her son, fully aware that this might be her one chance to assure him of her love and that everything was okay.

"Boo Boo," she said calmly, "I just want to tell you that we love you, sweetheart. We're proud of you, and don't be afraid." She made kissing noises into the phone as she always did when speaking long-distance with her son.

Elizabeth knew he wasn't breathing. She knew he had no heartbeat. But with a mother's sixth sense, she knew that Morgan could hear her.

Because she kept her composure and spoke in English, Cyril remained unaware of the gravity of the situation. He reached for the phone to say hello to his son, but Elizabeth shook her head. By then, Colin had taken the phone back. When he came on the line, he sounded utterly stricken. "I don't think there's anything else we can do for him, Mrs. Boisson."

At that exact moment, Elizabeth experienced a sensation like none she had ever felt before. It is one she will never forget, one that changed the tenor of the days to follow and carried her through a parent's worst nightmare.

She felt her son hug her from inside.

The sensation was so real that she finally exhaled, after having held in her breath for what seemed like an infinite stretch of time. That oh-so-real embrace told her what she already knew in her heart: Morgan was gone. But that special hug from heaven also let her know that he would be with them forever.

She laid the phone down and turned to Cyril. "*Les nouvelles ne sont bonnes,*" she said. "The news isn't good. *Je pense qu'ils ne peuvent pas le sauver.* I don't think they can save him."

Caught completely off guard, Cyril fell to his knees.

When they were able, they called Alix and Christine, their teen-aged daughters, who immediately came rushing home, accompanied by their friends. As reality set in, the house turned chaotic, the entire family brought sobbing to their knees.

Awash in emotion, Elizabeth dimly recalled that the family was scheduled to travel together to France. A wish flashed through her head that the plane might crash and they could all be with Morgan. But no—she immediately recognized that such a thought was insane. Their beautiful and talented daughters had far too bright a future to deserve such a fate.

This deep grief was an alien feeling. Her mind raced as panic constricted her chest. *What if I become that crazy lady of Cave Creek curled up on the bed all day with a big bottle of vodka?*

Then she remembered the hug.

She knew in that moment that she had come to a fork in the road. Each path led in a different direction; it was her choice which to take.

Gathering her wits, she stood and announced firmly, "Get up. We cannot fall apart."

Startled, the family ceased crying, following her orders to gather together on the couch.

"Listen," she said, lovingly yet decisively, "Morgan wants us to be strong."

She deliberately spoke in the present tense. "He wants us to move forward. We're going to be okay."

The path was clear. With Morgan's help, and the memory of his embrace, she had chosen the fork of their destiny. Even though they now existed in two different worlds, the Boisson family would move ahead together.

CHAPTER 5

Message from a Dove

MORGAN AND KYLE MUST SURELY have heard the music rising in their honor as the sun set over Mariposa Hill. I understood the reference to "our 'Freebird'" on Kyle's plaque when Lynyrd Skynyrd's hit song by that name wafted across the desert from a portable speaker held by Glenn Erickson, Kyle's father. His mother Nita later related how that popular tune often comes on the radio with impeccable timing when she thinks of her son.

The Boissons chose the upbeat song "Smile" from a memorial video put together by Morgan's cheerleading team. *"You're better than the best. I'm lucky just to linger in your light,"* sang Uncle Kracker from the little speaker. The crowd smiled and swayed to the music, and I clearly felt the strong presence of both young men.

By then Cyril had handed out the white dove balloons to everyone in attendance. A testament to her caring nature, Elizabeth had purposely chosen biodegradable balloons and strings so as not to harm the environment. At a sign from our hosts, we released the strings to the enthusiastic cheers and whistles of all in attendance.

The unusual shape and color of the balloons produced a magical effect. Like a flock of white doves, they drifted up and away from us on the gentle breeze. The cheers faded as the crowd, mesmerized, followed the silent envoys carrying their message of love to Morgan, Chelsea, and Kyle.

As the ceremony concluded, I saw Susanne Wilson standing by herself and went over to introduce myself. We ended up hiking back to the parking lot together, chatting nonstop along the way. To our surprise, we learned we had more in common than our work as mediums. Our names were one letter apart, our age one year apart, and we both worked in linear, left-brained jobs before embarking on our current metaphysical careers.

We had each earned an MPA, specializing in Public Administration. We both married former military men with a bit of "seniority," and we both cherish our supportive husbands. Neither of us has biological children of our own, but we each have two dogs that we consider our babies: miniature dachshunds for me and mini schnauzers for Susanne.

Most important, we recognized in each other a kindred spirit. Mediums face unique physical and emotional demands, and finding a fellow spirit who could serve as a sounding board when future issues arose was a true blessing for us both.

At the parking lot, I asked if Susanne were going to the post-ceremony party. She had other plans, so we arranged to meet for coffee later that week.

"Did you get directions to the party?" I asked Ty as he held open the car door for me.

He sniffed. "Men don't ask for directions!"

Two months shy of our twentieth wedding anniversary, I understood that he was only half kidding.

"So how do we know where to go?" I asked.

"We'll follow the rest," he said, gesturing at the small parade of vehicles leaving the lot.

"Assuming they're all going to the party," I laughed. "Remember the joke about the guy in the fog following the taillights of the car in front and ending up in a stranger's driveway?"

The fog analogy proved somewhat prophetic, as the dust kicked up by a dozen cars on the dirt road ahead formed a thick brown cloud around our Honda.

"I'm so glad I washed the car today," Ty said dryly.

For the next ten minutes, we bumped and jostled over a maze of unpaved roads until we reached a modern southwest style home. Recognizing several people from Mariposa Hill, I breathed a sigh of relief.

"Beautiful place," I said, taking in the earth tones of the adobe walls and terra cotta roof. Soft lights illuminated a large patio and pool overlooking the vast area where we'd been hiking. Elizabeth had told me of their beautiful desert view, and I could see why they enjoyed living in Cave Creek.

The front door was open, so in we walked. "Make yourselves at home," Glenn Erickson called. "Drinks are in the back room."

I glanced around for our hosts, but Elizabeth and Cyril were nowhere in sight.

We wandered through the house admiring the décor. At the back room, my gaze was drawn to a decal on the wall: *Because someone we love is in heaven, there's a little bit of heaven in our home.*

Several large canvas photos adorned the walls, all featuring the same smiling, handsome young man. In some he was playing a guitar; in others, he wore an Army Specialist's uniform. These were pictures of Kyle, I realized, Nita and Glenn's son. I was momentarily confused. Wouldn't Cyril and Elizabeth have hung pictures of Morgan here instead?

Just then, Nita Erickson appeared at my side. "That's Kyle when he was in Iraq," she said, following my gaze. "He was over there for 15 months."

"Did you bring the photos here for the party?" I asked.

She looked at me, puzzled. "No. They've always been here."

Suddenly, I understood the disconnect. I hadn't realized that the Boissons and Ericksons were neighbors. I laughed to myself, grateful now that Ty had not had the Boissons' address to follow. The stream of cars had led us to the correct house; we just had no clue who lived there.

Rather than admit my mistake, I focused on Kyle. "What did he do in the Army?"

"He was in transportation," Nita answered. "He was slated to return to Iraq in the fall, but he had a one-car accident coming home from a friend's. He was only 23."

I shook my head. Even knowing that death merely represents a transition to a new chapter in our lives, the stories still sting. In the silence that followed, I noticed another quote stenciled on the wall.

"That's a good one," I said, indicating the words with a nod. *"Faith, the strength by which a shattered world shall emerge into the light."*

"It's from Helen Keller," said Nita. "Faith is what has carried us through. That, and these special people." She gestured at the party-goers around us.

"When we lost Kyle, I went crazy trying to find out where he was. I found out about Mark Ireland, who cofounded Helping Parents Heal. His book about the afterlife was the first thing that gave me hope."

Nita had emailed Mark, and he called her the next day to ask if he could give her number to Elizabeth.

"Of course I said yes. But I didn't know when Elizabeth called that she lived so close."

"Neither did I," I laughed, thinking of my mix-up.

"I just love her," Nita said, shaking her head. "She's such a pillar of strength."

"So you joined the group?"

She nodded, her face serious. "Meeting the other parents, going out to dinner, I saw that there was hope, that we could still have a life after losing Kyle."

"I love how you all acknowledge that we haven't really 'lost' our kids."

"Yes," she said, her voice soft, "but it's still hard."

She drifted off to talk with the other guests, and I spotted Ty across the room. Beer in hand, he was conversing animatedly with an unlikely couple. Both were equally lean and fit, but the woman stood a good twelve inches shorter than her husband.

Ty hooked an arm around my waist as I approached. "I want you to meet Jeff and Lynn Hollahan. This is my wife, Suzanne."

I was instantly drawn to the pair. Jeff's easygoing nature radiated from his warm eyes and welcoming handshake. Lynn reminded me of a pixie with her intriguing "I've-got-a-secret" smile. Had Ty been telling stories about me? Or maybe she always had that devilish grin. After a few minutes of chatting, I knew it was the latter.

Before long, our conversation turned to the subject we all shared. Being at a gathering of bereaved parents, especially in such a festive atmosphere, was a new experience for me. Unlike shallow cocktail party talk, with questions like "Where are you from?" and "What do you do?" within minutes we found ourselves sharing our greatest joys and deepest sorrows. Such candor engenders instant intimacy, and our hearts quickly opened to these dear new friends.

The Hollahans, we learned, had two children, Kelsey and Devon. Kelsey was 27 and married for two years to her husband, Matt. Devon had left our physical world at the age of 22. Lynn and Jeff owned a house down the road from Cave Creek in Scottsdale, but after Devon's passing, they bought a second home in Denver.

"We go back and forth now depending on the season. But at first we just needed to get away from our memories here," Jeff said.

We nodded in understanding.

When Lynn began to tell us how Devon passed, I held up my hand. "If you don't mind, I'd rather not hear the details right now. I'm a medium, and if I give you a reading sometime, I don't want to know too much in advance. I'd rather Devon tell me himself."

Lynn tilted her head and gave me that enigmatic smile. "Okay. Sure."

We noticed the crowd thinning out, but our little foursome kept talking. Soon we were joined by Elizabeth Boisson.

"I see you've met two of our closest friends," she said.

"We get together for dinner at least once a month," Lynn said, "and I go to Elizabeth's yoga classes."

"You teach yoga?" I asked.

"Yes. I find it so helpful for healing grief."

"Oh, I wish we were staying around longer," I said.

"Why don't we have dinner at our house before you leave?" Jeff suggested.

Ty and I exchanged glances, mentally running through our schedule for the coming week. I had several speaking engagements and dinners lined up on each night I wasn't working.

"What if we stick around an extra day, after your last event?" Ty asked me. I could tell he felt as drawn to the Hollahans as I did.

"You're the scheduler," I said.

"I think we can make it happen. How about next Sunday night?"

Amazingly, the date worked for all three couples. We said good-bye to the Hollahans, gave our thanks to the Boissons and Ericksons, and made our way back to the campsite.

The following evening we headed for Mesa, 40 miles south of our campsite, for dinner at a Mexican restaurant with members of the local International Association of Near Death Studies. IANDS, whose members are interested in credible information about life after death, has welcomed my work as an evidential medium and was hosting my workshop later that week.

With traffic, the trip took about an hour but was well worth the time. I loved hearing the magical accounts of those who had crossed to the other side and come back to tell about it.

During dinner, Ty and I sat at different ends of the table. As we headed back to Cave Creek at the end of the evening, I shared one of the more scintillating stories I'd heard. The woman seated at my right had lapsed into a coma after an accident a few years back. When her heart stopped, she witnessed everything happening in her hospital room from a vantage point near the ceiling.

"When she came out of the coma," I told Ty, "she recognized the nurse taking care of her as the same woman she saw while out of her body."

"Oh, my God!" Ty exclaimed, his eyes wide with shock.

I cocked my head at his overreaction. The story was interesting, but didn't warrant such a dramatic response.

"Did you see that?!" he asked excitedly, gripping the wheel and glancing quickly over his left shoulder.

He wasn't reacting to my story, I realized, but to something that had just occurred.

I swiveled to look behind us but saw nothing amiss.

"What was it?"

"I can't believe it. That's impossible!" he said, shaking his head, his eyes still wide.

"What was it? Tell me!"

"One of the dove balloons from yesterday's ceremony. It flew right over our hood and up our windshield!"

"You're kidding! No way!"

"I'm serious! It was inches off the car!" He shot me a stunned but knowing look.

Listening to another's near-death experience is one thing. Experiencing a miracle yourself is another. My work as a medium brings me into daily contact with the other side, but most of my encounters are purely mental. This was one of those magical events for which no explanation exists but the hand of Spirit at work.

"How far are we from Morgan and Kyle's benches?" I asked.

"Forty miles, easily," Ty said.

I looked at my watch. "We released those balloons well over 24 hours ago."

I glanced at the cars spread over eight lanes of traffic. Thousands of vehicles must travel this stretch of the highway every hour. I looked up at the clouds, wondering about the wind direction and speed that had guided the balloon to our precise location at that exact moment. Then I caught myself —physical facts didn't matter. The appearance of the dove balloon had nothing to do with the weather, and every-thing to do with delivering a heavenly message of love.

I checked my watch. I was hesitant to call anyone after 9:00 PM, but this was too special not to share. I picked up my iPhone and texted Elizabeth: *"You won't believe what just happened!"*

She replied immediately: *"What?!"*

My thumbs tattooed a rapid response: *"We are 40 miles from Spur Cross on 101, and one of Morgan's balloons just flew right up over our windshield!"*

She responded with the expected *"OMG!"* A second text followed shortly: *"He does things like this for us every day!!!"*

I read her reply to Ty and texted back: *"See you Tuesday at Unity and Sunday at Lynn & Jeff's."*

She replied with a flurry of heart emoticons that I returned in kind.

Filled with gratitude at how Spirit works in our lives, I closed my eyes for a moment of communion with my Team above. Yes, we would see our new friends on Sunday, and if Morgan and Devon heeded the special request I tacked onto the end of my prayer, our kids would be there, too.

CHAPTER 6
Visitors

§

EVER SINCE I DISCOVERED MY abilities as a medium, people have asked if I've seen *The Long Island Medium* television show. I have not, but I know that Theresa Caputo is the real deal. I've been told that what makes the show both interesting and amusing is that Theresa approaches unsuspecting strangers in public places to deliver messages from their deceased loved ones.

This makes for great entertainment but also leads people to assume that all mediums see spirits around them like Theresa does. I do not, and I'm grateful not to be hounded by visitors from the far side. The occasional drop-in is most welcome, but my guides know me well: if the veil were lifted 24/7, I would be "on" all the time, accountable to whoever happened to show up. I depend on my Team in spirit to help me keep the balance between work and play.

Okay, Boris, I said silently, addressing my main guide as we pulled into the driveway of the Hollahan's Scottsdale home. *I know I'm off duty tonight, and we're here to enjoy dinner, but I also know how much it would mean to these couples to hear from their sons.*

I focused on my heart and sent a wave of gratitude to my beloved gatekeeper. *Please let me sense Devon and Morgan just enough to let their parents know they're around.*

It had been a week since the bench dedication party, but when Lynn and Jeff opened the door to greet us, they felt like old friends. Perky and cute in a blue and white striped t-shirt dress, Lynn could have passed for a woman her daughter's age. The gray in Jeff's goatee betrayed the fact that the two college sweethearts were now in their fifties.

We stepped into the entry hall and shared hugs with all, including Elizabeth, elegant in a flowery sundress and gold chains. The three led us through the kitchen to a side door that opened onto a bright and cheerful patio. A high wall enclosed a large backyard, creating a grassy oasis for Kirby, the Hollahan's adorable Cavalier-Bichon mix. The bundle of white fur scampered playfully at Cyril Boisson's feet.

Cyril approached us with a broad smile. I leaned forward to hug him, and in true French style, he graced me with a kiss on each cheek.

The greetings over, we gathered at a round table set with six fluted glasses and a tray of fresh grapes, apples, and strawberries. Jeff picked up a gold-labeled bottle and began twisting the wire cage holding the cork in place.

"Thank Cyril for this," he told us. "It's not a party without the Boissons bringing champagne."

The cork burst up with a satisfying pop, and Jeff filled our glasses. "To new friends," we said in unison and laughed, intertwining our arms to ensure that each goblet touched.

The conversation flowed easily as we caught up on each other's activities of the past week. After twenty minutes, Jeff got up to light the grill, joined by Ty and Cyril. Lynn excused herself for some final dinner prep, waving off Elizabeth's and my offers to help. I'm glad she did. Had I left the table at that moment, I would not have seen Morgan Boisson standing at his mother's left shoulder.

I blinked in surprise. Even though I had set the intention of tuning in to the boys, I was unaccustomed to seeing spirits in a social setting. I leaned in and squinted to be sure of what I was sensing. When I work, I see images of objects much more clearly than physical characteristics. I could not have described Morgan if someone had asked me to, but I clearly picked up the image of a hot-air balloon he projected onto my mind's eye, followed by the repeated image of a finger pointing downward, as if to say, "Now, now, now."

"Elizabeth," I said with a smile, "Morgan is standing right beside you."

Her face brightened. She turned to look where I indicated.

"He's showing me a hot-air balloon that you saw recently."

"Oh, my goodness!" she said. "A big balloon flew over our house this morning. It was so beautiful that I took pictures of it."

I gave a gentle victory pump with my fist. "Way to go, Morgan!"

I tuned in to see what else might be coming through. Just then, Lynn stepped back onto the patio. As she took her seat, I sensed a slight shift in the energy. I waited a moment to allow the feeling to settle in, then I looked her way and smiled with delight. "Devon is standing right beside you," I told her.

Startled, she pulled in her chin, then grinned. "He is?"

"Morgan is here, too," Elizabeth said.

I focused inward. "Devon is showing me ears of corn and pointing at the table, as if we're having corn on the cob for dinner."

Lynn shook her head, but continued to grin.

I frowned. There had to be a reason Devon chose this image. As I started to ask him why, Lynn pulled out her phone and flipped through some photos, then held it towards me. "My son-in-law sent me this today from the farmer's market, but I decided on something else."

I looked at the close-up of three perfect ears of corn on the cob and laughed. "That's exactly what he showed me! When I connect with those on the other side, I ask for specific types of evidence— things going on in your life right now, and photos you will recognize. Devon and Morgan each showed me a recent memory and a photo. They are so *right here!*"

I knew that neither woman expected a full reading, so I downshifted my attunement, and we returned to our previous conversation.

As we chatted, I passed along little tidbits the boys shared with me. They were so clearly present that the only thing missing was their physical bodies.

When Jeff announced that the grilled salmon was ready, we moved to a larger table.

"Morgan and Devon are here," I announced to the men as we filled our plates with fish, fresh vegetables, and the fluffy couscous that Lynn brought in from the kitchen.

"I'm not surprised," Jeff said with a big smile.

Elizabeth and Lynn filled them in on the images of the hot-air balloon and corn on the cob that had cued us in to their presence.

Cyril cocked his head with curiosity, as did Ty. He knew how rare it was for me to sense spirits when I was not giving an actual reading to a client.

"I guess they didn't want to miss the party," Ty said.

Just then, I felt a familiar presence: Susan, standing to my right with her hands on her hips. *What about me?!* she asked with mock indignation.

My eyes widened. Susan has her own life to live on the other side. It doesn't keep her from dropping in to help with my work, but I hadn't expected to hear from her that evening. I felt a stab of guilt for not imagining she would want to join the fun, but this was quickly eclipsed by the joy of feeling her near.

I had no doubt that it was Susan, but I didn't want anyone to take my word for it. Knowing the power of a good piece of evidence, I silently asked, *Tell me something about your dad that I don't know.*

Susan rolled her eyes dramatically and replied, *Ask him about his toothache.*

I whipped my head to the left. "Ty—you have a toothache?"

The question caught him off guard. He had no idea that I'd been conversing with his daughter. He blinked and brought a hand to his cheek. "Yes, but I didn't say anything about it. It started this morning."

I pumped my fist for a second time. "Susan's here, too!" I announced. I reached over and squeezed Ty's knee. "And she knows about your sore tooth."

"How wonderful that all our kids showed up," Elizabeth said.

"This doesn't usually happen," said Ty, still rubbing his cheek.

Most of my drop-ins, I explained, occur when I'm replying to emails from those I've given readings to or when I wake up in the middle of the night.

Ty rolled his eyes dramatically, mirroring his daughter's gesture. "Our bed can get a little crowded at times."

The others laughed. I shrugged. "I sleep with a pad of paper by my pillow, and if Ty hears me writing, he stays quiet so I don't break the connection."

"This all must be quite a switch for you," Jeff said to Ty.

"It is," Ty agreed, "but with all this evidence coming through"— he spread his palms— "you can't deny that it's real."

"My friends call him 'Saint Ty,'" I put in.

Appreciative laughter greeted my remark. Ty deflected the attention. "Tell them about your reading last week with Gary Schwartz."

I nodded. "That was cool."

Each time we'd traveled through Tucson over the past few years, I'd had the honor of doing a research reading for Dr. Schwartz in his Laboratory of Human Consciousness at the University of Arizona. On our most recent visit, he brought in one of his students as the sitter. The young woman sat across from me on a couch while Gary filmed the session from behind me.

With no prior knowledge of her wishes, I successfully connected with the spirit the young woman wanted to hear from. The young man across the veil told me correctly how he had passed and I was able to accurately describe his personality and character. He went on to provide obscure details that left no doubt of his presence. When he showed me large black birds, like ravens or crows, as signs that he was around, the girl's eyes widened and she nodded vigorously in confirmation.

I made two fists, held them with knuckles facing, and rocked them back and forth in opposite directions, showing how the spirit directed the birds as if by remote control. The birds, he told me, find it fun to be used this way.

"That was the first I ever heard this from a spirit," I told the dinner guests, "but it wasn't the first time for Dr. Schwartz. He interrupted the reading and asked, 'What did you just say?'"

"I repeated, 'The birds think it's fun.' And Gary said, 'Susanne Wilson said the same thing in her reading for me last week!'"

Everyone at the table was familiar with Susanne's work as a medium. They all murmured in delight.

"As you know," I continued, "those on the other side often use nature to let us know they're around. With Susan, it's butterflies, and Morgan sent you the deer," I said, addressing the Boissons. "For others, it could be dragonflies or any variety of birds."

Many people, when they witness these signs, believe mistakenly that our loved ones have come back as a bird, insect, or animal. Since the purpose of life in human form is the evolution of the soul, it would not make sense for a human soul to incarnate as a less evolved being. I explained that what we are witnessing when we receive these signs from nature is the blending of their consciousness with one of God's creatures in a beautiful act of cooperation.

"And it's wonderful that the birds think it's fun," Elizabeth said.

Jeff looked at Lynn and raised his eyebrows. "Should we tell them our blackbird story?"

Elizabeth clapped her hands. "Oh, yes! Tell it!"

Lynn wrinkled her nose. "It's a long story, and you two have heard it before."

"You could tell it a hundred times and I wouldn't get tired of it," said Elizabeth.

"It is all right with me," Cyril agreed.

"But Suzanne told me last week that she doesn't want to know too much about Devon in case she gives us a reading someday," Lynn countered.

I gave a dismissive wave of my hand. "Don't worry about that. He proved his presence here this evening. I'm sure he'll still have plenty to tell me in a reading."

"But this has to do with how he passed," Lynn said.

I shifted my awareness to our unseen guests and tuned in. *What do you think?* I asked Devon silently. In my mind's eye, I saw a big thumb's-up.

"He says, *'Go for it.'*"

Lynn and Jeff regarded each other. Neither spoke as a mix of emotions flashed across their faces. In perfect unison, they took a deep breath.

"Do you want to start?" Lynn asked.

"No," Jeff said, shaking his head, "you go first. It's your bird."

CHAPTER 7

Devon

§

Lᴙɴɴ Hᴏʟʟᴀʜᴀɴ ʜᴀᴅ ɴᴇᴠᴇʀ sᴘᴇɴᴛ any time around little boys. Pregnant for the first time, she was sure she was having a girl. She was wrong. She and Jeff brought baby Devon home from the hospital and laid him on the bed to remove his wet diaper. As she reached for a dry one, a warm wet stream hit her in the chest. The new mother fell to the floor, half laughing, half crying.

What have I gotten myself into? she wondered. *What am I going to do with this boy?*

To her surprise, she learned how much fun boys could be, and Devon was a joy. As early as two, he displayed a wicked sense of humor and soon became the clown of the family. As he grew older, he balanced his antics with a keen intellect. He loved to tease his parents and younger sister Kelsey with games of mental jousting. An expert debater, he reveled in challenging his family at the dinner table. He could easily play both sides of any issue, no matter his personal beliefs.

When it came to school, Devon had little interest in busywork. If he felt a teacher were giving him an assignment just to keep him occupied, he earned C's. Give him a challenge, and he buckled down. In college, he chose to major in economics, figuring there were worse things in life than a degree from the University of Arizona's Eller School of Business. But his heart was never in it. Recognizing Devon's potential, his professor offered him a position as teacher's assistant. After mastering the initial challenge of putting on a tie, Devon embraced his new teaching role.

Fresh from college, but with no real interest in the business world, he moved back home to figure out his next step. Lynn suggested the possibility of TEFL—Teaching English as a Foreign Language— but this seemed to be just one of several options.

In June, she and Jeff left with three couples for a ten-day trip to the British Virgin Islands. When they returned, Devon surprised them by announcing, "I've made a commitment to a TEFL program in Prague."

The abruptness of his decision startled his parents. The family had always enjoyed traveling, however. Lynn and Jeff had visited the Czech Republic two years earlier and shared their experiences and photos with the children upon their return. To Devon, Prague sounded like a lot more fun than hanging out in Arizona.

Fully supportive of their son's decision, Lynn and Jeff bought him a round-trip ticket to Prague. "If you love it and want to stay," Jeff told his son, "we can blow off the return portion of the ticket. Just do what your heart tells you."

Devon flew to Prague and rented an apartment with two fellow students in the TEFL training program. He fell in with a great group of friends and truly blossomed. The date of his return flight came and went. He completed the six-week course and remained in Prague, doing what he'd been trained for.

As a private English tutor, he juggled several jobs, often asking his mother for advice about handling his sometimes rambunctious students. When two friends from Colorado visited him on a trip to Europe in early November, they reported to Jeff and Lynn that Devon was happier than they'd ever seen him.

Twice a week, Jeff and Lynn either called or Skyped with their son in Prague. Lynn remembers their conversation on the Thursday before Thanksgiving. It was a typical chat—sharing the latest news and what they'd each been up to, nothing out of the ordinary. Devon mentioned that the cousin of one of his friends was in Prague.

"His name is Josh," Devon said. "He invited me to a concert in Frankfurt this weekend. It's an American band called 'Portugal the Man.'"

"That's a strange name," Lynn said, "but it sounds like fun." She told him she loved him as they said goodbye. And then, just as Jeff had when he and Devon spoke the day before, she told him how proud they were of him.

When Lynn and Jeff placed their weekly Sunday call and Devon failed to answer, they thought little of it, figuring he might have stayed in Frankfurt, or perhaps was out with friends. They went back to watching the Denver Broncos game with Jeff's mother.

When the phone rang in the fourth quarter, Jeff answered. The voice on the far end was so garbled he almost hung up, assuming it was a prank. Instead, he walked outside, and the reception improved. The voice was not one he recognized. The young man on the line then identified himself as Devon's new friend, Josh.

"Mr. Hollahan," Josh said, "I have some bad news."

A squiggly feeling ran through Jeff's body. He waited.

"Devon and I came to Frankfurt last night for a concert," Josh went on. "After the show we went to dinner with the band. We were heading back to our hostel, and I walked on a little ahead. When I turned around, Devon was gone."

"What do you mean, 'gone'?" Jeff demanded.

There was a pause, and then Josh explained. "I looked, but I couldn't find him. I thought he might have gone back to the hostel, but by morning there was still no sign of him. I came back to Prague, thinking he might have caught a different train, but no one had seen him."

Jeff thanked Josh for the call and returned to the den. He refused to allow himself to believe that anything bad might have happened to his son. Calmly he shared the news with Lynn and his mother. They immediately thought of their good friends, Franz and Monica, who lived in the house behind theirs. A native German, Franz had worked for Marriott Hotels as head of their European and Middle East divisions. He was very familiar with Frankfurt, the location of his corporate office.

Summoned, Franz and Monica came right away, and Franz placed a call to the Frankfurt Police. Lynn and Jeff stood beside him, listening in from their end, but could not understand a word of the conversation. When Franz hung up, he condensed the ten-minute call into one brief, discouraging message: "They say that since Devon is an adult, if he chooses to disappear, he can disappear." Franz shook his head. "I'm afraid they won't be much help."

The policy of the police was understandable, but they didn't know Devon. He had no reason to simply disappear.

"Don't worry," Franz said to Lynn and Jeff. "We'll call Hugo. He has connections in Frankfurt."

Franz and Monica had hosted the ten-day sailing trip in the British Virgin Islands that Jeff and Lynn were on when Devon signed up for the TEFL program. On that vacation they were joined by two other couples. One of the men, Franz's friend Hugo, was a prominent political writer for a German publication, splitting his time between Frankfurt and Berlin, and had friends in high places, including Frankfurt's chief of police.

Hugo called the police chief's personal number and made a case for Devon. "I know these people," Hugo said. "They're not fabricating a story. This is not normal behavior for their son. I would take it as a personal favor if you would do some investigating."

The phone calls completed, there was little more could be done this late on a Sunday night. Lynn left Jeff searching the Internet downstairs and crawled into bed. Sleep would not come. By now they should have heard from Devon.

As she stared wide-eyed at the ceiling, a ball of bright white light entered the bedroom through the decorative glass above the door. Her eyes followed the glowing orb as it moved from right to left across the room. It was unlike anything she'd ever seen, as solid as a miniature sun. It flew with direction and purpose, exiting the bedroom through the outside window.

Had the experience been only visual, Lynn might have chalked it up to her imagination. At the same time that she saw the light, however, the word "river" popped into her head. She searched her memory. Nothing in her recent experience concerned a river. With a sinking feeling that she could not explain or deny, Lynn understood why she'd heard it: Devon was gone, and he was in a river.

She got out of bed immediately and went downstairs. "Jeff," she said without preamble, "where's the river?"

He gave her a puzzled look. "What are you talking about?"

"Is there a river in Frankfurt?" She had no idea. She had never been to Frankfurt or studied its geography.

Jeff nodded towards a map of the city he had already pulled up on the computer screen. "Yes, there's a river. Why are you asking?"

"Devon is in the river," Lynn replied. She described what she had just experienced in the bedroom.

Jeff shook his head and pointed at the map. "Here's the Main River, and here's where the concert was. Devon wasn't even close to the river. It's not an option."

"Devon is in the river," Lynn insisted.

"How could you know that?" Jeff asked. Lynn shrugged, her lips a thin line.

"I just know."

She returned alone to the bedroom and somehow fell asleep. When she awoke in the morning, reality set in: The phone hadn't rung. Her son was missing.

That's when the shaking started. And the pacing. Her adrenaline flowed nonstop. Walking back and forth was how she coped with it.

Jeff became a man on a mission. He paid no heed to Lynn's intuition. He hadn't seen the ball of light or heard the ominous message about the river. He still believed that Devon was out there—that something had happened to his son, and that Devon needed someone to rescue him.

It did not occur to Jeff to call a radio or television station, but Devon had a friend in Prague whose mother worked for a CBS news affiliate. The friend put her mother in touch with Jeff, and she along with a reporter friend advised him to get the word out on a local level. If the story got picked up by the national news, they told him, it had a chance of spreading to Europe.

Jeff had no wish to be in the limelight. But he wanted as many eyes as possible on the lookout for his son. He and Kelsey gathered photos of Devon and details of his disappearance, distributing them as directed. As predicted, the news media came to the rescue.

It might have been the time of year, the fact that Thanksgiving is all about family. Once the story of a family whose son had gone missing the week before Thanksgiving hit the local airwaves, it spread like a western wildfire to the national outlets.

Jeff spoke with CBS and ABC. The day before Thanksgiving, NBC did a phone interview with him. When they asked to send a film crew to the house the next day and film Lynn cooking a turkey, she and Jeff agreed, hoping it might help their cause.

That Wednesday, while Jeff was dealing with the media, Lynn followed a hunch. She had never consulted a psychic, but something nudged her to call a local metaphysical bookstore which happened to be hosting a psychic that day. With a photo of Devon and a piece of his clothing in hand, she headed for the store.

The psychic held Devon's things and said, "Your son will be fine, but it will take you four weeks to find him."

Lynn took the man's words to mean that Devon was alive. It was the first glimmer of hope she'd had in days. In spite of her experience with the ball of light, she wasn't ready to accept what the inner voice had told her. From that moment, *Devon is fine* became her mantra.

Having the camera crew in her house on Thanksgiving Day didn't upset Lynn; on the contrary, it gave her something to do. The close-up as she put the turkey in the oven didn't capture her trembling, nor could the microphone pick up her nonstop mental monologue: *We'll find you, Devon. You're fine. I don't know where you are, and I don't know what happened, but you're fine.*

After early morning appearances on all three networks Friday morning, Jeff spoke with the head of security at his firm, Morgan Stanley, where he worked as a financial analyst. His company, he learned, was in daily contact with various law enforcement organizations in Europe, including Interpol and the police in Frankfurt and Prague.

"You've probably done as much as you can to help spread the word through the media from here," the chief of security told Jeff. "It's time to get you over to Frankfurt."

Jeff arranged to fly out the next day. The last-minute flight proved costly, so Lynn and Kelsey agreed to join him a few days later when they could get a more reasonable rate.

For the seven days since Devon had disappeared, Jeff had filled every waking moment trying to find his son. Once aboard the flight, with no phone or Internet connection, he fell asleep before the wheels left the runway, awakening only when the jet touched down in Germany.

Television viewers across Germany who watched the news that evening saw a tall man in a black jacket with a small backpack and gray ball cap walking through Frankfurt airport. Accompanying him on each side was a government official.

"The father of missing American Devon Hollahan has come to help the Frankfurt Police find his son," said the announcer. The camera then zoomed in on a headshot of Jeff with microphones thrust in his face.

"I'm here to do whatever I can to help find my son," he said. "There's still no word as to where he might be. I'm hoping to get an update today. At this point I feel I've done all I can back in the States to get his picture and description out over the airwaves."

A camera panned the nightclub where Devon had attended the concert one week before, while the newscaster described his last known activities. Once again Jeff's face filled the screen:

"After this long a period of time you think the worst. You think that something has happened to him, that he may not be in a good place, so we're all terrified. We're scared, and confused, and looking forward to getting some answers."

The cameras showed a silver sedan leaving the airport as the announcer reported, "Before leaving for the US Consulate, Hollahan gave an emotional plea for Devon to get in touch."

"Devon," Jeff said, looking at the camera, "if you see this, I hope you're well, and just know that we're doing everything we can to bring you safely home."

He paused for the briefest of moments, ending with, "Your family is really ready to see you."

The State Department official escorted Jeff to the Marriott. After years of working for the J.W. Marriott Company, his friend Franz had recommended the hotel as the best place for Jeff to stay. Feeling scruffy and bedraggled after his long trip, Jeff knew that he didn't present the best of appearances. At the reception desk in the hotel lobby, he identified himself and handed over his credit card, prepared to stay as long as it took to find Devon, no matter the cost.

"Welcome, Mr. Hollahan," the clerk said, and held up a finger, "If you will kindly wait a moment. . . . "

The clerk walked away, returning a few minutes later with a man in a dark suit and a hotel name tag. He came around the counter and shook Jeff's hand. "Welcome to the Marriott Frankfurt, Mr. Hollahan. I am the hotel's general manger. I'm very sorry for the circumstances that have brought you to our hotel, and I want you to know that as long as you are here, you and your party are guests of the Marriott."

He returned Jeff's credit card unused and escorted him to the top floor of the hotel. He then gave Jeff a key to the Club Lounge and explained that the entire floor had been cleared of guests and would henceforth serve as the command center in the search for Devon.

Such acts of kindness became commonplace. Word spread throughout the hotel, and once Lynn and Kelsey arrived two days later, the Hollahans and the staff of the Marriott became like family.

Until she could join him, however, Lynn continued to pace the floor and repeat her mantra, "Devon is fine. Devon is fine." And yet all the while, her mind kept taking her back to the ball of light and the word "river." Try as she might, she could not reconcile the fact that if Devon truly were fine, he would surely have called.

She made a Skype call to Jeff the night he arrived in Frankfurt. As he spoke she noticed a peculiar gesture: he kept raking the fingers of each hand from the center of his brow outward toward the temples. She had never seen him do such a thing, and she asked about it.

"What are you doing to your forehead?"

"I don't know. Why? What am I doing?" Jeff asked.

"With your fingers. You keep making this funny gesture."

"I didn't know I was doing it," Jeff said, dropping his hands to his lap.

An hour later, the phone rang at the house. When Lynn answered, a woman on the line stated, "Hello, my name is Debra Martin. I'm a medium, and your husband's father is trying to communicate with him through his forehead."

Lynn did a double take. She had never spoken with a medium, though she knew that mediums communicate with those who have passed, and indeed, Jeff's father had crossed to the other side. When Debra mentioned Jeff's forehead so soon after Lynn noticed her husband's unusual gestures, she gave the medium her full attention.

At the time of Debra's call, Kelsey was in the house, as was Lynn's sister. Wanting privacy, Lynn took the phone into her bedroom closet, closed the door, and crouched on the floor.

Debra explained that Lynn's friend Pam had come to her for a reading the day Devon disappeared and told her about the family's tragic mystery. She didn't mention any communication with Devon, and Lynn didn't ask. Mediums, as Lynn understood it, only connected with dead people, and the psychic had told her, "Devon is fine." The two women talked for a while, exchanging stories about their children and family life. Debra ended the call by letting Lynn know that she would stay in touch.

"And there's something I'm supposed to tell you," Debra added. "The blackbird will tell you the answer."

Lynn let out a little nervous laugh. "Okay . . . " She let her voice trail off, but inside she wondered, *What's that supposed to mean? . . . some bird is going to tell me the answer.*

She thanked Debra and hung up. In the darkness of the closet, with nothing to distract her, she could no longer deny what her heart was telling her—the same as the light had done a week ago. Devon was in the river.

She crawled out of the closet, but the darkness stayed with her. Sensing her distress, Debra Martin had suggested she contact her doctor for some anti-anxiety medicine. By this point, Lynn knew that she was incapable of taking care of herself, and she complied. Fortunately, the pills were in her purse two days later when she and Kelsey checked in for their flight to Germany. A normal glitch with their luggage that she would have handled easily any other time set her off and she began to sob. Once she started, she couldn't stop.

Stunned by her mother's very public meltdown, Kelsey whispered, "Mom, where's your medicine? You need one of those pills."

Lynn took the tablet and boarded the plane with her daughter. The next thing she knew, she was debarking in Frankfurt. She remembered nothing of the flight from Phoenix. She had no recollection of changing planes in Philadelphia. She was functionally unconscious for the whole trip, which was exactly what she needed.

Debra Martin became her long-distance lifeline, a compassionate listener with whom Lynn could safely share her deepest feelings and fears. Unwilling to let her family and friends see what a dark place she was in, she resisted talking to them about Devon. Instead, she and Debra spoke and emailed regularly.

Over the following weeks, life for the Hollahans took on a rhythm. Members of the press followed Jeff around, asking for interviews. He appeared on the local news or in the newspaper almost nightly. His sister Beth, who had spent most of her life working overseas and had a network of colleagues and friends in Frankfurt, flew in from Kazakhstan and settled into the room across the hall.

They designed flyers and found a shop to print them. It was hard not to look at Devon's boyish face on the posters with his big grin and bright round eyes and not feel a clench in the gut. A group of volunteers showed up in the Marriott lobby on the first night the flyers were ready. Armed with tape and pushpins, they began posting bills on their way home. Every night thereafter, eight to ten people would stop by to pick up flyers and post them along a different route through the city.

Jeff visited the corporate office of Morgan Stanley in Frankfurt and introduced himself. The managing directors, by now familiar with Devon's story, offered their assistance. "We think what makes sense is to get search parties to go out at night," they said. "Let's talk to the young people face to face and share what we know."

Their generosity stunned Jeff. In early December, the sun would not rise in Frankfurt until nine in the morning and would set by three. A heavy cloud covering gave the skies a perpetual pall and left the temperatures frigid. Sixty high-level employees and their spouses, including one of the senior Morgan Stanley executives in Europe, showed up in the Marriott lobby that first night to head out into the bitter cold, not returning until 2:00 AM.

No one complained about the low temperature or the late hour. Instead, many returned night after night to join in the search. Several volunteers stopped by the hotel in the mornings to grab more flyers. Those who took a train home from work would jump off at each stop to post a bill on the platform, then jump back on the train before the doors closed. During the day, Jeff went out with his sister and others to canvas different parts of town. After a short while, it was hard to go anywhere in Frankfurt without seeing a picture of Devon on a light post or street sign.

Lynn and Kelsey spent their days differently. With each hour that passed without hearing Devon's voice, their anxiety increased. Sensing their need to escape the constant stress, new friends would call and take them out to eat, to visit museums, to shop. One American couple smuggled their pup into the hotel to give them a sorely needed "dog fix."

Some of those who called to offer their help sounded other-worldly to Lynn. The only way she knew to describe the callers was that to her, they sounded like angels.

Two friends of Devon's arrived to help with the search. His roommate Carrie from Prague stayed the better part of a week. An Irishman named Domhnall, who graduated from the same TEFL class, heard that Devon was missing and flew in at his own expense from New Zealand.

Domhnall preferred to stay at a local youth hostel rather than accept the Marriott's hospitality. Each morning he showed up at breakfast and stayed till he bid the Hollahans goodnight at 9:00. He had the uncanny ability to know when someone needed a hug or when they just needed space to be by themselves. Some days his only job was to take Lynn and Kelsey out to the countryside as a diversion from the relentless uncertainty of Devon's absence.

The days turned into weeks. Lynn maintained regular contact with Debra Martin. Nearly every time they spoke Debra reiterated her prophetic statement: "The blackbird will tell you the answer."

Lynn still didn't understand what the phrase meant. Walking the streets of Frankfurt, she saw very few blackbirds. When she did, she would look at it and ask, "Are you my bird? Are you going to tell me the answer?" When no response came, she would shrug and say, "Not my bird."

She had always loved birds, and the fact that a bird would deliver the answer she sought seemed significant. Over the years, she often talked about getting an African Grey parrot. Raised in captivity, the breed can live as long as 50 years. It became a private joke with the kids. Each time Lynn announced, "I'm going to get a bird," Devon would reply, "I'm not taking that bird when you die, you know!" The kids had even begun to tease her with, "Mom's going to become The Crazy Bird Lady!"

She knew Jeff and Kelsey questioned her sanity when she talked to the birds on the streets of Frankfurt, and she couldn't help but notice the irony. *Have I already become that crazy lady, talking to birds?* She felt her life spinning out of control, but Debra's cryptic message gave her something to hang onto.

Mediums who learned of Devon's disappearance started calling out of the blue. They called from the United States and as far away as Poland and Russia. Contrary to anything Josh had seen, all the mediums reported sensing three to four people around Devon the night he disappeared. They all said that at least two of them were men. Even Debra's young daughter, not yet ten years old but born with the same gift as her mother, reported seeing four people approaching Devon in the dark that night. All had visions of him either falling into the Main River or being pushed.

Lynn received a call from a man who identified himself as Chuck Bergman, a former police officer in Florida who now worked as a medium. Chuck used his abilities to help with missing persons cases. He was the first medium to inform the Hollahans that Devon was indeed gone.

He mentioned family memories in New Jersey and in Boston that he could not have known about. He said Devon was showing him a birthday cake. Kelsey's 21st birthday and Lynn's 50th were both weeks away. Chuck said that Devon's body would be found, and the news would come in the morning, not at night.

By then, the Hollahans knew in their hearts that Devon would not be found alive. The supporting evidence that Chuck provided gave them reason to trust that he had connected with their son not from Germany, but from across the veil.

He referenced a stone wall with a river, and said that a bird was able to watch what was happening. "And one final thing," Chuck said as he ended the conversation. "The raven will tell you the answer."

Shortly after this prophetic call, Jeff attended one of his regular meetings with the Frankfurt police. The detective in charge of Devon's case ominously asked Jeff what size shoe Devon wore. Jeff couldn't help but recall that Chuck Bergman had mentioned something about Devon's footwear. The information meant nothing to them at the time. Now, the reference took on great significance when the police informed Jeff they had found a shoe that matched one worn in a photo taken of Devon the night he disappeared.

The shoe, the detective said, had been found in the river.

An investigator hired by Morgan Stanley had told Jeff that until they found a body, not to give up. Ever. They still hadn't found a body, but Jeff could not ignore the mounting evidence. With broken hearts, he and Lynn decided to start wrapping things up and head home. To return to Arizona without Devon was unthinkable, but their lives had been put on hold for too long.

Seeking closure and wanting to feel closer to Devon, Jeff, Lynn, Kelsey, and Domhnall flew to Prague. There they endured the painful process of packing up Devon's belongings from his apartment. Later, they spent a bittersweet evening with a group of Devon's friends. They shared laughter and tears over stories that provided much-needed healing to all who had been deeply touched by knowing the young man.

Before leaving the city, Jeff, Lynn, Kelsey, Carrie, and Domhnall climbed the hill to the medieval castle overlooking the city. There they entered the nave of St. Vitus Cathedral. The sun shining through the stained-glass windows sent dappled rays of blue, red, and yellow onto the massive stone walls. In hushed wonder, they soaked up the holiness of the sacred surroundings. It was the perfect balm for their aching hearts.

As they prepared to leave and begin their long journey home, Jeff's cell phone vibrated in his pocket. Recognizing his sister Beth's phone number, he stepped outside to answer.

"Jeff," Beth said, "I got a call from a woman who saw the flyers."

Jeff held his breath. "What did she say?"

"She said she saw what happened that night."

"Say that again."

"She said she was there, Jeff. She called from an untraceable number, and she wouldn't give her name, but she said she was there and that there were two guys—"

"And?"

"And that Devon either fell or was pushed into the river."

Until that moment, even though he knew it was highly unlikely, Jeff had believed in his heart that they would be bringing Devon back home. The phone call provided the most unwelcome of news. To receive it on the holy grounds of St. Vitus Cathedral made it somehow bearable.

He walked back into the nave and shared what he had learned. The small group cried and hugged and cried some more, then headed down the hill.

Once the decision was made to return home, the Hollahans couldn't leave quickly enough. Friends arranged their flight to the United States two days after their return to Germany. On their final afternoon in the country, Lynn suddenly announced, "I want to go to the river. I need to go there before we leave."

It was a dark, dreary, typical December day, perfectly befitting the mood of the family. They made the somber fifteen-minute walk completely in silence.

Kelsey stayed at street level while Jeff and Lynn crossed from the sidewalk down to the stone wall at the river's edge. They stood about ten feet apart, lost in their thoughts. Suddenly a large blackbird flew down and landed three feet from Lynn. She stared at him and felt her heart stir when the bird stared back.

In that moment, she knew. *You're my bird,* she said silently, *and you're telling me the answer.*

In response, the bird looked at the river, and Lynn did the same. With tears rolling down her cheeks, she prayed that Jeff was watching their exchange, unsure whether what she was experiencing was real or her imagination.

Jeff was, indeed, taking it all in. The photos he took memorialized a magical event that did not end with one serendipitous glance at the water. The blackbird continued his back and forth glances. He looked at Lynn, and then he looked at the river. Again he looked at Lynn, and then looked at the river, repeating the robotic motion as if remotely controlled.

She and Jeff lost track of time until, crying hard now, Lynn announced, "I have to go touch the river. I have to put my hand in the water."

She walked about twenty feet to a break in the wall where three steps led down to a small platform at the river's edge. There, she knelt down, reached out, and dipped her trembling hand into the cool water. As she did so, the bird flew to within a wing's length from her side. He dipped his beak into the ripples caused by her fingertips, and took a drink.

Chuck Bergman had spoken of a stone wall with a river and a bird that was able to watch what was happening. The bright white orb that flew through Lynn's bedroom the night Devon disappeared spoke to her soul about the river, but it planted questions in her mind. The blackbird took those questions away once and for all.

The psychic in Phoenix had told Lynn, "*Your son will be fine, but it will take you four weeks to find him.*"

Lynn had interpreted "your son will be fine" to mean that Devon was alive. Perhaps all the signs, the synchronicities, the evidence from mediums, and the surreal behavior of the blackbird were Devon's way of showing her that he was, indeed, fine, albeit in another dimension.

The blackbird will tell you the answer.

She stood and rejoined Jeff. Arm in arm they walked back to Kelsey, knowing now with certainty that their lives were forever changed, that they would have to learn to live as a family of three. Without telling Kelsey what had just transpired, they began to walk back to the hotel.

A loud whooshing sound drew their attention skyward. In all the days that Lynn had been looking for her bird, blackbirds of any type had remained strangely absent. Her bird had come to her and brought her the answer she sought. In an unforgettable encore that seemed choreographed from above, hundreds of blackbirds lifted off the rooftops from both sides of the broad boulevard. They swooped in from left and right, converging directly overhead, and flew in formation to the river.

The police found Devon's body while the Hollahans were on their flight home. They pulled him out of the river, four weeks to the day after he disappeared.

CHAPTER 8

Take the Ride

§

EVERY GOOD STORY HAS ITS highs and lows, its joys and sorrows. The aspect of the story one chooses to focus upon determines one's peace.

Each of us listening to Devon's story at the Hollahan's dinner party had experienced every parent's greatest fear. We nodded empathically as Jeff and Lynn spoke of their son's passing; then we each chose to focus on the magic.

"The blackbirds were definitely a miracle," I confirmed.

"Tell them your definition of a miracle," Ty urged.

"It's when the physical and non-physical worlds merge in a way that strikes us powerfully, deep in our inner being. When the veil lifts enough to reveal a greater reality, and we recognize how we are all part of it."

Elizabeth agreed. "Devon's story is one of the most validating ones I've heard."

"I'm sure Morgan has sent you your share of miracles," I said, "and that you hear about them from parents in your group all the time."

"Like the butterflies in your book," she replied. "I know how you and Ty appreciate the sacred quality of the events that occurred after Susan passed."

Ty nodded seriously. "Definitely."

I caught his eye and gently rubbed my cheek, reminding him of Susan's presence tonight. He smiled his understanding.

"Those miracles that happened after Devon disappeared," Lynn interjected. "I had to be the one the mediums came to. Jeff and Kelsey would not have been open to it."

"How about now?" I asked, turning to Jeff, but Lynn answered with a laugh.

"Now he's more into the spiritual path than I am."

Jeff shrugged. "Buy the ticket, take the ride."

I cocked my head. "Where did I just see that?"

Everyone chuckled at once and pointed in unison to a spot over my right shoulder. When I turned, I had to join in the laughter. A four-foot marble slab stood no more than ten feet behind me with the words "Buy the ticket, take the ride" painted in large black letters across the face. The word "Believe" adorned a smaller slab that served as a base for the unusual monument.

"What's that about?" Ty asked.

"Lynn's dad is a sculptor," Jeff said. "He wanted to create a memorial for Devon, and the phrase is one I used in his Celebration of Life."

"Is it something Devon used to say?" I asked.

"No, I found the quote after he passed. But it has a double meaning that's relevant to all of us."

"Who's it attributed to?" Ty asked.

"Hunter S. Thompson," Jeff replied, "from his book *Fear and Loathing in Las Vegas.*"

Ty shook his head. "I'm not familiar with him."

Jeff laughed. "I shouldn't think you would be, Captain. His books are a record of his wild travels and drug-soaked adventures. He's credited with popularizing 'gonzo journalism,' where the writer inserts his own opinions into the news he reports."

Ty rolled his eyes. "What I wouldn't give to go back to the days of Walter Cronkite."

"Devon was into that kind of thing?" I asked, confused by Jeff's mention of drugs and wild adventures. The spirit of their son standing with us at the party didn't match the character Jeff was describing.

Jeff shook his head. "He was a voracious reader, and he liked all kinds of literature. You never knew what was going to show up in his backpack. He loved Shakespeare and Stephen Hawking. He was reading a popular economics book by Nassim Taleb when he left for Germany."

"Anything he could get his hands on," said Lynn.

"I was going through his effects, trying to figure out what to say at his Celebration of Life," Jeff went on, "and I saw the Hunter S. Thompson book. I hadn't read it, and I wanted to know more. I searched him online, and when the quote *'Buy the ticket, take the ride'* came up, I thought, *Oh, jeez, that's perfect.*"

"Because—" Lynn prompted him with a wave.

"Because Devon loved roller coasters. That's the double meaning for us."

"It wasn't just Devon," said Lynn dryly.

Jeff shot her a tolerant smile. "It started when we took the kids to Busch Gardens, in Florida. Devon was about 10 or 12. He wanted to ride this big steel roller coaster called The Manta. I knew neither of the girls would go with him, and I didn't want him to go alone. It sure wasn't my first choice, but I took the ride with him. And I was hooked."

Recounting the memory, Jeff's face brightened like a twelve-year-old's. He went on to share how the family spent the next eight years traveling the United States and beyond searching for the biggest and fastest roller coasters they could find. They went to Australia, New Zealand, China, and Japan, where they rode one of the country's biggest roller coasters in Tokyo.

"That part of the quote reflects Devon's love of hanging over the edge of the world on a ridiculously fast and tall coaster."

He gazed across the patio, suddenly miles away. Accustomed to sensing others' thoughts, I could almost hear the clickety-clack of wheels as he and Devon ascended to the crest of some frightening first incline.

"It sounds like that phrase has become your philosophy of life," said Ty.

Jeff and Lynn locked eyes. "We've talked about how grateful we are that we didn't put things off," said Lynn.

"Yes, it was expensive," Jeff added, "and yes, I missed a lot of work, but we took advantage of what was given to us. We always took the opportunity to travel with the family instead of leaving the kids at home."

"Sounds like you two," Ty said, glancing at Cyril and Elizabeth.

"Yes, our children are very comfortable traveling overseas," Cyril affirmed.

"You've seen a lot of the world, too," Elizabeth said. "I know from your book that you even sailed across the Atlantic Ocean."

"Really?" Jeff said as we nodded.

"How cool is that!" Lynn exclaimed.

I smiled. "I have to admit, it was quite an adventure."

"You're sailors, too," Ty said, referring to their charter trip to the British Virgin Islands.

Jeff scoffed. "A week in the BVI doesn't compare to sailing across the ocean."

"I love sailing," said Elizabeth dreamily.

"Me, too," Lynn agreed.

"And Cyril is a sailor," Elizabeth added, patting him on the knee. "He grew up waterskiing on a lagoon in Ivory Coast."

Cyril simply smiled and nodded.

"You travel around by bus now," Jeff said to Ty. "Do you miss the boat?"

"Sometimes," Ty admitted, "but I love the mountains, too."

Ty was being modest, I told them. Fourteen of his 26 years in the Navy had been spent at sea. He was more at home on the water than on land. As much as he loved hiking and backpacking in the mountains, I knew that he would be quite content to still be cruising full-time on a sailboat.

After Susan passed we took a temporary hiatus from sailing, but fully planned to return to it full-time. When I discovered my abilities as a medium, our lives went off in an unexpected direction. Traveling around the country these days to help people through my work didn't leave much time for sailing.

"We chartered a boat in Nice once," Ty said to Cyril. "It was one of the best vacations we ever had."

"And our first charter trip was in the BVI, just like yours," I said to Lynn and Jeff, "but we sailed on a monohull, not a catamaran."

We launched into a discussion of the merits of twin-hulled boats with their inherent stability and roomy staterooms. We agreed that sailing a catamaran wasn't as exciting as a monohull, but the comfort and space were incomparable.

Ty suddenly raised his wineglass high. "I think we should all charter a catamaran in the BVI."

I turned in surprise. Our schedule was packed, and a charter vacation would be a major expense. Certainly we had enjoyed talking about sailing, but suggesting a vacation with four relative strangers was the last thing I expected him to do.

Then I remembered one of my prime workshop teachings: We tend to take credit for thoughts that pop unexpectedly into our mind. Few of us realize how many of those thoughts are put there by our guides and loved ones on the other side.

I had to agree Ty's idea was a fine one, but was it the wine speaking or had our kids in spirit put him up to it?

As everyone else responded to Ty's suggestion with enthusiasm, I shifted my focus, tuning in to Morgan, Devon, and Susan. In my mind's eye, I saw a giant thumbs-up—my unmistakable sign for "yes." The image came with a *zing* of encouragement and joyous excitement.

I smiled at the group, "This is a setup."

Conversation stopped as all eyes turned to me. "From our kids. They think it's a great idea. In fact, I think it's their idea to begin with."

Elizabeth clapped her hands. "Oh, my goodness! Of course! And they'll come with us, I'm sure!"

Lynn and Jeff looked at each other. "Count us in."

"We should do it," I agreed.

"Of course we should," Ty replied, looking proud of himself for suggesting it. "It'll be great."

I turned to Lynn, "You had four couples on your trip, right?"

"That's right. Plus a captain and cook."

"We won't need a captain with Ty onboard," said Elizabeth, and my heart swelled.

Ty dodged the praise. "We'll have room for a fourth couple. Charter catamarans usually have four cabins, each with its own head."

"Oh!" I said, clapping my hands like Elizabeth, "I know the perfect couple: Irene and Tony Vouvalides!"

"Irene!" Elizabeth exclaimed with equal excitement. "Perfect! She's the one who led me to you—I just love her!"

"Wait until you meet her in person," I said. "You'll all love her, and Tony is a real sweetheart."

"A sailor, too," Ty said. "In fact, he's building a sailboat in his garage."

The air buzzed with high-voltage energy as we discussed dates, weather, food options, and potential anchorages. By the end of the evening, what had seemed like an offhand remark felt like a done deal.

"You're all really serious about this, right?" I asked, with fingers crossed. "Because I know Ty. He'll leave here tonight and spend the next month planning every single detail."

Everyone nodded their heads and responded in unison.

"Absolutely!"

"You bet!"

"Of course!"

"Mais, oui!"

"Buy the ticket, take the ride," Jeff recounted. "We never pass up an opportunity to travel and connect with others."

"For us," Lynn said, "it's all about being with friends, making new friendships, just getting out and being engaged in life." She raised her glass.

"Sounds good to us," Ty said, as the rest of us lifted our glasses in the air.

"I'm ready to buy the ticket!" I said.

"And celebrate our kids," Elizabeth said.

"Since it was their idea," I said with a grin.

We bid everyone goodnight and headed back to the bus. I checked the time on the dashboard and did a double take. Four hours with our new friends had seemed far shorter. The bonds we had formed in such a brief period were unparalleled in my experience.

On two separate occasions, Ty and I had spent a week sailing with friends we thought we knew well. Both times, I realized within the first day that we'd made a grave mistake. It's one thing to enjoy someone's company; quite another to be confined on a sailboat, where dissonant energies amplify and quickly become apparent. With no easy escape route, relationships can deteriorate faster than the weather.

Despite these two challenging experiences, I felt no trepidation at the thought of spending a week on a catamaran with the Boissons and Hollahans. On the contrary, I couldn't wait to get to know them better. I harkened back to a comment Jeff had made earlier that evening: the friendships he and Lynn had forged through Helping Parents Heal were deeper and more meaningful than any they had known prior to Devon's passing.

I knew they would feel the same way about Irene and Tony. Their daughter Carly had brought us together through the reading I gave

Irene, and we subsequently became fast friends. I smiled to myself. I hadn't felt Carly's presence that evening, but she was a frequent drop-in for me, thoroughly lovable and delightfully brazen. I had a sneaking suspicion that she was the ringleader behind the idea of the trip.

Irene and Carly enjoyed one of the closest mother-daughter bonds I'd come across in any of my readings. Knowing how deeply her mom had suffered because of her passing, Carly goes to great efforts to let Irene know she's still around.

It was too late to call Irene about the charter, but I knew without asking what her answer would be. If Carly had anything to do with it—and I clearly sensed that she did—heaven and earth would come together to get Irene and Tony onboard.

CHAPTER 9
Carly

§

THE APGAR IS A SIMPLE test performed at birth to determine if a newborn is prepared to join the world without medical assistance. The acronym refers to five indicators of health: Appearance, Pulse, Grimace, Activity, and Respiration. Carly Hughes slipped into the waiting hands of the obstetrician red-faced and howling with indignation. The doctor turned to the nurse. "No APGAR needed on this child."

Back when Carly was born, babies weren't kept in the hospital room with their mothers. On Carly's first night in the nursery, the nurse called Irene on her room phone. "Mrs. Hughes," she said, "we're going to bring Carly to you. She's screaming so much, she's keeping all the other babies awake."

A teddy bear named Sebastian—a gift from Irene's co-worker—helped baby Carly sleep. Sebastian became her nightly companion and would remain so through college and beyond. Havoc ensued one night when the little bear was nowhere to be found. Irene, her husband Richard, and Carly's grandparents stayed up late searching for Sebastian, locating him at last in the kitchen cabinet, where three-year-old Carly had forgotten she had hidden him.

A sweet and kind child who played well with anyone, Carly nevertheless never lost the vocal tendencies she displayed at birth. When her parents announced their upcoming move around the block from their Haworth, New Jersey, home, Carly let her feelings be known.

"No one asked my opinion," announced the four-year-old. "This is the house I was born in, and I'm not moving."

The family survived the move, and Carly continued to voice her desires. At the check-out counter of the local grocery store one afternoon, a colorful balloon caught Carly's eye. "This isn't a day for a treat," Irene told Carly gently but firmly. In response, her daughter threw a familiar tantrum. "Out of all the mothers in the universe," she demanded, hands on her hips, "why was I born to *you*?"

Carly's strong will was matched by her brains and beauty. A natural leader, she excelled in school from her earliest years. One day when her daughter was in second grade, Irene received a summons to the principal's office. Carly's teachers, noting the girl's fierce drive and perfectionism, were worried that her parents might be pressuring her to do well in school. Irene assured them that her daughter's ambition and focus were entirely self-generated.

In high school, Carly consistently placed in the top ten percent of her class. Her strong academics earned her partial scholarships at several universities. When she and her parents toured Boston College, Carly knew she'd found her new home. Yes, she loved the architecture and academic feel of the campus, but BC tipped the scales by meeting a critical requirement: it was the only university on the East Coast within a five-minute drive from Bloomingdale's.

Carly had no trouble making friends at Boston College, where she majored in mathematics and education. A young man who shared her last name, Mike Hughes, was taken by Carly's intelligence, vibrant energy, and striking good looks. They dated briefly, but after just two weeks, the shy freshman was overwhelmed by Carly's strong personality.

Carly and Mike remained friends. They grew closer when Irene and Richard, Carly's father, divorced. Mike's parents had recently separated, and he and Carly openly shared their conflicted emotions. During this time of disappointment and sadness, Carly remained extremely close to her mother.

As part of her education curriculum, Carly spent four semesters student teaching, during which she discovered a passion for special education. For a week during winter vacation she traveled to Natchez, Mississippi, to volunteer at the Holy Family Early Learning Center, the oldest African-American Catholic school in the United States. On her return home, she told Irene, "Mom, it feels like home there."

She had fallen in love with the children at Holy Family, affectionately referring to them as her "babies." In return, they fell in love with her. Stunned at the lack of basic supplies and instruction for children with such eagerness to learn, she kept in touch with her young friends and returned with Mike Hughes for a second week the following year.

Each time Mike turned around, Carly had another child in her arms. She sang and danced with the children and helped them with arts and crafts. On her return to BC, she organized several successful fundraisers for the school.

In Carly's sophomore year, Irene met Tony Vouvalides, a sweet and gentle widower. When Irene began dating Tony, Carly welcomed him into the family circle with her customary openness and love. She shared common ground with her mother's new beau, an elementary school principal, and often called him to discuss her student teaching lesson plans.

Tony had never witnessed a relationship as close as Carly and Irene's. Mother and daughter spoke every day, twice a day. Carly would call Irene on the way to school, and again as she prepared for bed, no matter how late.

"Does she have to call at midnight?" Tony would ask.

"She wants to say goodnight," Irene replied with a shrug.

Often on weekends Carly would return to New Jersey. The father of a grown son and daughter of his own, Tony watched as Irene carried Carly's breakfast up to her on a tray. "You're not still doing that," he would ask, shaking his head, but Irene continued to pamper her daughter.

Making no headway with Irene, he challenged Carly. "I don't get this. You're too old to be letting your mother wait on you hand and foot."

Carly pretended not to understand his concern, simply smiling sweetly and giving a little shrug, just like her mother. "She likes to do it for me."

Each time Carly returned home from Boston, she piled several Hefty bags filled with dirty laundry into the trunk. Her stated goal was to get through college without ever having to do her own laundry.

"These smell awful!" Tony complained good-naturedly as he carried them in from the car.

"I was down to three pair of underwear, so it was time to come home," Carly called over her shoulder, running into the house ahead of him.

Seeing how deeply Irene and Carly loved each other, Tony never got too upset when Irene doted on her daughter. It was easy to understand her motherly devotion. With her bubbly enthusiasm and positive attitude, Carly lit up any room she entered.

Shortly after Carly's twenty-first birthday, Tony and Irene announced their plan to get married. Carly responded by telling her mother, "You've done this before, so this wedding's not going to be about you. It's going to be about me—about my dress, and my shoes, my hair—"

In hindsight, Irene wondered if somehow Carly knew she might not get to experience a wedding of her own.

The wedding was Carly's opportunity to live out her shopping fantasies. "Come on, Mom," she said, dragging Irene into Neiman Marcus, "play along with me!"

She headed resolutely for the footwear department and requested the most expensive shoes in the inventory. Out came the Jimmy Choos, the Manolo Blahnicks, the Christian Louboutins. A dental hygienist, Irene nearly choked at the thousand-dollar price tags. But Carly played it cool. Tall, thin, blonde, and beautiful, she had the salesmen fawning over her as she test-drove the pricey pumps.

"I just can't make up my mind," she said, sitting amid the open boxes with a hand theatrically on her chin. "I'll have to come back when I have my dress, and we'll do this again."

Irene kept mum until they reached the sidewalk, at which point Carly threw back her head and let out an unrestrained squeal. "Oh, my God!" she cried. "That was so exhilarating!"

Before and after the wedding, Carly demonstrated love for Tony and quickly bonded well with his grown son and daughter. During the ceremony, she, Irene, Tony, his children, and his grandchild stood side by side.

Despite her stepfather's encouragement, Carly didn't immediately seek a teaching job after college. During one of her student teaching stints, she'd been assigned to an inner-city high school. Since she looked barely out of high school herself, the students gave her a hard time. She decided to eschew teaching for a while and use her math skills in the business world first.

She landed a job as an analyst for Visible Measures and made friends quickly with her young, hip colleagues. Irene and Tony helped her move into an apartment in Boston. But not long afterwards, she started to complain of not feeling well. Her legs kept cramping, she was losing weight, and her hair didn't feel quite right.

Irene thought her daughter's symptoms might be the result of her recent breakup with her on-again/off-again boyfriend. When their regular doctor couldn't find anything wrong, Irene sent her to an orthopedist. But the specialist had no answers, either.

Meanwhile, the family was preparing for a special trip to Hawaii. Knowing that Carly was on the Pill, Irene worried about possible blood clots and insisted that Carly be checked more thoroughly before the long flight. She sent Carly to Massachusetts General Hospital, where an ultrasound showed nothing of concern.

"I think the person who did the test was a trainee," Carly told her mother afterwards.

The pain in her legs didn't keep Carly from enjoying their vacation in Hawaii, but by the time they returned, her calves were rock hard. When a business trip to New York came up for her in August, Irene stepped in. She called a mutual friend of hers and Richard's, Dr. Roman Nowygrod, the chief vascular surgeon at Columbia Presbyterian Medical Center.

"I can't imagine what this is," Irene told Roman. "Do you think you could have a look at her?"

Irene was at work at the dental office when the doctor called. "Irene," he said grimly, "you'd better get here right away."

Tests at Columbia had revealed blood clots in Carly's leg from her ankle to her hip. One large vein was completely blocked. She was admitted immediately to the hospital. When she complained of being short of breath, X-rays of her chest showed clots in her lungs as well.

Initially the doctors felt that Irene's concern about the Pill might be valid. The long flight from Hawaii could also have exacerbated the clotting. The decision was made to surgically remove the clots in her leg and to start Carly on blood thinners.

Instead of returning to Boston when she left the hospital, Carly remained in New Jersey with Irene and Tony. She needed to use a walker to move from room to room. Every morning before leaving for work, Tony performed the unenviable task of injecting an anti-clotting serum into Carly's midsection.

Carly did her best to remain upbeat, but to Irene she admitted, "I just don't feel good, Mom."

Roman visited nightly to check on her. When she showed no signs of improving, he re-admitted her to the hospital. Tests revealed more clots; she underwent surgery in her other leg. Concerned, a team of specialists joined the search for the cause. "This is just like an episode of *House*," joked one of the interns gathered around her bed. "We're all trying to figure out what's going on with you."

A hematologist was the first to suggest they look for a tumor.

Carly's father Richard finally lost his cool. "This is really bad stuff," he uttered grimly.

In full "Mom mode," Irene waved a dismissive hand. "Don't be ridiculous. She's 23 years old and she's always been perfectly healthy. She's in the best hospital in the country and her surgeon is world-class. She'll be fine."

Released from hospital after yet another surgery, Carly went home with Irene and Tony, and Richard returned to Florida. Back and forth from home to hospital mother and daughter traveled for further testing. A PET scan showed nothing unusual. The medical team ordered an endoscopy.

On their way to New York once again, Carly looked at Irene and asked, "I *am* coming home tonight, aren't I, Mom?"

"Of course, you are," Irene replied. "They're not going to find anything."

Tony and Irene sat in the waiting room while Carly underwent the procedure. Irene prayed nonstop. Finally a nurse called them into Recovery. Carly lay on a bed in one of the far cubicles. Irene and Tony stood at her side and awaited further instructions. With each passing minute Irene's anxiety increased.

"Just a little longer," the nurse told them. "The doctor will be out shortly to talk with you."

Oh, my God, Irene thought. For the first time, she felt a shiver of real fear. *Why is everyone else getting dressed and going home?*

Dr. Markowitz, the gastroenterologist, emerged from behind a closed door, dressed in green scrubs.

"I'm afraid I have some significant news," he said.

Standing beside Carly's bed, Irene and Tony stiffened, unprepared to hear anything "significant."

"We found a tumor," Dr. Markowitz announced.

Carly grabbed Irene's hand. The words hung in the air like an ominous thundercloud.

"I don't want to say much more at this point," the doctor continued. "We need to wait for the lab results."

Irene's we-can-handle-anything attitude dissolved into full-fledged panic. All she wanted was to go back to life as they knew it. Instead, she found herself in Roman's hospital office barely able to think as Carly was readmitted for further testing.

There can't be anything wrong, she told herself silently, to keep more frightening thoughts at bay. *There can't be anything seriously wrong.*

"You'd better call Richard and tell him to come back," Roman said. "Hopefully it's just Hodgkin's."

Irene fought the urge to completely break down. Here she had been trying to convince herself that all was well, and suddenly Hodgkin's lymphoma was a best-case scenario.

"Whatever it is," she asked Roman, "can't they just operate and take it out?"

"Let's wait for the results," Roman advised.

The results came the next day: esophageal cancer.

"How can I have esophageal cancer?" Carly demanded unbelievingly. "I've never even smoked."

The family support team that gathered with Carly the following day included Irene, Tony, Carly's Aunt Judi and Uncle Bill, her Grandpa Sal, and Mike Hughes, who had become a daily presence in her life. Richard joined them by speakerphone as he drove back up to New York from Florida.

The medical team no longer consisted of interns. Now the hospital's big guns took charge: Dr. Markowitz, Roman Nowygrod, and renowned surgeons Joshua Sonett and Marc Bessler. Although the oncologist, a critical member of the team, was equally respected and qualified, his dour demeanor led Irene and her sister to refer to him privately as "The Grim Reaper."

The group met in a beautiful lounge overlooking the George Washington Bridge.

Trying to keep the mood light, the medical team described the road ahead: they would map out the tumor the next day, followed by possible surgery the day after that. The family nodded their agreement. *Do whatever it takes to make Carly better.*

Irene resumed her prayers during the tumor mapping procedure. She envisioned the tumor as a flower, mentally plucking the diseased petals away one by one. The scene took on a life of its own as the flower became a beautiful field of blossoms with Carly standing in its midst. At first, Irene imagined that she was glimpsing a vision of Carly's wedding. With sudden horror, her perception shifted, and she intuitively recognized the scene as Carly's memorial service. When she shared her premonition later with Judi and Bill, she learned that her brother-in-law had experienced an identical vision.

By the end of the week, the tumor had been mapped and the lab results were in. As the family gathered for the full report, the tension was palpable.

"I'm so sorry," intoned the Grim Reaper. "The tumor is the size of a bottlecap. It's located at the junction of Carly's esophagus and her stomach."

A mass so small didn't sound particularly scary to Irene. But when the oncologist further identified it as an adenocarcinoma, Roman exhaled and shook his head.

"I'm so sorry," he said.

"Why is everyone so sorry?" Irene asked, uncomprehending. "Tomorrow is Carly's twenty-fourth birthday. She's going to be fine, isn't she?"

Tony reached out and squeezed her leg.

The doctors shared a look, then explained Carly's predicament in greater detail. Hodgkin's lymphoma would have been a best-case diagnosis. An adenocarcinoma was the worst-case.

Irene fought to hold herself together. This kind of disaster happened to other people, not to her daughter.

Richard followed the oncologist down the hall to speak with him privately. Irene watched with horror as her ex-husband crumpled against the wall in response to what he had heard. When he approached with tears on his cheeks, Irene held up her hands.

"I don't want to hear it, Richard. She will beat this."

"You don't understand," Richard tried to reply.

Irene turned and hurried away in the opposite direction. "Keep it to yourself. Our daughter's not going anywhere!"

The doctors agreed upon a course of action: daily radiation combined with weekly chemotherapy. The goal was to shrink the tumor as much as possible before performing surgery to remove it. They held back from the family the news that adenocarcinomas are generally so deadly that surgery is not an option.

Most cases of esophageal cancer occur in men over fifty. A true girly-girl at 24 years of age, Carly became the youngest case on record.

A month of torture ensued, with daily trips to the bottom floor of the hospital for radiation. Countless times, often in silence, Irene and Carly crossed the bridge they'd viewed from the hospital lounge. Despite constant nausea, needles, and not knowing what lay ahead, Carly remained upbeat and optimistic.

When Halloween arrived, and Carly had no strength to go out, her best friend Kayla brought a private party to her. With red tutus over their pajama bottoms and devil's horns on their heads, they danced around the kitchen, poking each other with their plastic pitchforks, singing along with the stereo, acting silly and giggling as only grown girls can.

Mike Hughes continued to visit daily, whether Carly was in the hospital or at her parents' home. The strong young woman who had proven too much for him in his freshman year had become the most important person in his life. Soon neither could deny that they had fallen in love.

Carly's treatments concluded in December, allowing her to return to Boston and her apartment while she regained her strength. She came back to New Jersey to spend the holidays with her family. Irene and Tony did everything they could to maintain as much normalcy as possible.

Mike took Carly to Boston for New Year's Eve. No longer needing to endure daily radiation treatments, Carly felt better than she had in months. Filled with hope, they rang in the New Year with friends.

The surgery to remove Carly's tumor was scheduled for January 9. Everyone tried to keep the mood light. Irene and Carly bought colorful bed linens to brighten her hospital room. As a special treat, Roman arranged for a room on the ward reserved for celebrity patients. Irene dubbed it "the rock star floor."

On the night before the operation, Tony stayed at home while Irene and Richard slept on cots next to Carly's bed. The irony of spending the night with her ex-husband was not lost on Irene. Mike curled up beside Carly, sleeping upright as Carly's condition would not allow her to lie flat.

The following morning, Tony arrived with the rest of the family. Irene smothered Carly with kisses, holding back tears as they wheeled her daughter to the operating room.

Three hours into the surgery, Roman came out and addressed the waiting group. Pulling down his mask, he informed them, "The cancer is confined to the local area. But because of the amount of node involvement, we need to remove Carly's stomach."

The news hit Irene like a punch to the gut. *Remove her stomach?* She caught herself and immediately shifted gears. *Okay. That's a good thing. They'll get all the cancer out.*

After eight agonizing hours, the surgery concluded and Carly was sent to recovery for the night. After initially telling the family no visitors would be allowed, the staff relented and let Irene sit by her daughter's side. For the entire night, Irene bargained with God: *please let Carly come home and live the life she loves.*

The next day her family gathered around Carly's bed. Only then was she given the complete news of her surgery. Still groggy, Carly turned to Irene's sister and asked, "Aunt Judi, if I don't have a stomach, what's going to growl when I'm hungry?"

The stomach, the family learned with relief, is nothing more than a holding tank, where gastric juices are used to break down food. Eventually Carly would be able to eat like everyone else, albeit on a highly restricted diet.

Discharged from the hospital, Carly returned to her mother's house. The frustration of losing her independence and dealing with her many physical issues led to heated arguments between her and Irene. Tony did his best not to get caught in the crossfire. He had lived through his late wife's battle with cancer, one which she ultimately lost. Now he found himself in a marriage with challenges most couples never have to face. Instead of doting on him, Irene's attention was naturally focused on Carly. But Tony couldn't feel sorry for himself for long. Seeing the two women he loved in such pain only motivated him to do whatever he could to make their lives easier.

A week after Carly's surgery, more bad news arrived: the biopsy results from the lymph nodes surrounding Carly's stomach indicated that her cancer was now stage IV, considered incurable. Hearing this, Carly finally broke down. Her tears cut Irene's heart like a knife. The mother who had always been able to give her daughter whatever she wanted now felt completely helpless. Silently, she railed at God.

After a few minutes, Carly regained her composure and dried her tears. "Okay. I'm going to make it. I'll do what I have to do."

Mike's visits provided much-needed relief. He took over giving Carly her shots and helped with her feeding tube. He cracked jokes and acted as if these were the normal tasks of a new boyfriend.

The new couple planned to get their own apartment when Mike returned from a pre-arranged climbing trip with his father to Mt. Kilimanjaro. He considered canceling his plans, but Carly insisted that he go. Strong enough to drive the two men to the airport, Carly grew serious when it came time to send them off. "It's not goodbye," she told Mike, "just 'see ya later.'"

On February 13 Carly resumed chemotherapy. She and Irene returned to New Jersey to wait for any side effects to kick in. Thankfully, she passed a relatively easy evening. An unexpected chat with Mike, who had found an Internet café in Tanzania, lifted her spirits.

Never lacking for company, she enjoyed spending the following day with Marni, a friend from high school who was attending law school in New York City. When it came time for Marni to return to the city, Irene accompanied the girls, but Carly insisted on taking the wheel for the trip home.

"Oh, Mom, it feels so good to drive!" she exclaimed joyfully as she sped through heavy traffic. Irene fought the urge to comment on her daughter's aggressive driving, keeping her eyes closed as well as her mouth, wanting nothing to spoil her daughter's brief happiness.

When they arrived home, they stayed up late, snuggled together on the couch watching back-to-back episodes of *Hart of Dixie*. After months of turmoil, an evening with no talk of the dreaded C-word came as blessed relief.

Irene had gotten into the habit of climbing into bed each night with Carly. Since she was still unable to lie flat, they had purchased a special inclining Posturepedic.

"Mom," Carly said, "why don't you sleep with Tony tonight?"

Reluctantly Irene agreed. As she left the room, Carly called out, "I am so in the mood for pancakes. Can Tony make them for me in the morning?"

"Of course, honey," Irene said, turning back in delight. "He'll make you whatever you want."

"And will you go to Valentino's and buy Italian bread and make me prosciutto and melon?"

Irene smiled. "Anything your heart desires, Mama will get for you."

It would take hours, they knew, for Carly to get the food down, ounce by ounce, but none of that mattered. Irene felt so good to see her daughter's appetite coming to life.

Carly held out her arms. "Give me a hug."

Irene crossed the room and embraced her. As grateful as she was for this special moment, she held back, afraid to bump Carly's feeding tube and chemo port.

"Not that kind of hug," Carly said. "A real hug!"

How did I get so lucky? Irene thought, as she squeezed her daughter tightly. "I love you, Carly," she whispered.

"I love you too, Mom."

That night Irene slept better than she had in weeks. At 7:30 she got up, peeking in Carly's room as she headed downstairs. Carly was sound asleep. Irene went into the kitchen, made a cup of coffee, and carried it to her computer. A few minutes later the house phone rang. Who could be calling so early? she wondered. She was stunned to hear Carly's voice on the line, coming from her cell phone upstairs.

"Come quickly!" Carly implored. "Something is terribly wrong."

Her heart in her throat, Irene flew up the stairs. She found Carly in the bathroom, clutching the pole that carried her feeding pump. As she cried, "What's the matter?" Carly collapsed in her arms. Carefully Irene lowered her daughter to the floor, then screamed for Tony.

Hearing her distraught calls, Tony came running. Irene cushioned Carly's head with the rug. She had no idea whether the situation was serious or if Carly had simply fainted.

"Should I call 911?"

Tony took one look at Carly. "Yes, call now!"

While Irene dashed for the phone, Tony knelt beside Carly and cradled her head in his lap. "Stay with us, Carly, stay with us," he begged. She looked up at him with eyes that seemed miles away, then her head rolled to the side. At that moment Tony knew that things would never again be the same.

The next few minutes passed in a blur. Help arrived quickly, and the house was soon filled with police and EMTs. They instructed Irene to disconnect Carly's feeding tube, which she did with trembling hands. She continued to pray that Carly had simply passed out. Tony knew differently. When one of the police officers gave him a questioning look, Tony shook his head. Things did not look good.

As the EMTs worked on Carly, Irene called Roman. He recommended they take her to Englewood Hospital.

"She's not going to make it to Englewood," one of the medics said. "We have to get her to the local hospital. It's only five minutes away."

The EMTs would not permit Tony or Irene to ride in the ambulance. They followed behind, stopping when the ambulance pulled over several times during the short ride.

Forced to remain in the waiting room outside the Emergency Department, Irene paced in circles. Round and round she walked for what seemed like hours. Family and friends, summoned by frantic phone calls, arrived one after another.

Finally a doctor emerged from the double doors of the treatment area. One look at his face told them more than they wanted to know. He approached Irene and said gravely, "We need to talk."

"No!" Irene screamed, "No!"

"I'm so sorry," the doctor said, "but she's gone."

Irene whirled and began to run down the hallway. Tony went after her. The hallway seemed to spin around her. Faces and objects blurred.

"I can't do this," Irene gasped, looking beseechingly at Tony. Never, even at Carly's worst, had she allowed herself to imagine life without her daughter. Suddenly she was faced with her worst nightmare. "I can't. I just can't go on."

Tony shook his head, truly concerned about her state of mind. He knew that she meant her words literally, that she was in danger of slipping away from a reality too agonizing to bear. Desperately he searched for something to bring her back.

"What about us?" he asked. "What about our life together?"

Irene leaned into him, unable to think, taking what comfort she could from his strong frame and his arms around her. "What do we do now?" she murmured into his chest. Her mind was a fog, her future an unfathomable blankness.

From faraway she heard his answer: "We persevere. That's what we have to do. For Carly's sake, for her legacy."

Over the next painful days and weeks, the family channeled their grief into creating something positive from Carly's passing. Instead of flowers, they requested that donations be made to a fund they set up at the hospital for vascular research.

Going forward, they decided they needed something more permanent. Recalling the joy Carly found in helping the children at Holy Family Early Learning Center in Mississippi, they founded "Carly's Kids," with a twofold mission: to ensure the continued operation of the school and to raise money for digestive cancer research.

Despite their best efforts to carry on, little could fill the tremendous void caused by Carly's absence. The thought of never seeing her daughter again was unbearable for Irene. Each night she crawled into bed clutching Sebastian the Bear, Carly's lifelong companion. She held him to her nose and breathed in Carly's scent. All she could think of was joining her daughter. Fighting to maintain her sanity, she thought of her conversation with Tony in the hospital and came up with a new mantra: *Tony can't be widowed twice.*

Two months after Carly passed, Irene's former neighbors Sally and Bob came to visit. Their daughter Jane had been Carly's playmate since childhood. They presented Irene with a small package, brought back from a recent trip to Hawaii. Inside she found a letter and a delicate bracelet strung with beads and tiny crystal angels.

Dear Irene, the letter began, *My name is Beth D'Angelo, and I work at the resort where your friends Sally and Bob are staying.*

Beth explained that Sally and Bob had told her about Carly's passing and expressed their concern for Irene.

My heart is heavy hearing about your loss, Beth wrote. *There is nothing more difficult than experiencing the death of a child. It's backwards and out of order. I wanted to write to you and give you one of my angel bracelets. It's to honor Carly and to remind you of the connection you will always have with each other. Nothing can break the bond that you two have. Nothing.*

It's been nine years since our lives changed when my son died in an accident. No one could convince me then that I would one day feel or see the colors in the sunset, or want to eat again, or get out of bed to do much of anything. I did feel one thing, however—it was my son—sitting down with me when I couldn't take another step. It was a sense of Sean who stood up when I was ready to move again; he inspired me to write in a journal, and I felt him with me when I had to pull over on the highway to cry. I could feel him trying to tell me that what I was experiencing was the love I had for him.

Someone told me something that I held onto. At first it was just words; now there is a meaning that has helped me survive: "The edges will soften," maybe not today or tomorrow, but one day they will. Trust me on this, Irene. If there is anything I can do or share with you, I am here for you. In hope and promise, Beth.

Tears flowed down Irene's cheeks as she tucked the letter back into the envelope and slipped the bracelet onto her arm. Beth was the first mother who had also lost a child that she had heard from since Carly had passed. As loving and supportive as her friends and family were, connecting with someone who had experienced what she was going through brought a newfound wave of relief. It also brought an emotional shift.

She felt as if someone had thrown her a life preserver. Until then, she had been treading water, surviving from minute to minute.

Maybe I can do this, she thought for the first time since Carly had passed. *Maybe I can find a way to live on this earth without Carly.*

She contacted Beth, who became her lifeline. They spoke on the phone and emailed frequently. Still unable to sleep much, Irene spent her nights on the Internet, researching everything she could find out about the afterlife. She knew in her heart that Carly still existed somewhere. All that love could not simply evaporate. Almost immediately after Carly passed she had decided to find a medium who could connect her with her daughter.

Determined to avoid sensationalist and unreliable psychics and palm readers, she ordered a book by the highly respected medium George Anderson. Reading Anderson's *Walking in the Garden of Souls* gave her hope that she might actually be able to connect with Carly. Anderson's credible stories of communicating with those who had passed led her to schedule an appointment with him at his New York office.

Accompanied by her sister Judi, Irene took her copy of *Walking in the Garden of Souls* to the reading. She wanted to know that Carly was okay, that she wasn't frightened, and that someone was there for her when she passed.

Once the reading began, Irene found herself incapable of speaking, choked with emotion as George addressed each of her unspoken concerns. Judi had to answer George's questions for her sister.

"She wants you to stop obsessing about her passing," he said. "It was as easy as stepping through a doorway."

Before leaving, George signed Irene's copy of *Walking in the Garden of Souls*. From that day forward, she carried it with her always, coming to refer to it as her bible.

Her reading with George gave Irene the hope she had been seeking, and fueled her desire to learn more about life after death. At an hour when most were snugly tucked into their beds, she continued scouring the Internet. Early one morning, she came across a book that grabbed her attention: *Messages of Hope*, by Suzanne Giesemann.

She recognized Suzanne as the coauthor of another book on mediumship that she was familiar with and immediately downloaded the electronic version of the book. After only a few pages, she stopped and ordered hard copies for Judi and Beth.

Messages of Hope brought Irene more than the title promised. Feeling a connection with the author that she found hard to put into words, she looked up Suzanne's website online. When she learned that long-distance readings were available by phone, she clicked a link and began composing an email to request an appointment.

As she hit "enter" and the form disappeared from the screen, she had a strange premonition of the future. She knew she would get a reading with Suzanne Giesemann, but more than that, she was somehow aware that after their phone reading, she and Suzanne would meet, and if what her heart was telling her was true, they would become good friends.

CHAPTER 10
Aha Moment

§

I PRESSED THE GREEN TELEPHONE app on my iPhone and selected Favorites, followed by the familiar name. "Hello, my friend," I said when Irene answered.

"How was your dinner with Elizabeth?" Irene asked without preamble. I knew she would have given anything to have joined us in Arizona.

"Wonderful," I replied. "She and Cyril are delightful, as are Lynn and Jeff Hollahan, who hosted us. You would fit right in with everyone. Which"—I paused for effect— "is the reason I'm calling."

"Really?" Irene's curiosity was evident. "What's up?"

"Hold on a minute." I put the call on speakerphone.

"Hi, Irene!" Ty shouted from across the living room of our bus.

"Hi, Ty!" Irene called back.

"How's Tony doing?"

"He's doing great."

"What's he up to?" Ty asked.

Irene laughed. "He's out in the garage working on the boat. What else?"

For at least a year Tony had been building a wooden sailboat in his garage. When we stopped to visit the Vouvalides on our way through South Carolina the previous winter, we oohed and aahed at the superb craftsmanship. Irene good-naturedly rolled her eyes and let it be known that she was looking forward to being able to park her SUV in the garage again someday. From the tone of her voice, I could tell that her car would remain in the driveway for quite a while longer.

"Funny you should bring up the boat," I said. "The six of us got to talking about sailing last night. We decided to charter a sailboat together in the Virgin Islands and we want you two to come with us."

"You're kidding!" Irene exclaimed.

Her surprise that six people who had just met would decide to make such big plans was not unexpected. But her next words revealed there was more to her response.

"We just put a deposit down on a BVI charter yesterday."

"No!" Ty and I exclaimed in unison.

We learned that she and Tony planned a week's sailing trip on a catamaran in the BVI, accompanied by two couples with whom they had shared a similar trip on their honeymoon.

"Sounds like a crowded honeymoon," Ty quipped.

"We had so much fun," Irene said, "we decided to do it again."

"You'll just have to cancel your plans," I said, only half-joking.

Irene gave a singsong half groan, half whine. "We can't. We already paid for our flights."

"Talk about timing," I said. "You must have been calling the airlines the same time we were hatching the idea."

"Actually," Ty interjected, "the kids came up with the idea. Remember?"

"Yes, Irene," I told her. "Morgan, Devon, and Susan all showed up at the dinner party last night. It was great. And I know they're going to be with us on this trip. That's why you have to come."

Irene groaned again.

"I'm sure Carly will come if you do," I prompted.

"Oh there's no doubt about that," Irene said. "She wasn't happy to be excluded from our honeymoon. I promised her we would do it together one day."

"You see?" I said gently, noting a hint of sadness in her voice. "Come on this trip, and you'll get to fulfill your promise."

I knew that Irene still missed Carly greatly, but no one could deny how far she'd come in transforming her grief. Carly's strong communication skills had helped bring her to the point where we could talk in a lighthearted manner about Carly joining us from the spirit world, knowing full well it was more than wishful thinking.

I thought back to the reading that offered Irene much-needed relief from the trauma of Carly's passing. The desperation she expressed in her first email to me made it clear that I couldn't keep her waiting. Within days of her reaching out, we set up a telephone session.

Before I began the reading, we chatted briefly. She mentioned that she had read *Messages of Hope* and knew we were sailors. Her husband, she told me, was also a sailor. As for the one she wished to connect with in the reading, I knew only that it was a daughter, and that she had passed from cancer.

Irene's voice on the phone was timeless; I had no way of guessing her age or that of her daughter. Such details don't matter; my work is not about guessing. My job is to serve as the voice for those who can no longer physically communicate, and Carly Hughes came through loud and clear. As I learned rather quickly, she would have it no other way.

§

"So with gratitude," I said as I began the session, "let me just tune in here."

The connection started out a bit sketchily, as sometimes happens when I settle in. Working under the assumption that Carly had stepped in to join us, I shared a few first impressions, though I couldn't immediately confirm that she was there. Irene gave me no feedback as I rattled off generic words of greeting.

Let me feel you, I urged Carly silently. In response, I sensed powerful character traits that let me know in no uncertain terms that I would very much enjoy this new connection.

"There's a feeling of maintaining good spirits, even when she was sick. There's a feeling of strength, and just doing her best to keep a smile on her face. Would that make sense to you?" I asked.[3]

"Yes, absolutely," Irene replied.

"Okay. All right. There's a feeling of openness and loving everybody." I spread my arms wide as I spoke, as if Carly wanted to embrace the whole world, and described the gesture to Irene on the end of the line. "I'm not feeling someone who was closed off at all. She feels very open and magnanimous. Does that match her?"

"Absolutely," Irene confirmed a second time.

"I just now got a pain in the left side at the waistline," I reported. "And now the pains are across my whole ribcage, so I'm not just focused on the stomach."

Feeling actual physical pain didn't concern me. Those on the other side often let me know how they passed by giving me their symptoms as if they were my own. The discomfort disappears as soon as I report it, so I welcome this excellent way of validating a spirit's presence and proving that I'm not simply reading my client's mind.

"She had to have surgery to remove her stomach," Irene told me.

I blinked in shock. I had never heard of such a procedure.

With Irene's validation of Carly's personality and symptoms, I had no doubt that her daughter was present. Any pity on my part would only bring down the vibration and interfere with the link, so I sent out a wave of compassion to Irene and shifted back to Carly's energy.

"The word 'teacher' keeps coming up," I reported.

"Her degree was in education."

---

[3] All words in quotes are taken verbatim from the transcript of Irene's reading.

"Okay. She may have done more in administration, because as you say that, I hear 'administration.'"

"Yes, she did," Irene confirmed. "She didn't get a chance to become a teacher. Her initial job out of college was in an office."

"Okay." I raised my hands to cup my ears and winced. "I just got some shooting pains in my head. I'm lightheaded and dizzy all of a sudden." The pains disappeared, and I added, "And February comes up."

"Yes," Irene said, "she passed in February."

"She's wearing this beautiful gown. It's kind of flow-y. It looks like a wedding gown, and she says, *'I'm with the angels now, Mom. It's beautiful here. Don't worry about me. I'm fine.'*"

I was keenly aware that Carly's message was one that any mother would want to hear. I also knew there was no way to definitively prove whether the information truly came from her disembodied spirit. Silently I thanked Carly for bracketing her comforting words with facts that her mother could validate and would lend credence to the message.

"There's a purity about her that's unusual . . . an acceptance of others . . . an all-inclusiveness. Make sense?"

"Yes."

Carly flashed a scene before my eyes that caused me to cock my head. It perfectly supported the sense of connection she had wordlessly communicated to me.

"I'm seeing little black boys," I reported. "Did she work in a system that was somehow racially inclusive? There's something about race here."

"Absolutely," Irene said, with growing excitement. "She did service trips to the oldest African-American Catholic school in Mississippi."

"Oh, my God," I said, thrilled for both mother and daughter at this crystal-clear connection. "That's beautiful, isn't it?"

"Yes!"

Still celebrating, I clapped my hands. "Yay, yay, yay. Thank you, thank you, thank you, Carly. Good job. Oh, oh, oh!" I added as I received yet another hit. "You may be wearing it now: she's talking about a necklace, and I'm fingering a necklace, so—"

"We had the exact same necklace," Irene said. "I wear hers, and I gave mine to my sister, her godmother."

"She's showing me binoculars, like she looks right in on you. If you could see me, I'm holding two binoculars to my eyes."

"Okay," said Irene.

Carly continued showing me various images, some of which made sense to Irene and others she couldn't confirm. As if to get me back on track, a stabbing pain suddenly shot through my midsection.

"Ow, ow! All right. I just saw a bunch of red, and it's like a vessel filling up with red like she bled out."

"Yes, she did."

I didn't really enjoy sharing painful memories and was relieved when Carly quickly followed this vivid imagery with something more positive. "Oh, she's just so happy because she wants you so badly to know that she's right here. She's clapping and saying, *'I'm right here, Mom, I'm right here.'*"

"So keep it coming," I prompted Carly aloud.

"Oh, she loved kids. She loved people. She loved *you.* There's a feeling that at times she couldn't hold it all in." Carly's love was intoxicating. "I don't feel that too often from people."

"Everybody called her a lovebug."

"But she's saying, *'Two peas in a pod, chip off the old block.'* You have this grief that gets in the way of the love, but it's the love that just takes you back to ground, like Ground Zero. Like, *'I know that's what it's all about, if I could just get past this pain. I know I'm supposed to be here to love,'*" I said, referring to the image of Irene that Carly was showing me.

"It's like you're an old soul, like she was, and you have a calling to help other people know this. Does that make sense to you?"

"Absolutely."

I instructed Irene to cross her fingers, as if making a promise. "That's what Carly's doing. That means how tight you were."

"Oh, absolutely."

I put my hand to my head again. "Why did I just get really lightheaded?"

"That's how she passed. She fainted in my arms."

"She says she was met by big angels. *'It's just incredible, Mom. It's beautiful. I'm surrounded by light. Don't worry about me.'*" I spoke directly for Carly now, then added, "It feels like she was cremated. Is that right?"

"Yes."

Once again, I cringed at bringing up painful memories, but then Carly showed me something so unusual that I knew she was again backing up her comforting words with hard-core evidence: "It's almost like I feel the ashes. I don't know if you actually sifted . . . I've never seen this. . . . It's like your fingers are in the ashes."

"Not mine," Irene said. "My husband sifted through the ashes to give some to Carly's boyfriend when he climbed the highest mountain in Russia."

"Wow." I shook my head. "I don't know where Kathmandu is, but that comes up, even though you just mentioned Russia. Kathmandu. Or 'K.' There's a K sound with that mountain."

"Her boyfriend was on Mount Kilimanjaro when she passed."

"Oh, okay, okay. *'The mountain with a K,'* she says. *'He shouldn't feel guilty for not being there. I love him.'*"

"Oh, gosh," Irene said. "He struggles with it so much."

"He might have had a beard at some point." I rubbed my chin, even though Irene couldn't see me. "She's showing me *'scruffy.'*"

"Yes. When he does his climbs, he doesn't shave."

The reading provided a wonderful mixture of hearing, seeing, and sensing what Carly wanted me to share with her mom. Now I picked up on some differences of personality between Carly and her boyfriend. "There's a feeling that she'd like to be more adventurous, but she . . . not quite matching him."

"Oh, yeah, she wasn't."

"Okay. I just want to curl up on a couch with a nice soft blanket and be snuggled in. That's where she's comfortable." Once again, Carly and I merged, and I simply needed to report how I felt.

"Yeah, that's what she did," Irene confirmed.

Carly shifted gears and brought another man into my awareness. "She loves her stepdad like a dad. He feels equally open, and friendly, and smiley, and talkative, and enthusiastic, and they just feel like a nice, energetic match. Does that make sense?"

"Oh, yeah. People have said Tony's the nicest man in the world."

I sent silent thanks to the Universe for this delightful reading. Even though her passing had been traumatic for her mother, Carly brought a lovely upbeat energy to the session that kept the mood light. With the information that followed, I understood her purpose.

"*'You did everything you could,'* she says, and there's this feeling of you frantically searching the Internet."

"Yes, we were," Irene said. "It was such a horrific cancer. We were just trying—"

"She shows it like a fire, like it just spread really quickly, and now she says, *'Talk about that fire, it's significant,'* like it started with a burning, like heartburn and her stomach burning."

"Yes. She had esophageal-gastric cancer, so it was reflux and heartburn."

"Perfect. This is the kind of connection I pray for," I said, once again giving thanks. As I did so, another image flashed through my mind.

"So, I just got a picture of the Bible, but then it turned into another book that was signed inside the cover. Is there a signed Bible?"

"No," Irene replied. "I'm sitting with it right now. My 'bible' I call it. It's George Anderson's *Walking in the Garden of Souls,* and he signed it for me."

I smiled, recognizing the title of the book I was reading when Susan turned on the television in our Venetian hotel and later sent us the butterflies at sea. Both events occurred with uncanny timing relative to the words I was reading. Those incidents forever changed my own view of the afterlife.

I had no idea that Carly's mention of Irene's "bible" would have the same effect on her.

"And then there's something about signing it inside the cover on the left side. Most people sign on the right, but there's . . . I'm supposed to look inside the cover on the left side. Does that make any sense?"

"Yes," Irene replied with even greater excitement. She confirmed that George had annotated the pages inside the cover on both left and right sides, but his actual signature was on the left.

I had autographed thousands of books and owned quite a few given to me by other writers. All were signed on the right side, not the left. I pumped a fist at this wonderful validation of such a specific detail.

I had no idea that prior to our session, Irene had asked Carly to specifically mention George Anderson's book. When I spoke of her "signed bible that was not really a bible," Irene experienced her greatest "Aha!" moment since Carly's passing. That pivotal instant confirmed the revelation that Carly was truly still with her, just as if she were curled up on the couch next to her mother.

"That's so beautiful," I repeated. "Let's just keep going. It's about the joy of connecting, so, *go ahead, Carly. . . .* "

She showed me balloons going up in the air, and I reported this to Irene.

"At the school in Natchez, on her birthday, they release balloons," Irene informed me.

"Wow. Okay. I love this! She says she got to hug some of those kids, and it was her greatest joy."

"Oh, yeah. The pictures on the website are her holding the children, and I have pictures of her hugging them."

"Oh, my gosh. So one of the things I always ask those in spirit to show me are pictures that are significant. When we're done, please tell me where I can find those pictures so I can see, okay? And those kids drew posters or something. I see hands, those little handprints."

"Yes, I have those. I have those posters."

Carly shared a few more fun details, and then I felt a slight shift.

"I just sensed a momentary presence of your mother here, but this feels like this reading is all about Carly," I said, not realizing that my words revealed even more of Carly's personality.

"She loved school," I continued. "She did really great. I see A's, A's, A's, like she was an A student."

"Absolutely. She was a straight-A honor student."

"Yeah," I said, as the feeling lingered. "And it wasn't about pleasing you. She had to do that for herself. There's self-imposed perfection in that regard."

Carly continued showing me aspects of her personality that included a great curiosity about the world and its people. "It feels as if money was not that important to her. It was a means to an end, she just—"

Here Irene had to interject. "I don't know. She loved to shop."

I gave a little snort. "When you said she loved to shop, she laughed and said, *'Especially shoes.'* Is that true?"

Irene joined in the laughter. "Yes!"

"She's pointing from her to you and you to her, back and forth as if you wear the same size and that you can wear some of her shoes now. Is that true?"

"No, no."

I knew not to let the "no's" throw me. "Back and forth, so maybe you both went shopping together."

"We went shopping together all the time."

Carly passed along more reassurance of her continued presence, not just during the reading, but anytime Irene thought of her, and many times when she visited in between.

"She's showing me sailboats, because you mentioned your husband is a sailor. I asked her, *'Does he have a boat now?'* and she shows me her hands starting out wide and going smaller, like he downsized or he has a smaller boat now. Does that make any sense?"

Irene laughed again. "Yes, we gave away the boat when we moved from New Jersey to South Carolina, and he's now building a smaller boat."

"Excellent. And there's a sense that you're not as into it as he is."

"Yes," she replied, and I sensed Carly giggling along with us. "She says *'You're happier with your feet on the ground, but it's hard to keep your feet on the ground.'* There's a double entendre there—that you would be lifting off in spiritual-type things. You have a hard time staying grounded. I think you know what I mean by that."

"Yes."

"Okay. *'You also feel a calling to help others,'* she says. It's something you shared. This foundation that you brought up . . . it feels like that could become all-consuming for you. It's what helps you feel close to her, and helps you feel good, and that's okay, that's okay. Does that make sense?"

Irene confirmed that it made great sense. She told me that she volunteers in a shelter and works on the foundation. She had, in fact, just returned from the school in Mississippi.

"Let's get back to Carly now," I said. I shifted my awareness and linked in again. "Yep. Talk about a good girl! There are no vices with her. Others might have said she was a goody-two-shoes."

We chuckled together.

"I just can't impress upon you how happy she feels. There's nothing but lightness around her. She shows me the only low point is feeling your pain, so if you would just realize that she's okay and know that she would like you to feel more lightness in her heart, that will actually be easier for her."

I waited to see what else Carly wished to communicate, and for the third time she showed me a wedding gown. "It seems extremely important for her to get across to you: '*I'm still living. I'm right here.*' It's like, '*I get to wear that gown. No regrets, Mom. You did everything you could for me. I'm—I'm happy. This is where I belong now. I'll be back.*' That comes with a feeling that you'll always be able to connect with her soul, no matter what. Okay?"

Irene gave a small hum.

Carly then raised the energy by talking about her love of music. She let me know that she liked to sing but couldn't carry a tune. Irene confirmed how they would joke about Carly's tone-deafness.

"Good," I said, "Excellent. She had this desire to sing because she has this joy inside of her that just wanted to come out. I'm seeing blonde hair. Did she have blonde hair?"

"Yes, white-blonde hair."

"Just beautiful."

"Gorgeous," Irene said wistfully.

A surge of love filled my heart. "She says, '*Everybody would call this a tragedy, but don't see it that way. I left my mark, you're carrying it on, and I couldn't be happier. What more can I say than that?*' And then she puts a ring on your hand, on the right hand. I don't know if you're wearing a ring that's special to her."

"I'm not now," Irene replied, "but I do wear one of her rings on my right hand."

I could tell that Carly had shared the most important information she wanted her family to know, but she gave me one final image.

"She shows me that you hold a teddy bear up against your chest, like snuggling with this. There's something about you getting comfort from a stuffed animal."

Irene sighed. "She had a bear that she got when she was born . . . Sebastian. She slept with it every single night, and I hold it now."

I shook my head. "I could not be more grateful for this connection today," I said. I paused and took a long, slow breath as I asked Carly for her parting words.

"She says, '*I love you so much, Mom. You couldn't have changed this. Please don't feel guilty. I'm okay. I'm right here. I'm going to keep talking to you.*'"

I brought my hands into prayer position and thanked Carly and my team of helpers. Just as with a cell phone, a clear signal is never guaranteed, but we had enjoyed a five-bar connection.

Irene and I spent a few minutes further discussing interesting and enjoyable details about the evidence that had come through. She suggested I check out the website of the foundation they'd set up in Carly's memory.

We said goodbye, and I immediately got online and typed in "CarlysKidsFoundation.com." When the homepage opened, I sucked in my breath. The banner displayed a collage of images exactly like those Carly had shown me. Anyone unfamiliar with the value I place on integrity might have suspected I'd Googled Irene before our reading. The collage of photos portrayed gorgeous, blonde-haired Carly holding little African-American children, hugging them, and helping them paint colorful posters.

Way to go, Carly, I said with reverence.

Irene emailed me shortly after the reading and forwarded photos of Sebastian the bear and a closeup of her right hand bearing Carly's ring. She shared with me that after our reading, she slept through the night for the first time since Carly had passed. I was stunned to learn that until the reading her insomnia had become so severe that she needed to seek medical help after seven days and nights with no sleep at all.

"Sleep comes easily now," Irene wrote, and her closing words explained why: "I'm no longer lost."

"So, what do you say?" I asked Irene. "You can't skip this boat trip."

"Really, Suzanne, we finalized everything just last night."

"Well, either change your plans or plan to do both trips."

I kept my tone light, but I wasn't joking. The adventure would not be the same without Irene and Tony along. It wasn't only that we loved them and greatly enjoyed their company. They were part of The Club.

"I'm not sure how Tony will feel about two weeks on a boat."

"Like that would be hard to take," Ty drawled.

Irene moaned as if being tortured.

"Listen," I said, "our kids have got this covered. It's all going to work out."

And indeed, it did. We already had a date in mind when we called Irene and Tony, the only time slot that worked for all three couples. It so happened that Irene and Tony would be in the BVI the week immediately preceding our plans.

Eager to make it work, Irene contacted Delta airlines about changing their tickets. Delta was charging $200 per ticket to change their reservation. By sailing with our group, Irene and Tony's return to South Carolina would be delayed by one week, and each fare for the following week's return was exactly $200 less.

Those in the spirit world know that perfect order is a pure and permanent condition. We are not always capable of noticing, much less appreciating, this perfection, especially when it comes with apparent pain, but in the greater scheme of things, order reigns.

Tony agreed to suffer through two weeks in the Virgin Islands.

The trip was a "go."

PART II

CHAPTER 11

Surprise!

§

THE LOGISTICS INVOLVED IN BRINGING four couples together for a week of sailing might seem daunting to some. Not to Ty. Working his way up the Navy's leadership ladder to captain he had held many positions aboard the ships and dealt with a spectrum of details large and small. The rest of us were more than happy to defer to his expertise.

Once he determined the dates in mid-January that would allow Tony and Irene to transfer directly from their first boat to ours, he researched the optimum charter company, boat, and departure port. His final recommendation involved a Moorings 4800 out of Road Harbor on the island of Tortola. The spacious 48-foot catamaran offered four identical cabins with queen-sized berths and private heads. It turned out to be the same type of boat that the Vouvalides were chartering with their group.

Ty handled the contracts, figured out the finances, recommended ports of call, and distributed a proposed list of provisions. The ease with which everyone agreed on even the smallest details portended smooth sailing once the trip began.

Emails zipped back and forth with increasing frequency as the new year approached. Emoticons of smiley faces, hearts, thumbs-up, and clapping hands adorned each enthusiastic group text. When Tony and Irene's departure date arrived, the rest of us vicariously followed their trip.

"We're flying in style," read the caption beneath a selfie Irene took onboard their Boeing 737 out of Atlanta. In the photo, she and Tony held up a pair of glass goblets instead of the typical plastic cups offered in coach. Whether Carly had a hand in her mother and stepfather being upgraded to first class or the perk was awarded for their many trips to visit Tony's family in Los Angeles didn't matter. We all shared their happiness as they winged their way to the Virgin Islands.

The night before our departure for Tortola from Orlando, I calculated the time I would need to get ready the following morning. No matter how early I had to get up on any given day, I always added an extra half hour to meditate. Those thirty minutes of communion with my guides are sacrosanct.

With my bags packed and my alarm set, I set about completing one final task before bed. Sitting at my computer, I opened a blank Power Point Slide, clicked "insert photo," and selected a favorite portrait of Susan from a folder bearing her name. In it, she is glancing back at the camera over her left shoulder with a Mona Lisa smile, her dark shoulder-length hair framing her face.

Next, I browsed through a folder on my hard drive that contained a good selection of photos of Carly. After Irene's first reading, I had asked her to send me several for use in my workshops, citing the wonderful evidence Carly gave us as proof to others of how healing evidential mediumship can be. Now I selected a particularly sassy photo of Carly standing with arms crossed in a sexy bare-shouldered black dress.

I adjusted the position of the two photos, setting Susan in the lower right corner and Carly in the upper left. Then I went in search of photos of Morgan and Devon. Rather than relying on Google, I headed for the Helping Parents Heal website. I knew it contained a database of tributes to members' children and I guessed that the Hollahans and Boissons would have chosen a favorite photo for such an important purpose.

The kids' pages are arranged by birthday or angel date. Knowing neither for the boys, I went to the main directory and entered "Morgan." Just above the listing for Morgan James Pierre Boisson I found Chelsea Boisson, whose birthday and angel date are one and the same. After copying down Morgan's special dates, I went first to Chelsea's page.

A photograph of a beautiful hummingbird with a striking purple crown adorned the tribute. The text beneath the photo radiated Elizabeth's loving energy:

> *"I have always wished that I could have been able to know my sweet Chelsea; it is so difficult to lose a child at birth. The one shining light that pulled me through was my wonderful Morgan; he was the reason that I continued to move forward and he helped me to heal. I am so happy that Chelsea was there to meet Morgan when he transitioned. I have been told that she is very beautiful. She has always been my guiding angel; I now have two. I love you, Chelsea, and I know your brother will help you celebrate (your birthday/ angel date) in a BIG way. Love always, Mom"*

With a few clicks, I found myself gazing into Morgan's sparkling eyes in two side-by-side photos. The one on the right showed him posing with arms outspread at Mt. Everest Base Camp. The iconic mountain towered in the distance. I chose the head-and-shoulders shot on the left, but both photos showed how Morgan lived up to his nickname of "Big Bear," not only in size, but through his wide teddy bear smile.

Morgan's tribute was lengthier than Chelsea's, ending with this special recognition of Alix and Christine:

> *"He is missed by all of his friends and family, but especially by his two younger sisters, who miss his gentle teasing and kind good nature. He was the protector of the weak, the life of every social event, the*

sunshine that glowed warmly in every room he entered. Morgan was everyone's friend. He was nicknamed 'Big Bear' because of the amazing bear hugs he gave. He had a positive impact on everyone he ever met. His friends and family were blessed by every moment they had with him. I feel fortunate to continue to feel his presence every minute of every day. He hugs me on the inside whenever I feel down. Thank you, Morgan, for being such a wonderful son."

I next looked up Devon's birthday and found him in the May listings. The photo on his tribute page showed Devon looking every bit the world traveling adventurer I knew him to be, sporting a blue bandana over his wavy hair. I read the tribute before copying the picture for the collage:

"Perhaps his friend Ali said it best: 'I was in awe of the simplicity in which he led his life. Never before had I met someone so un-materialistic and content with the people in his life – and making lasting memories. This… was his greatest gift!' While we mourn the loss of his physical being, we take comfort in the presence of his spirit, we celebrate his joy of life and we do our best to emulate his sense of adventure. Devon, we love and miss you! We live every day as if you're here with us . . . and we truly believe that you are! Love, Mom, Dad and Kelsey."

I positioned the two boys' photos in the center between the girls and chose a complementary blue background. Finally, I drew a text box and inserted the three words that conveyed the reason for my efforts: in big white letters, the four kids announced, "We're here too!"

While our LaserJet printed up the color photo, I pulled an unused 8" x 10" frame from a shelf in the closet. A sailing trip called for soft-sided luggage, so I removed the glass before inserting the picture, which I intended to display prominently in the main cabin. Seeing our four children's smiling faces together each day would remind us of what we already knew: that they were as much a part of the crew as the rest of us.

Our alarm went off precisely at 5:30 the next morning. Excited about the trip, we both rose without complaint. While Ty set about getting the house in order for our dog-sitters, I headed to my study to meditate.

Each day for the past six years my guides have dictated an inspirational message during my meditation period. I enter into the silence and invite Sanaya to join me, saying, *"Please share with me something that someone who reads your words needs to hear."* At that point, either my right index finger twitches or I hear the words, *"Pick up your pen."* I do as directed, and become the spirit world's scribe, taking down the nonstop flow of words without analyzing or questioning. Always, the messages speak directly to the heart and carry a wisdom far beyond my own.[4]

Not knowing if reliable Internet access would be available in the islands, I had asked my assistant Bev to choose a favorite message from Sanaya's archives each morning of our vacation and post it for me. Due to our early departure, Bev had agreed to start the "reruns" that morning.

I wasn't expecting visitors from the spirit world today, so I felt a jolt of surprise when I heard my stepdaughter Susan's familiar voice.

"Hey, Suzanne."

My arms erupted in goosebumps. When I hear from a sitter's loved ones in a reading, their words sound like my own thoughts. Whenever Susan or my father show up, I hear them speak with the same tone and inflection as when they were here in their earthly bodies.

I welcomed Susan and thanked her for coming. Even though I'm a medium, I can't summon my own loved ones in spirit at will. Those

---

[4] Messages from Sanaya dating back to August 2010 can be searched by subject at http://www.suzannegiesemann.com/category/sanaya/

who have passed are busy on the other side. They choose when to show up based on many factors, most especially how it impacts our own soul's growth.

We shared a few pleasantries, all without any need for me to speak aloud. Communication among those in the spirit world happens by thought, and so it often is when we connect across the veil from our physical dimension.

Susan's message for me that morning was short and to the point: *There will be surprises for you on this trip*, she said. I could feel her customary enthusiasm as she added, *and upgrades.*

I flashed back to the photo of Irene and Tony enjoying their upgrade to first class, and I felt a flutter of excitement. *Surprises and upgrades.* What fun! But then I remembered that we would be flying on Jet Blue Airlines. Like other budget carriers, they didn't offer a first-class section.

How can there be surprises or upgrades? I asked silently. *The airline only has coach, and the sailboat is a standard 48-foot catamaran.*

She sent a *Just you wait* thought through my soul and faded from my awareness.

I shook my head. Communicating with those in the spirit world is rarely as clear as a phone call. Had I imagined the visit? No. There was no mistaking Susan's presence, but her prediction seemed off the mark. Still, I picked up the pen and notepad I reserved for Sanaya's messages and jotted down, *"Surprises and upgrades"* before heading for the shower.

Our flights from Orlando to San Juan and on to Tortola went smoothly. After a few hours of travel we found ourselves in a tropical wonderland, jostling down a narrow, rutted road in the airport shuttle. As much as Ty and I had traveled both during our Navy careers and on personal vacations, we nonetheless still marveled at how quickly one can transition from the familiar to the exotic.

The van deposited us at the Moorings main base in the town of Road Harbor. I blinked in wonder at the sheer number of huge catamarans lining multiple docks. I had regarded the 46-foot sloop we lived aboard for five years as a large cruising boat, but these charter vessels looked like floating palaces in comparison.

"We're taking one of those?" I asked Ty incredulously.

"Yep," he replied. "See the 4800 on the hulls? Those are the 48-footers."

"They're almost as wide as they are long," I said, still gaping.

If I had been excited about the trip before our arrival, I now felt euphoric. Even two couples on a monohull can feel crowded, but from the looks of these floating condos, the eight of us would have as much togetherness or privacy as we wished on our sailing vacation.

Our six-day charter was due to commence at noon the following day. With all of us coming from different locations, the Hollahans and Boissons had made their own arrangements at other hotels. Due to our late-afternoon arrival, Ty had reserved a room for the night at the marina hotel.

The open-air lobby in which we stood had reception desks on two sides. A sign on the desk to our left indicated check-in for boat charters. We turned to the right and approached the registration desk.

"We're the Giesemanns," Ty told the pretty islander seated at a computer.

"Welcome to Paradise." She smiled at us, repeating the same phrase we had heard from our shuttle driver. Her fingers moved deftly across her keyboard. Then she squinted at her screen, tilted her head, looked up at us, and grinned. "I have a surprise for you," she said, emphasizing the word "surprise" by playfully raising her eyebrows.

The word registered in my brain with a jolt as she finished her announcement: "We're upgrading you to a suite."

I whipped my head to the right and gaped at Ty. I had told him of Susan's visit that morning. "Did you hear what she said?" I asked.

"An *upgrade*. To a suite. And did you hear how she put it? She said, 'I have a *surprise* for you'—Susan's exact words!"

I threw back my head with a quick laugh of delight.

The receptionist looked at me a little strangely, but I didn't care. Instead, I gazed skyward and said, "Good one, Susan! Thank you!"

Ty shook his head in wonder and smiled. He had come to expect these special validations, but I think he still didn't know quite how to handle them.

Our room wasn't yet ready, so we left our bags in a designated corner of the lobby and went for a stroll on the docks. Cleaning crews were busily readying boats for their next guests. Maintenance men shimmied up masts, filled water tanks, and tidied up mooring lines. Ty and I did our best to stay out of the way, pointing out to each other some of the more imaginative names on the hulls.

"Most of these boats look great," I commented, "but a few are a little rough."

"Charter boats get a lot of use," said Ty. "After about five years, Moorings often sells them to companies that charge less."

"I hope ours is a nice one," I said.

"It should be," he replied. "We paid a little extra to get one under two years old."

"Let's go see if they'll tell us which one is ours," I suggested.

We returned to the lobby and approached the registration desk across from the hotel check-in.

"We're scheduled to take out one of your 4800's tomorrow," Ty said.

"Power or sail?" asked the young attendant.

"Sail," Ty replied, and gave the man our last name.

"Yes, I see you here," the clerk replied, "but you can't go aboard your boat until noon tomorrow."

"We know that," I told him, "but can you tell us which one is ours?"

He glanced back at the list. "Hull number 4026."

I gave the man a puzzled look. "No name?"

"It hasn't been given one yet. It's brand new."

I thought about the boats we'd just seen on our tour of the docks. All of them had a name.

"How did we luck out with a brand-new boat?" I asked him.

He shrugged and replied, "I guess you can consider it an upgrade."

I turned to Ty, beaming. I've learned that the higher perspective of those who have passed allows them to view events coming down the road that we can't foresee.

"Susan knew," I said with delight.

"What a *surprise*," he replied with a happy grin.

The trip was off to a good start.

CHAPTER 12

Underway

§

NINE MONTHS AFTER WE—OR MORE accurately our children— had conceived of the idea, our boat trip commenced. Ty and I looked up from our post-breakfast stroll around the marina to catch sight of Elizabeth and Cyril walking toward us. We'd spent no more than a few hours in their physical presence, yet we greeted each other like long-lost friends. Walking back happily together to the lobby, we came face to face a few moments later with Lynn and Jeff. We all hugged and kissed—the men included—indulging in Cyril's French tradition of a peck on each cheek.

"I can't believe we're finally together!" Elizabeth exclaimed.

"All but Irene and Tony," I said. "We're picking them up in Soper's Hole tomorrow."

The Vouvalides' back-to-back boat trips overlapped by one day. The plan called for them to disembark in St. Thomas and take a ferry to the western end of Tortola. We three couples would get underway from Road Harbor and anchor off nearby Peter Island for the night, then sail back to Tortola and pick up Irene and Tony in the morning.

"Where's your luggage?" Ty asked the group.

"This is it," Jeff replied, indicating two small bags no larger than a standard carry-on.

"Wow!" I said. "You guys travel light."

"We're used to it," Lynn said.

"Oh, my goodness," Elizabeth exclaimed with a sheepish expression, glancing at the two oversized duffels and two smaller bags at her feet. "We do a lot of traveling, too, but I still pack for every possible occasion."

"Your duffel bags are bigger than the seabag my sailors packed for a six-month deployment," Ty cracked.

Cyril rolled his eyes, and the rest of us burst into laughter.

A Moorings official approached and summoned Ty to the registration desk. He returned a few minutes later holding several folders and announced, "We're allowed to board now. Our boat is on 'A' dock, slip 32."

Ty and I had already checked out of our room, so the six of us loaded our luggage onto a cart and paraded down the nearest dock. "Oohs" and "aahs" filled the air as we took in a first glimpse of our floating home for the next six nights. As the craft was moored stern to the dock, we stepped easily onto the port-side pontoon's built-in steps that led to a spacious aft cockpit. A hard awning covered a four-foot square dining table with integral seating. Another set of stairs led from the starboard side of the cockpit up to a two-man padded seat at a large helm station.

Two sliding glass doors separated the cockpit from the main cabin. One by one we stepped into the sunny salon. A second dining table of equivalent size with padded bench seats took up a quarter of the space. A well-equipped navigation station occupied one corner, and the galley filled the remainder of the space.

"It's so bright!" I exclaimed, marveling at the difference between this floating palace and our cruising boat. The 360-degree view of the water through the wraparound windows gave the craft a completely different feel from the interior of a traditional monohull. The white bulkheads, cream-colored upholstery, and cabinetry added to the sunny ambience.

"Who gets which cabin?" Lynn asked, peering down a set of five steps leading into the starboard pontoon. An identical ladder descended into the port-side passageway, with one cabin at the end of each pontoon.

"Take your pick," Ty answered. "They're all the same."

"Not quite," I called back to the salon as I peered into the forward cabin on the port side. "This one has a hatch at the foot of the bed that opens into a cramped little space at the bow with a single berth."

I recognized the space as the crew's cabin for those groups who hired a paid captain or chef, but Ty offered up his own idea: "That's for husbands who don't keep their wives happy."

A flurry of guffaws was followed by silence as we chose our cabins and set about unpacking. When we gathered again in the main salon, we found several large crates filled with groceries that had not been there a few minutes earlier. Two young men with shirts bearing the logo of the local caterer stood in the doorway.

"Here's the food you ordered," the taller one announced. "Be sure to inventory everything as you put it away. If anything is missing, you must let us know before you leave."

He placed a three-page grocery list on the table, and the two left as quickly and quietly as they had arrived. We stared at the crates. No one moved.

"That's a lot of food," Elizabeth said, wide-eyed.

"We signed up for what they call 'split provisioning,'" Ty explained. "The package includes six breakfasts, six lunches, snacks, and three dinners with dessert for eight people. I did the best I could based on the food preferences you all gave me."

Lynn bent down and picked up a large ripe mango. "It all looks wonderful."

The rest of us simply stared at the intimidating stacks of boxes, jars, frozen meals in aluminum foil, and what looked like enough fresh fruit for a wedding reception. The professional chef that Tony and Irene enjoyed on their boat now sounded like a luxury we should have considered.

Finally, Jeff reached over and picked up the list. "I guess we'd better start going through this if we ever want to leave the dock."

Just then, a woman in a blue Moorings polo shirt with a no-nonsense demeanor and a thick Caribbean accent stepped into the cockpit from the dock and asked curtly, "Who is the captain?"

All eyes turned to Ty, who stepped forward and answered, "I am."

She reached out, shook his hand, and said, "I'm going to go over the systems with you. Once you sign off that you are taking responsibility for the boat, you can get underway."

Without further ado, she whipped open the glass cover to a high-tech electrical panel on the bulkhead and began rattling off a rapid-fire series of instructions.

"This is your AC panel. The generator carries 50 amps. Don't overload it. If the generator trips, you'll have to go into the forward locker and reset it. This breaker for the bilge pump on the DC panel must remain in the ON position at all times. There are two shore power cables which you will disconnect and stow in the transom locker before getting underway. Any questions? If not, follow me and we will go over fuel systems and engine starting procedures."

Ty and I had been around cruising sailboats for years. The woman was speaking our language, but when I glanced at our friends, I noticed a distinctly glazed look in their eyes. I had hoped to relax in total vacation mode, but realized now that I'd better listen in on the boat briefing in case anything happened to our captain.

I tagged along with Ty while the others inventoried and stowed the food. It turned out that quite a few items were missing from the provisions list, including four dozen eggs. After several trips down the dock for last-minute supplies such as ice and the critical ingredients for island rum drinks, we were ready to get underway.

I could feel everyone's excitement as we left the marina, but I held my breath as Ty took the helm. Every vessel handles differently, and wind and current always add a measure of unpredictability when leaving a dock. To me, the boat felt massive as Ty eased it out of the narrow slip, yet he turned the behemoth in its own wake and headed down the fairway as if he'd done so a hundred times.

"Greased it," I whispered to him with pride as I passed the helm. In typical humble fashion, he merely smiled and kept his focus on getting us safely to our first anchorage.

Freed of my deckhand duties by Jeff and Cyril, who busily stowed the fenders and dock lines, I ducked below and retrieved the surprise I'd put together. Elizabeth and Lynn broke into broad smiles when I placed the *"We're here too!"* collage of our kids on a shelf in the main salon. Not a hint of sadness clouded their reaction. Each of us knew that the special words were not just wishful hoping, but actual fact.

"After Irene and Tony join us, I'd like to do a group reading and let the kids make their presence known," I said.

"That would be great," said Lynn with her beautiful crooked smile.

"You don't have to do that," Elizabeth said sweetly. "This is a vacation for you, too."

"Believe me," I reassured her, "connecting with our kids is not work."

We stepped through the single glass door by the navigation table and joined Jeff and Cyril on the foredeck. Irene and Tony had kept us updated on the high winds that daily produced nine-foot seas in Drake's Channel, the main thoroughfare between the islands. Happily, that weather front had moved on to the north, leaving us with blue skies and little more than a light breeze. No one complained as we motored across the channel to Peter Island, not even bothering to put up the sails.

Within an hour of arriving at our first anchorage, the six of us clambered into the rigid-hull inflatable that came with the boat. A hike amid the flowering bushes and palm trees on Peter Island held far more appeal to each of us than a dip in the ocean. Our six pairs of feet competed for space on the floor of the dinghy as we motored ashore. Ty and I wore Tevas while Jeff, Cyril, and Lynn sported running shoes. Elizabeth's elegant feet stood out in a pair of strappy gold sandals that seemed more suited to a fashion model's runway than a tropical island hike.

I pointed at her feet and raised my eyebrows. "Didn't you say you packed for every occasion?"

Lynn laughed. Elizabeth tilted her head and replied without a hint of defensiveness, "You wouldn't believe how comfortable these are. I should send you both a pair when we get home."

Indeed, once ashore, she marched off so quickly that the rest of us had a hard time keeping up with her long-legged stride. We started out together and then flowed naturally in and out of groupings of twos and threes and back into six, chatting happily as we went.

The main paved road bisected the island, heading up a long, steep grade. Ever-improving views provided a rest from the vigorous climb. We stopped frequently to snap photos of the sparkling turquoise water and colorful resort homes dotting the hillside and beach below.

"The water is the same color as in Bali," Elizabeth said.

"You are well traveled!" I commented.

"Cyril and I visited as part of a Club Med vacation two years after Morgan passed."

"We met a woman there who knew Morgan," Cyril added.

"In Bali?" Lynn asked, surprised.

"Yes," Cyril said. "Every morning we went to yoga class, and one day I asked a young Chinese lady next to me if she was from China. She answered yes, and I asked her, 'And you are from what town?' and she said, 'Nanjing.' So I said to her, 'My son was in Nanjing University,' and she looked at me then very carefully, and she asked me, 'Are you Morgan's father?'"

"You're kidding," said Jeff said as the rest of us responded with equal surprise.

Cyril nodded. "The woman told me, 'You know, everybody cried when Morgan passed away. We all signed a poem for him.'"

"And we had that signed poem and a letter from the students back at our home in Arizona," Elizabeth put in.

"You were sitting next to this woman in Bali?" Ty asked, incredulous.

"It's true," Elizabeth said. "In a yoga class."

"You teach yoga now, don't you?" I asked.

"She's wonderful," Lynn said before Elizabeth could answer. "I go to her classes as often as I can."

"I highly recommend yoga for people who are going through grief, because it's a fantastic way to heal," said Elizabeth. "Yoga and meditation are what really saved me after Morgan passed."

"How so?" I asked.

At the time of Morgan's passing, Elizabeth explained, she had been training to teach yoga, and regularly doing at least two periods of practice a day.

"Yoga teaches you how to breathe and practice heart-openers that expand your lung capacity," she said. "You know how you get constricted by grief. It's like you have this stone on your chest."

We all nodded our understanding.

"I still had that stone on my chest, but it lasted a lot shorter time because of my practice."

"I'm terrible at yoga," I admitted. "About the only pose I can do is the one where you lie down and relax at the end."

Everybody laughed.

"It's called 'savasana,'" Elizabeth said and smiled. "As a matter of fact, as soon as Morgan passed, I stopped doing yoga, because I was afraid of savasana."

"Afraid?" Jeff asked.

"I thought I'd start crying, because yoga brings so much emotion to the surface."

"Were you avoiding those feelings?" I asked.

"Oh, no!" she said, not breaking her brisk stride up the hill. "I don't think it's wrong to cry at all. It's a wonderful thing, but grief is private. I didn't want to cry in the middle of a room with 20 other people."

I knew all too well how she felt. I flashed back to Susan's funeral, when I felt the need to stay strong in front of Ty. He had cried unabashedly in our hotel room, but I knew if I let down my guard, it would only add to his suffering.

"I stopped doing yoga," Elizabeth continued, "but Cyril and I did lots and lots of hiking."

"I can tell!" I said, struggling to keep up with her flashing gold sandals. "We hike, too, but there aren't a lot of hills in Florida."

"When you haven't climbed in a while, it's hard," she agreed, "but we hiked the hills around our house every day."

Two years earlier, she told us, on Morgan's birthday, the family had climbed Black Mountain together. "It's a very steep incline. I kept thinking, 'I've got to make it up, I've got to make it up,' and my daughter Alix told me she saw Morgan sitting on rocks ahead of us, laughing at me. Alix said, 'Morgan, push your mom up the mountain.'"

Elizabeth got her second wind, and when they reached the top, they discovered a mound with thousands of heart-shaped rocks they had never noticed before.

She smiled at the memory. "It was the best birthday present ever."

"When we see the deer or other wild animals," Cyril said, "it's when I say, 'Hey, thank you, Morgan.'"

Elizabeth nodded. "Every time we hike, we always see something beautiful, and we always thank Morgan for it."

"Following when he passed away, I ran a lot," Cyril said, "because when I run, I can release all the stress, and sometimes I am tired when there's a hill, and I say, 'Okay, Morgan, push me,' and I start to sing, 'I Believe I Can Fly!'"

"That's his song?" Jeff asked.

"Yes," Cyril replied. "We have a recording of him singing it on his telephone the summer before he passed."

"I love that we all still talk to our kids," I said. "So many people don't do that."

"I truly believe our kids work hard from the other side to let us know they're still here," Elizabeth said. "Not in the physical, but in a much bigger sense. If people could understand how their kids on the other side are with them every step of the way, the connection would be so healing."

Cyril nodded. "I knew in France a family who lost a kid, and these people were completely destroyed. We did not speak about death. We didn't speak about the memory. It's why I say that what Elizabeth did at the beginning was wonderful: she told us to focus on the good things and to talk about Morgan."

"I talk to Susan when I'm out hiking," Ty said. "It's when I feel closest to her."

"Susan put her fingers on his arm while he was on a trail that they had hiked together," I told the others.

"I'll never forget that feeling," Ty said wistfully.

"I've heard so many people say that you never, ever get over the death of a child," said Elizabeth, "but I questioned that from the beginning. I mean, why should that be the case?"

None of us answered, caught up in our own memories.

"Our kids want us to be happy and to experience joy," Elizabeth insisted. "Why should we not be able to heal? Of course, those of us who are left behind to grieve are sad, because we don't have them physically here, but the thing is, they're in such a beautiful place, and they still share in every special event of our lives."

Gazing out at the azure sea beyond the lush tropical foliage, it was hard to imagine a more beautiful place, yet we all nodded in solemn agreement.

"So that's how we've lived our life since then," Elizabeth said as we reached the summit of the long hill. She stepped beside Cyril and touched his arm.

Standing at the highest point on the island, I thought of the inscription on Morgan's bench: *He went to the top of the world to be closer to heaven.*

With her next words, Elizabeth confirmed my thought that the children in heaven could not have chosen a more appropriate spokeswoman.

"It's our job now to go forward and make something of their legacy in our own lives," she said. "To honor our kids."

CHAPTER 13
Healing

§

Lynn, Jeff, and Cyril scrambled from the dinghy onto the rickety finger pier at Soper's Hole marina. Pastel buildings lined the main dock, beckoning shoppers with racks of t-shirts, hats, and island gear. I looked for a place to secure the dinghy, but other boats' tenders filled every available dock space.

Ty's voice crackled on the handheld radio in my pocket, letting me know I didn't need to worry about tying up.

"Irene and Tony just got off the ferry," he announced. "They're going through customs now."

I shared an excited smile with Elizabeth, sitting across from me on the dinghy's pontoon.

"We're on our way," I replied.

"*Au revoir!*" Elizabeth called to the others on the dock. "See you in a little while!"

Ty had stayed on the catamaran to talk with the Moorings about a mechanical issue with the boat, so I had volunteered to pick up Tony and Irene. Seven years had passed since I'd steered with an outboard motor. I backed away from the dock a bit clumsily, then shifted the gear lever into forward position. The dinghy left a serpentine wake as Elizabeth and I crossed the harbor to the industrial side.

I throttled back as we approached the ferry landing, putting the motor in idle just far enough out to allow us to drift into the dock. Before the bow could even kiss the pier, Elizabeth bounced up from her seat and stretched out one long leg. In one quick motion, she stepped onto the pontoon and leaped across to the dock. The unexpected motion and resultant dip at the bow caused me to yelp in surprise, startling her.

"I'm so sorry," she laughed. "That's how we do it with our boat on Bartlett Lake."

"No, *I'm sorry*." I laughed. "Ty trained me to be super cautious. You're still dry, and that's all that matters."

We tied off the dinghy and headed for the customs house a short distance away. Taxis and a few cars were lined up at the far end of the building. The tropical sun beat down on us, and we quickly found a shady spot under an awning within view of the exit to wait for our friends to emerge.

I buzzed with excitement, grateful to be present when Irene and Elizabeth finally met in person. Irene, after all, had been the one to introduce me to Elizabeth, having met her herself online when she joined Helping Parents Heal. After six months of reading the group's newsletter and following their Facebook page, Irene had reached out to Elizabeth with the idea of starting her own chapter in South Carolina, though not without some trepidation. New to the Moss Creek community in Hilton Head, she was uncertain whether people would be open to a bereavement group that accepted candid discussions of the afterlife.

"You've been such a great help to Irene," I told Elizabeth as we waited. "She was worried at first that no one would show up for her meetings. She's told me how much your encouragement meant to her."

"Of course people came." Elizabeth beamed. "I told her that Carly would help her, and that's exactly what's happened."

As travelers began emerging from the customs building, our anticipation increased.

"I know the two of you chat a few times a month, but have you ever done any video calls?"

"Never," Elizabeth replied.

"So, you've only seen photos of each other." I rubbed my hands together. "Oh, this is so exciting!"

Finally I recognized the familiar faces of my dear friends. Irene locked eyes with mine, we grinned, and then she turned to Elizabeth. Tony stepped aside as I raised my camera and captured the moment. The two women wrapped their arms around each other in a heartfelt embrace, rocking back and forth and murmuring joyfully.

When they finally separated, I claimed my own hug from Irene, and then turned to give one to Tony. Stepping back, I took in the "Foxy's Bar" logo on his blue t-shirt.

"I see you've 'been there, done that, and got the t-shirt,'" I said to him. "Ready for another week of fun in the sun?"

"It's a tough job," he grinned, "but if somebody's gotta do it, it might as well be me!" He looked around. "Where's Ty?"

"Back on the boat. There's an issue with the inverter."

Tony rolled his eyes. "Sounds like a boat."

"Cyril is across the harbor with Lynn and Jeff," Elizabeth said. "They're all looking forward to meeting you."

"It might be a little crowded in the dinghy with your luggage," I said, "so we'll get you out to the boat, then Ty will pick up the others."

As we approached the stern of the big cat, Ty greeted us at the port-side steps. "Welcome aboard!" he called out as he offered a hand. "Great to see you, Mate!" He clapped Tony on the back. "Long time no see!"

"Yeah, what's it been?" Irene said after a hug.

"A whole five weeks," Ty answered, referring to the happy get-together we shared in Florida to celebrate his and Tony's December birthdays.

I swept a hand out, motioning forward. "Is this anything like the boat you just chartered?"

Tony and Irene stood under the cockpit awning and looked around.

"It's the exact same boat," said Tony.

"Only newer," Irene added, nodding with pleasure.

I asked which cabin they had.

"Port side, aft," Tony replied.

"That one's ours," Ty said, "so you'd better not come wandering into the wrong cabin at night, Shipmate!"

We all laughed and then Tony said, "I hear you have a problem with the inverter."

"Yeah," Ty replied. "I don't think the boat has one."

"You're kidding," said Tony, clearly aware that an inverter is standard issue on most cruising boats.

"I wish I was," Ty said. "The boat's so new my guess is they haven't installed one yet. It's not a big problem, though. The only 110 appliances we need are the coffeepot and microwave, and we can run the generator when we have to use those."

Tony and Irene shared a glance, and then Irene said, "We need power for Tony's C-PAP machine. He needs it for his sleep apnea."

"It's not a problem," Tony said, waving a dismissive hand.

I shot Ty a concerned look. "Sounds like a problem to me if you can't breathe."

"We'll get it figured out," Ty assured him, "even if it means running the generator at night. But first things first. Let's get your luggage below so you can get settled in, then I'll go pick up the others."

He and Tony stepped aside to allow the ladies to go first. Elizabeth and I led the way through the double glass doors. Irene took two steps into the salon and stopped. She stared down at the fiberglass floor and made a face.

I cocked my head. "What's the matter?"

"Um," she hesitated. "The floors. They're kind of messy."

I looked at the mosaic of footprints caused by six pairs of wet feet and shrugged. "It's almost impossible to keep a deck clean with this many people onboard."

Irene stifled a shudder and then mustered a brave smile. "I don't want this to be everybody's first impression of me, but I have a thing about dirty floors. I clean mine once a day at home."

"Once a day?" I blurted. "Just the kitchen, right?"

She looked sheepish. "The whole house. It's like therapy to me."

"Oh!" Elizabeth said, reaching for a rag by the sink. "We'll keep it as clean as we can!"

Irene smiled modestly. "No, it's okay. Really. I'm fine."

I felt my heart open. After what she had had to endure with Carly's illness, nobody on this boat would judge her. If anyone were entitled to have "issues," it was Irene. A fixation on clean floors was a minor quirk; Irene was as well adjusted, after the trauma of her daughter's passing, as anyone I knew, thanks to a special healing miracle . . .

§

I loved knowing Irene was in the audience when I told her story as part of my presentation at the annual conference of the International Association of Near Death Studies. She had given me permission to discuss certain details of her evidential reading as part of my effort to help others through their grief. I accompanied my talk with several slides of her and Carly that backed up the evidence that had come through in our session. When I asked her to raise her hand so that others could acknowledge her, I felt my heart stir. In person she appeared even more kind and approachable than in her photos.

As soon as my presentation concluded, we found each other in the crowd and immediately embraced.

"Thank you for allowing me to share your reading," I said.

"Thank you for honoring my daughter," she replied, her lashes still wet.

I laughed. "From what I know of Carly, I'm sure she enjoyed the attention."

Following a hunch, the next day I tracked her down and made a special offer. "What do you say we go up to my room and connect with Carly?"

Her eyes lit up. "Okay by me!"

I tilted my head. "Didn't you tell me that your father had passed since our reading?"

"That's right."

"Hopefully he'll show up, too. Come on up to room 832 in about ten minutes."

"You don't have to ask twice!" Irene replied.

Exactly ten minutes later, Irene settled on the couch in my room, and I pulled a chair over to sit across from her. We joined hands and I mentally connected our hearts, giving thanks for the opportunity to reach across the veil.

"Okay. Let's see who's here," I said, releasing her hands and shifting my focus to the spirit world.[5] Within seconds I felt the familiar lightheaded sensation that indicated the presence of someone in spirit. My head was pulled toward my right shoulder.

"That's not what I expected. I thought we might hear from Carly first, but fathers always come in over here on the right. This may be your dad."

I stumbled a bit, picking up on some issues that Irene could not identify, and then we locked in the connection.

"He's sending great admiration to your husband. I know Tony has a boat, but there's a feeling your dad is interested in it too, or he used to go boating."

Irene smiled and nodded. "My dad had a boat, but he and Tony were building a sailboat together."

"Okay, and there's a George somewhere in the family."

"Tony's father."

---

[5] The dialogue is taken verbatim from Irene's reading.

"Oh, nice," I replied, not having realized that both fathers had stepped in.

An influx of bubbly energy where I most often sense a child let me know that Carly wanted to make her presence known.

"Oh, my head goes bouncing over here to Carly. She's clapping her hands, and then she throws her arms around you to give you a big hug. She's so happy you're at this conference. She says you're putting on wings—really taking off. You're really stepping into your own."

I rubbed the goosebumps on my arms, a clear validation of Carly's presence.

"She says, *'Mom, we're in this together.'* And there's something about you going through the airport. I sense you must be a big traveler, but she's showing me you being a little unsure on the way here. She takes your hand to show you she was in on the whole thing with you. There was some mix-up at the airport. She shows me the image of you looking up at the display boards with some dismay."

Hearing this, Irene sat up straight and explained excitedly, "At the airport on the way here I left my phone in the car. I looked up at the monitors, and I was crying. The gate agent called Tony, and Tony came back, and it was a whole big airport scene."

"Ahh," I nodded, pleased at how Carly had confirmed that she was truly "in on the whole thing" with her mom.

I shared a few things that Irene couldn't validate, and then Carly showed me a pair of footy pajamas.

"She loved footy pajamas," Irene confirmed.

"Really?" I asked, surprised. "As an adult?"

"Yeah."

I described an image of Carly snuggled up against her mother. I felt their love like a warm, soft blanket wrapped around me.

Next Carly showed me a bracelet. I had a simultaneous awareness of Irene's friend Beth, who wrote the heartfelt letter to Irene in her darkest hour. The two subsequently struck up a long-distance friendship. Beth had flown to the conference from Hawaii so the two could meet in person. They were sharing a room, and I made a mental note to offer her a reading as well.

"I know you're involved with some bracelets with your friend Beth," I said, "but now I'm seeing a baby bracelet with a name. Remember those? Do you know why she'd be showing me that?"

Irene nodded. "When I went through my dad's things, I found my baby bracelet with the name on the beads."

"Oh, good. Yeah." I paused and looked to my right. "He's so proud of you. He says there's nothing you can't do. Your foundation comes up, with a feeling that it's losing momentum, but it'll go like that, in spurts."

My head moved back toward Carly. "There's a feeling that you're going to move in a new direction to affect more people on a bigger scale than that."

I had no idea then that Irene had been in contact with Elizabeth about starting her own chapter of Helping Parents Heal. Carly made it clear that she knew all about it.

"I see the school over here to one side, but here come the wings again. You're ready to take off in a new direction, still related to Carly, still as a result of her passing. And she says the seeds have already been planted for this. She shows me you and Beth putting your heads together."

Irene laughed, but remained silent. I took her happy response as validation and continued. "She shows me that you two are cooking up a scheme, and it's going to involve pulling other mothers in. I think you probably know what she's talking about."

"I hope."

"That's good. All right. She's taking me now to exercise with you, like you've recently gotten into some kind of new exercise routine, and it involves stretching, and the moving is 'stretching' you."

We both laughed at Carly's pun.

"Are you doing something new?" I asked.

"I work out with a trainer now three times a week. It's pretty new."

"Perfect. Yay," I said. "They sure know what's going on, huh? Carly's laughing like, *'Look out, world!'*"

I could tell that this lighthearted banter between Carly and her mother was exactly what they had enjoyed before she passed. It felt as much friend-to-friend as a mother and daughter bond. The connection was so clear that I let Carly speak directly through me:

"Mom, this should show you that I'm still so much a part of your life, and I'm pushing you with this new stuff. I tried to calm you down at the airport, but I would have done the same thing."

Irene laughed and nodded.

I grew aware of a new presence, a woman smoothing down her skirt. She stood to my left, so I guessed Irene's mother had stepped in. I shared a few personality traits, some pieces of evidence and names, not all of which Irene could validate. The connection faded in and out as I tried futilely to fine-tune my antenna.

"She just feels so open and loving with you," I said, making sure to pass along the most important aspect of her mother's presence.

"Oh, absolutely," Irene confirmed.

"Okay, well let's move on." I shifted my awareness and reported, "February is a significant month."

"Both my dad and Carly passed in February."

"Okay, and your father is saying, 'Tony is a saint.' He shows me that Tony is very pleasant, and he laughs a lot. Oh, I want to meet him!" I squinted to clarify the image in my mind's eye. "I don't know if it's Tony with a strap around the chest . . . you know, those heart monitors that people wear for exercise."

Irene nodded. "He was just diagnosed with sleep apnea and has to sleep with all that stuff."

"The monitor around the heart? Oh, cool. It feels like it's his dad acknowledging that, and he's showing me that yours is a match made in heaven. He says, *'We mean this literally,'* because you could not have gotten through Carly's passing without him. And Spirit would never do this to you without providing you a life preserver, literally."

I leaned back. "Whoa. It's as if you'd have taken your own life, or you wouldn't have made it if you didn't have him to wrap around you like a life preserver."

I had only met Irene the day before. We communicated briefly when I contacted her for permission to share Carly's story at the conference. I had no idea of the role Tony had played in her life before or after Carly's passing, but from the tears in her eyes and her vigorous nods, I knew the information from across the veil had hit its mark.

"At a human level, Tony didn't know what he signed up for, but at a soul level, he was on a mission. He couldn't not be there for you. Wow. This transmission is to validate for him that this is part of what he came here for."

Often when I receive messages that we can't prove, those in spirit will follow them with a random piece of evidence as if to say, *"You see? I'm really here, and you can believe what I'm telling you."* As if to validate the message about Tony's mission, Carly put the image of a small stuffed lion in my mind's eye.

"I know about the teddy bear," I said to Irene, "but this is a lion. Do you recognize it?"

"She had a favorite stuffed animal that was a little lion."

"Oh, that's good," I said, pleased with the validation. "Okay. *'Transfusion,'* she says now. Did she need a transfusion?"

"Seventeen transfusions."

"Oh, my." I shook my head. The energy abruptly downshifted. "She's aware that each one of those transfusions hurt you." I concentrated. "There's an acknowledgment here that you are still carrying traumatic wounds in your energy body. You're doing a really good job of healing, but be aware that these energy blocks become lodged, so there will be healers that—"

I stopped mid-sentence and sat back, surprised. I had sensed initially that Irene would be working with energy healers to clear the emotional blockages that resulted from Carly's passing. The unexpected presence of my guides caught me off guard.

"Oh, really?" I said, looking upward and speaking directly to Sanaya. *"We haven't done this in a long time."* I turned to Irene. "Give me back your hands."

Irene looked as surprised as I was. I reached out to take her hands and said, "This is a healing, okay? So just feel whatever happens."

"Go ahead," I said aloud to Sanaya.

I had no formal training as a healer, but that didn't matter. All healers, I knew, are simply instruments of Spirit. I closed my eyes, visualizing my body as a conduit. I imagined a white light of healing energy flowing in through the top of my head, out through my hands, and into Irene's body. As I did so, I felt a powerful surge that traveled the path I envisioned, followed immediately by a second massive wave. Never in my life had I experienced anything like it.

With an intuitive sense that the two huge waves had done their job, I opened my eyes. "I don't know if you felt anything," I said to Irene, "but I sure did,"

She opened her eyes and shook her head. "Oh boy, did I. I felt it through my hands, and I heard this big *'whoosh.'* It was a rush," she said, wide-eyed. "It was amazing."

I told her that as the energy was moving through me, I heard the word *"bolus,"* which I recognized as a medical term for a substantial infusion of medication given in a single push.

I realized I was breathing heavily and forced myself to settle down. "That came from really high up, okay? There was some big block in you that was just pushed out, and this may sound silly, but I'm being shown that you're supposed to take a shower now."

Irene still had a dazed expression. "Okay."

I laughed nervously. I could no longer deny the presence of higher consciousness working in our lives. I didn't always understand it, but I had come to trust it.

"So you go stand in the shower, and visualize white light washing through anything that you've been carrying around that was broken loose. Allow it to flow down the drain." I paused to receive more instructions, and then reported, "You're supposed to stand there until you hear, '*It is done.*' Okay?"

"Okay."

We stood and I walked Irene to the door. The guidance continued as we stepped into the hall.

"You will feel a lightness that you have not experienced in a while, and you will sleep even better. And you will also be able to feel Carly's presence more clearly." I blinked. "They are saying, '*That is all,*' and I see Carly giving you a big hug and lighting up again because she's so aware of you taking flight now. It's going to be big," I said, referring to whatever project she was planning. "I don't know what it is, but you know, okay?" I reached out and touched her arm.

"Okay."

"They're serious about the shower," I insisted. "You're going to take one now, right?"

"Right now," Irene echoed.

"Good."

She turned and began to walk slowly down the hallway. I reached for the doorknob, but my Team gave me a final piece of advice. Startled but excited for her, I called after her, "And prepare to cry!"

Irene gave a nervous laugh and waved as she stepped onto the elevator.

Feeling a bit drained, I entered the room, picked up my purse, and went in search of dinner. Throughout the meal I kept replaying the reading and the unexpected guidance to take Irene's hands. I had so little experience with healing work that doubt kept creeping into my thoughts. Had the powerful surge of energy we both experienced truly healed some deep wound?

Two hours later, as I was returning to the hotel, my phone chirped with a new text message from Irene.

"Can we meet for coffee?"

I found her sitting in a quiet corner of the lobby. When I approached, her energy felt so drastically different that I gaped.

"You're glowing!" I said, without a word of greeting.

She spread her arms as if showing off a new outfit but said not a word, only shook her head in amazement and grinned.

"What's different?" I asked, slipping into a seat beside her.

"It's gone," she announced incredulously.

"What's gone?"

"My *Groundhog's Day* moment."

I recognized the name of the Bill Murray comedy in which his character gets caught in a time loop, endlessly repeating the same day over and over. "What moment is that?" I asked.

Irene explained. "A week before Carly passed, she turned to me and said, 'Oh, Mom, I just want to feel like myself again,' and I felt so bad that I couldn't do anything for her." She shook her head at the memory. "No matter what I did, there I was like *Groundhog's Day,* going back to that moment again over and over."

"Ahhhh," I said, understanding. "That's the blockage. Those in the spirit world knew you were stuck."

"Not anymore," she said, grinning.

"Did you do what they said?"

"Yes!" she replied adamantly. "My first thought when you told me to go take a shower was, *You mean I have to wash my hair again?*"

I laughed.

"But that whoosh of energy was so real," she continued, "I knew something big had happened. So I took the shower, and as the water ran down me, my hands just started moving on their own."

She waved her arms around her head and shoulders.

"I was shampooing, and I was scrubbing, and I was so glad Beth wasn't in the room, because I started to wail."

"'*Prepare to cry,*'" I said softly.

"Did I ever!" she said, but instead of appearing drained, as one might expect after such an emotional release, Irene looked vibrant. "I just scrubbed and cleaned my energy field until I felt, '*It is done.*'"

"I can tell by the way you look that something major has shifted."

She shook her head, not in denial but amazement. "I keep trying to put myself back in that spot that I was stuck in. I keep trying to repeat that trigger moment when Carly was so sick, and all I can do is smile."

"The difference in you is stunning."

"I know," she said. "And now I feel bad about smiling, because it was a very emotional time for me and Carly."

Her smile seemed so incongruent with her words that we had to laugh.

"Don't you see?" I said with excitement. "You're picking up on Carly's happiness. She knew you were stuck, and now you're free! She showed me how very much alive and happy she is in her new world, and all she wants is for you to be happy, too. She knows it's not the same as having her here physically, but she's moving on, and now you can both move forward together!"

Irene looked as if she'd won the lottery. We said goodnight and promised to meet in the morning. I recalled that the guides had said she would feel a new lightness. That much was evident. They'd also mentioned she would sleep even better than after our first reading. She seemed so high, I wondered if she would be able to sleep at all.

When we greeted each other the following day, Irene's eyes were clear and sparkling. Her broad smile continued to light up her face. Her words of greeting answered my unspoken question.

"I closed my eyes at eleven o'clock," she announced with wonder, "and didn't open them again until seven A.M."

§

"Hey, Irene," I said, as we stepped into the catamaran's main salon, "look who's here!" I pointed to the framed collage of our kids on the shelf next to the table.

She tilted her head to one side and gave a mother's proud smile. "*We're here too*,'" she read aloud. "I love it."

Tony stepped up behind her, holding a bag in each hand, and followed her gaze. "Carly may be here," he said with a smirk, "but I guarantee you she won't be doing any sailing."

Irene gave him a playful swat on the arm.

"She didn't like sailing?" asked Ty.

Tony guffawed. "I had a Pearson Triton 28 when Irene and I first got together. Carly asked me to teach her to sail, so I went out and bought her sailing gloves."

"Uh-oh," I said, recalling how Carly liked shopping and girly things. "I can guess where this is going."

Tony rolled his eyes. "Once we got on the boat, she decided, 'This is too much work. I don't like to do that.' I had to do all the sailing."

Everyone laughed. From across the room, Carly's smiling face seemed to join in the fun.

"You know what?" I said, flopping onto the dinette seat and crossing my arms to mimic their daughter's saucy pose, "I'm with Carly. Tony, it's great to have you aboard."

CHAPTER 14
Signs

§

Ty DINGHIED ASHORE TO PICK up Cyril, Lynn, and Jeff while Irene and Tony unpacked. When I heard the growl of the outboard motor approaching, I called down excitedly to the port-side cabin, "Here they come!"

Less than an hour before I had witnessed Irene's and Elizabeth's poignant first meeting. Now we gathered on the aft deck for yet another face-to-face first. No one expected the men to gush, but we girls had been a-twitter with anticipation for months. I lost count of the *I-can't-wait-to-meet-you*'s that passed between Irene, Elizabeth, and Lynn. Finally, our foursome as mothers was about to be complete.

Tony stepped down the transom stairs to take the line from Cyril as Ty maneuvered the dinghy in close. Lynn was the first to come aboard. I was peripherally aware of Cyril and Jeff greeting Tony, but my full attention was focused on Lynn and Irene. The two women embraced like long-lost friends.

This was no perfunctory hug between strangers. Irene and Lynn held onto each other and rocked back and forth, truly savoring the moment. Elizabeth stood to the side, beaming, her hands clasped to her heart. I raised my camera as they turned to face me, their arms still wrapped around each other.

The air vibrated with emotion and unspoken thoughts: *I know who you are, I know what you've been through. I've been there too, and I love you for being part of my journey.*

We stepped into the main salon. Irene picked up a small bag from the counter. "I brought you all a gift."

I immediately recognized the delicate bracelets she drew from the bag, nodding at me as she did so. "Suzanne, I know you already have one of these, but I didn't know if you'd bring it along. Beth wanted us all to have one for the trip."

I gratefully accepted a string of small orange beads separated by crystal angels. "My other one has black beads, so I'll wear them with different outfits."

Irene then related the history of her friendship with Beth D'Angelo to Elizabeth and Lynn. "She started making these after her son Sean passed at nineteen in a car accident. Beth lives in Hawaii. She met up with two of my friends there and they got to talking about me." She handed Lynn a bracelet adorned with brown beads.

"They told her about Carly?"

Irene nodded, picking out a bracelet with turquoise beads for Elizabeth. "Apparently they said something like, *'We're afraid Irene's not going to make it.'*"

Elizabeth looked shocked. "Oh, my goodness. But look at you now—how far you've come!"

Irene grinned and held up her right arm. "Beth sent me this bracelet, along with a letter. It was the first time I felt that I wasn't walking this path alone." She paused and glanced across the room at the collage of our kids. "We're pretty sure Carly and Sean brought us together."

"Of course they did," Elizabeth said, as the three of us slipped the delicate little angels around our wrists.

"Hey, Ty," I called to the cockpit. "Will you come here a minute?"

"What's up?" he asked, stepping into the galley.

"Look what Irene brought us."

"Very nice," he said, admiring our bangles.

I handed him my iPhone. "Will you take a photo for us?"

"Sure."

We put our creative heads together to determine the best shot. We ended up stacking our right hands atop one another from all four directions, then holding them over the bare floor so that no stray objects would mar the effect. Ty zoomed in from above, capturing a shot that spanned from our fingers to just above the bracelets.

The resultant picture is one of love, solidarity, femininity, and strength, as much a treasure as the bracelets themselves. It signifies both our membership in The Club That Nobody Wants to Join and the transcendence to be found through surviving and thriving in the wake of great loss.

Tony and Irene's arrival was cause for celebration. With provisions aboard for only three out of six dinners, we decided to splurge on our first restaurant meal that evening. The renowned Pusser's Restaurant, named for the popular island rum, lay within eyesight of our mooring ball. We crowded into the dinghy and headed ashore as the sun set over the islands to the west of Tortola.

A patio with picnic tables in front of an outdoor bar comprised the first floor of the restaurant. Loud Caribbean music assaulted our ears, and we agreed to seek refuge in the more formal dining room upstairs. Our hostess seated us at two long wooden tables in the center of the room. Stained glass lighting and scarlet life preservers hung from the ceiling, along with an old rowboat. A waist-high wrought-iron railing lined the front of the circular room, allowing us an unobstructed view of the harbor lights.

We took our seats and ordered drinks. The dining area was surprisingly empty for the high season, with only a few patrons seated at the bar. Our server informed us that high winds from the previous week had frightened away the tourists.

As we studied the menus, one of the overhead lights flickered.

Jeff raised his brows. "Devon?"

"Does he mess with your lights?" I knew no one in our group would find the question odd.

"Yes," Lynn answered. "He did so quite often in the beginning, usually when we were talking about him."

Jeff leaned forward and planted his elbows on the table. "I think our best story is the one that took place in Denver. We had quite a few witnesses. Do you want to tell it, hon?"

Lynn smiled. "Okay." She explained for Irene and Tony's benefit how after Devon passed, she and Jeff had bought a second home in Colorado in order put distance between themselves and the difficult memories back in Arizona. "Our first summer there, our next-door neighbors Teresa and Mark didn't know a lot about us, but they knew we had a son who died."

Lynn's tone was eager, not melancholy, as she went on. "Teresa came over and told me, *'I think Devon was in our house last night.'*

"*'Why?'* I asked her.

"*'Well, I've had these candlesticks in the same place for years. Late last night they suddenly fell over, and the first thing that popped into my head was, that was Devon.'*"

The rest of our group murmured thoughtfully, aware that unexplained phenomena often indicate the presence of those in spirit.

Lynn continued, "She came back several nights later and told me, *'Devon was here again.'* I knew then it was time to share our story with her, because he was always doing things like that—making things move and playing with the lights. So a few days later, they were at our house again—"

"You mean, you didn't scare them off?" Ty interrupted.

"They're really good people," Jeff remarked.

Lynn ignored the interruption. "This time we were on our patio with Teresa and Mark and two other couples from our neighborhood. We were telling the others about the lights, and I said, 'Devon knows what neighborhood we live in, he's just not sure which house.' And just as I said that, the dining room light came on."

"Great timing!" I said.

"Yeah," Lynn agreed, "and there was nobody in the house. I looked up and said, 'Oh, I guess you do know where we live, Devon.' And everybody was looking at me like, *Oh, my gosh, who are you people?*"

"And how many FOR SALE signs went up in the neighborhood after that?" Tony quipped, leaving us all doubled over in laughter.

"Devon was really active the year after he passed," Lynn said. "I was so excited every day to wake up and see what he had up his sleeve next."

"Then it slowed down," said Jeff.

Lynn sobered. "That's when reality hit. It was like, *Okay, they're signs, but he's not physically here.*"

Jeff chimed in, "Lynn was afraid that Devon no longer needed to be around us so much. But now we know better. We know that he's with us all the time."

Ty and I could relate to Lynn and Jeff's experience. Signs from Susan came rapidly the first week after her passing and then dwindled. Knowing she had gotten through to us with the magical butterfly encounters and the television that turned itself on in our Venice hotel, she then stepped back, allowing us to explore and discover our personal path to healing, much like a parent who allows her toddler to stumble as he learns to walk on his own. Today, Susan saves her signs for special moments that continue to confirm with certainty her presence in our lives.

Irene's story was different. "Early on," she told us, "there were no signs for me. I was too deep in grief, too out of my mind to pick up on anything, even if the signs were there."

Tony wrapped an arm around her shoulder and drew her close.

"But my sister did get a sign—a great one—early on," Irene continued. "Judi stayed with me the first few days after Carly passed. At one point she went home to get some new clothes. She was an emotional wreck, crying and worrying about me. On impulse, she texted Carly's cellphone: *'Carly, I know you're okay, but your mom needs help, and I don't know what to do. I wish there was something you could do, to help me help her.'"*

"She sent a text to Carly?" Elizabeth asked.

"Yes. Carly's phone was at my house, turned off. Judi fell asleep, and was woken up awhile later by the sound of an incoming text on her phone. When she checked her screen, there was no text, but an open Safari window. In the Google search bar she read the words, *Heaven Looks a Lot Like a Mall.*"

"No way!" said Lynn.

"That's outrageous," I said, thoroughly enjoying the creativity of the spirit world.

Tony rolled his eyes. "That's Carly."

Irene went on, "Judi asked out loud, *'Carly, is that you?'* And of course it was. Who else would compare the afterlife to a mall, long after closing hours? It was my shopaholic, shop-til-you-drop daughter!"

The remains of her New Jersey accent made Irene's delivery all the more entertaining, and everyone laughed.

"Do you get signs now?" Lynn asked.

Irene nodded vigorously. "Constantly."

"Irene has come so far that now she even tunes in to other people's kids," I told the others. "Tell them about Grace, Irene."

Irene glanced down modestly, then lifted her chin.

"A few months ago, while I was in the shower on the morning of our Helping Parents Heal meeting, I sent out a prayer. I had taken Suzanne's mediumship class, and she taught us that you have to set an intention; the spirits don't always just appear. So, I said, *Kids, I hope someone will give one of the parents who comes to the meeting today a sign. Please show up and give your parents some comfort.* And there in the shower I heard, *Please tell my mother to do my laundry. It's gross, and disgusting.*"

"Oh, my goodness," said Elizabeth, stifling a laugh.

"I know," said Irene. "And because Suzanne said you should ask who it is when a spirit shows up, I said, *Who is this?* and I heard, *Grace.*"

Grace, Irene explained, was the daughter of Heidi, one of the group's newest members. Heidi and her partner Kristen had twin daughters, Faith and Grace. Fifteen-year-old Grace had been killed in an automobile accident only a few months earlier, and the family was devastated.

"I'd only met Heidi twice, but I went up to her at the meeting that afternoon and delivered Grace's message."

"That was brave," said Lynn.

Irene shrugged off the compliment. "Heidi said she didn't know about the laundry, because Kristen took care of that, but she would check. That night she sent me an email—*You're not going to believe this, but Kristen hasn't been able to bring herself to touch the clothes in Grace's room. Her dirty laundry has been sitting in a basket since she passed!*"

"And Grace showed up in your shower to tell you her dirty laundry was gross," Jeff said, shaking his head.

"Sounds like something Carly would do," Tony joked.

The conversation halted momentarily as the server appeared to take our orders. When she had left, I turned to Elizabeth and Cyril. "How about Morgan? Does he send you signs?"

They both nodded.

"I think one of the best happened to Cyril when he was in Hong Kong on business," Elizabeth said. She turned to her husband. "Why don't you tell it?"

Cyril cleared his throat and paused for a moment, as if to get his emotions in check. "I was in the taxi on my way to the airport. I was feeling very blue about Morgan. Very blue. I still cry sometimes."

Elizabeth touched his arm.

"It was 5:30 in the morning, and the taxi's radio was playing Chinese music. But right as I started feeling so blue about my son, the song 'I Believe I Can Fly' came over the radio."

Elizabeth quickly explained. "That song was in a movie that featured Michael Jordan, one of Morgan's favorite athletes. I went to school with Michael for three years at Chapel Hill. Morgan idolized Michael and sang 'I Believe I Can Fly' into his phone's recorder. "

"It was the last thing he recorded on his phone. We were on vacation in the south of France," Cyril explained. "When he passed away, I had his phone, and I found the song with his voice."

"We both used that recording of him singing as our ringtone for a very long time," said Elizabeth.

"And that song came on a Chinese radio at 5:30 in the morning?" Tony asked.

"Yes. Just when I am feeling so sad for my son."

As the group murmured its appreciation, the sound of an acoustic guitar drifted over from the far side of the dining room. A singer clad in a t-shirt and shorts was perched sideways on a stool in front of a microphone. His long ponytail bobbed up and down as he plucked a few preparatory notes.

"Looks like we're going to have live music," said Ty.

"Maybe you can join him," Elizabeth said to Jeff.

"You play guitar?" I asked.

"He used to be in a rock band," said Lynn.

"No kidding," I said. "So was Ty."

The rest of the group turned to Ty in surprise. They had no idea I was playing straight man for one of his favorite stories. Ty followed my remark without missing a beat.

"I used to be a drummer with the Rolling Stones," he deadpanned.

I struggled not to laugh as I watched the others' stunned reactions. Even though Ty had retired from the Navy years earlier, he kept his hair trimmed to military standards. It was hard to imagine him hanging out with Mick Jagger.

Ty broke into a grin, "At least that's what I was able to convince my daughters. Until they were eight years old."

The others groaned.

Still smiling, Ty turned to Jeff. "What kind of music did your band play?"

"Oh, soft sounds of the 70's, folk, pop, light country. Easy listening stuff—kind of like he's playing now." He nodded toward the guitarist in the corner, who had begun his first set, far enough from our table to be well out of earshot. His first two songs provided a welcome relief from the canned Caribbean music that had blared through the speakers since our arrival. The softer tones allowed us to converse more freely.

There was a brief pause in the music, and a smattering of diners rewarded the musician with polite applause. When he started the third song, Jeff turned to Lynn. "There you go."

"What?" Tony asked.

"He's playing 'Blackbird.'"

"Oh, my gosh," I said, recalling their story of the blackbird that delivered a message to Lynn. "Is that Devon's song?"

"Kind of," she said, nodding at Jeff to explain.

He shrugged. "It's just one of those things. We tend to frequent places that play the kind of music I do. Invariably, at venues where there's acoustic guitars, 'Blackbird' comes up on the playlist two or three songs after we sit down."

"And this is his third song," I said, still struck with wonder, even though such incidents now occur routinely with my clients.

"It always happens," Jeff said, nonchalantly. "I can't explain it. It just *happens*."

"You can't make this stuff up," Ty said, gazing at the singer.

"And once you start noticing all the amazing signs our loved ones set right in front of us," I added, "you don't have to!"

"Carly plays 'Somewhere Over the Rainbow' for me," said Irene. "She loved going to Hawaii, and on one of our first visits, we heard that song played by a Hawaiian singer named Iz. I have a card she gave me when she was in college that plays 'Somewhere Over the Rainbow' when you open it. So it was always our song. It got to the point where if I heard it, I would call her, and if she heard it, she would call me. You know, 'Mom, the song's on!'"

She gazed wistfully out at the water. "I couldn't play it at her memorial service. I just couldn't. And for a while, when I'd hear the song, I'd be very sad. Then it changed to where I did want to hear it again, and I started noticing that it would play if I thought about her."

We could feel Irene's energy lifting as she described her transition. "Now, what happens is I will literally get this feeling that the song is going to play, or I will hear, *Put Pandora on*, and if a song is finishing up, the next song will be the rainbow song."

"Those in spirit put the thought in our head to listen to the music," I explained to the others.

"Right," Irene agreed. "Carly's not changing the playlist. She's letting me know it's coming up next."

The singer's voice trailed off as he came to the end of "Blackbird." In the silence we all glanced his way. Lost in his music, he remained unaware of our group. He moved his hand up to the headstock and tweaked the tuning keys. He gave a small nod, perhaps acknowledging to himself that his instrument was once again in tune. Or perhaps it was a subconscious nod to those in spirit.

He may never know what caused him to choose the song he played next. Those of us at the table, however, will never forget our shared delight when the familiar opening tones of "Somewhere Over the Rainbow" followed directly on the tail of "Blackbird". In gratitude to our kids and to our unwitting musical messenger, we raised our glasses in a toast toward the star-filled sky.[6]

---

[6] Every story in this book is true. The magical moments such as these two songs playing back-to-back when they did unfolded exactly as written. There is no need to fictionalize what those in spirit bring to us. When we have eyes to see and ears to hear, the interconnectedness of the physical and the nonphysical world becomes clear.

CHAPTER 15
Hugs

§

I REMOVED MY HEADPHONES AND opened my eyes. The morning sun streamed through the small ports and overhead hatch of our cabin, promising another glorious day. The murmur of voices and clinking of dishes drifted down from the galley, replacing the ethereal meditation music I'd been enjoying. I glanced at my watch; the time was 7:20. I pictured Ty on the aft deck enjoying a cup of coffee and wondered if everyone else was up and about.

I slid to the end of the berth and slipped my legs over the edge until my feet touched the deck. Dressed in t-shirt and shorts, and not bothering to put on shoes, I ducked into the head for a quick glance in the mirror and winced. Without a dryer, there wasn't much I could do about my flat hair, but my face was a different story.

I hesitated, wavering in my decision to go without makeup. It was far too easy for my human side to find fault with my eyes and skin. Then I reminded myself that the other women looked beautiful to me no matter how much or how little makeup they wore. I could only hope they felt the same about my vacation-on-a-sailboat look.

Five quick steps and I emerged into the sunny salon to discover I was the last one to come topside. Greetings rang out, accompanied by joyful hugs from the other ladies, followed by the same from their husbands. Not wanting to miss out, even Ty joined in what I sensed would become a morning ritual now that we were all aboard.

"Did you get this kind of greeting?" I asked him.

"Yeah," he laughed and shook his head. "I'm not used to being kissed by a Frenchman first thing in the morning."

I found the group's rapport almost addictive. *If only everyone knew this kind of unconditional acceptance, I mused, people would understand that heaven is right where we are.*

The men returned to the aft deck to chat and I glanced around the salon. Elizabeth had gone back to the table and resumed typing on her laptop. Lynn stood at the counter making a second pot of coffee. With a rag under each foot, Irene was shuffling around the deck on the far side of the salon like an energetic ice skater.

"What are you doing, Irene?"

"Cleaning the floor!" she responded cheerily. "This is how I do it at home. It's really efficient."

"Looks like great exercise!" I turned to the others, remembering my meditation. "Do I have time to type up Sanaya's message?"

Elizabeth looked up, her fingers poised on her laptop keyboard. "We have all the time in the world."

"You two do what you need to," Lynn said. "I'll start breakfast."

"I'll help as soon as I finish the floor," Irene said.

I took a seat perpendicular to Elizabeth and set up my iPad. "What are you working on?"

She glanced up long enough to flash me a pearly smile. "I'm posting today's tributes for our kids on Facebook."

I recalled seeing the "Today's Tributes" page on the Helping Parents Heal website when I was searching for photos of Morgan and Devon for the collage. I had no idea that Elizabeth personally copied each photo and write-up onto the group's Facebook page to honor a child's birthday and angel dates.

"You do those manually?" I asked, incredulous. With ten thousand members and growing, there must be well over a dozen tributes each day.

"All by herself, every day," said Lynn as she pulled a package of bacon from the small refrigerator.

"It's no problem, really," Elizabeth said, waving off our comments without looking up from her laptop.

"I'm sure you could easily get a team of volunteers to help you," I offered.

She gave a small shudder. "Oh, no—I missed a couple of posts once, and the mothers got really upset. They took it personally, as if I deliberately ignored their kids, and it only added to their grief."

I gaped. "But that wasn't your fault."

"I know, but I felt so bad for them."

"But you're on vacation," I said. "You shouldn't have to be tied to the website."

The moment I heard my own words I stopped and chuckled to myself. My guides often state that our "shoulds" and "have to's" are the ego's way of keeping us trapped in our stories. Wasn't I just as driven to post Sanaya's messages every day? My compulsion was no different than Elizabeth's with her tributes and Irene with her clean floors. We're all works in progress.

"I don't mind doing the tributes," Elizabeth added. "We're one family, more so even than some biological families. And our kids are all connected."

"The connections are incredible," Lynn agreed. "Just look at Mark Ireland. He's the co-founder of Helping Parents Heal—his eighteen-year-old son Brandon passed on a mountain."

"Oh, my gosh," I said. "Just like Morgan."

"Not exactly the same, but also due to a breathing problem," Elizabeth said.

"How long after Morgan passed did you start Helping Parents Heal?" Irene asked.

"I didn't call it that at the time," Elizabeth said matter-of-factly, "but I started a support group one week after Morgan's transition."

"One week!" Irene and I exclaimed in unison. The two of us shared a look, knowing that neither of us could think straight after our daughters passed, let alone start an organization.

Elizabeth explained that Morgan had helped her set up a Facebook profile before he left for China so that she could see the pictures he posted. After he passed, she searched without success for bereavement resources online and ended up forming her own parents' support group on Facebook. With a mission statement that aimed to "aid bereaved parents, helping them heal as they walk this difficult journey," she began holding monthly meetings in Scottsdale.

"I called the group 'Parents United in Loss,'" she said, "but I never liked the name. I realized very quickly that our kids are definitely not lost."

Irene pulled the rags from under her feet and joined us at the table. "How did Mark Ireland get involved?"

Elizabeth explained that Mark's father, Richard Ireland, was a famous psychic and medium who had authored several books on the topic. When Brandon passed, there was no question in Mark's mind that his son's soul continued to exist. For him, discussions of the afterlife were a part of everyday life. He had always known there was more to this life than our earthly existence.

A day before Brandon's autopsy was complete, Mark received a call from his paternal uncle, Robert Ireland, who shared the same abilities as Mark's father. His uncle reported that in meditation he had connected with Richard, Mark's father and Brandon's grandfather. Mark's father in spirit stated that he was there when Brandon passed, and that Brandon's death was due to a lack of oxygen that caused his heart to fail. The autopsy report arrived the next day, listing the cause of death: a severe asthma attack that caused his blood oxygen level to drop and his heart to fail.

With this confirmation, Mark found himself drawn to share his awareness of the afterlife with others, just as his father had done throughout his own life. He penned the book *Soul Shift* about his personal journey. Mark also found an old manuscript of his father's on psychic development that had never been released and had it published. A short time later, a friend of his, Tina Powers, a well-respected evidential medium in her own right, informed Mark that she sensed that one of his main callings in this life was to help parents with children on the other side of the veil. Mark took Tina's words to heart.

He first thought of forming a support group that focused on what he had always known in his heart: that death is not the end. He was well aware that most bereavement groups avoid this critical point. Mark wanted to be part of an organization that incorporates hope into their efforts to alleviate the suffering of those dealing with the passing of a loved one. Hope was the one element that seemed to be missing from other support groups.

He began to speak from his unique perspective at events featuring well-respected mediums in the Phoenix area. At one of these events Mark met the medium Susanne Wilson. Shortly thereafter, Susanne offered to introduce him to Elizabeth Boisson. Intrigued about this woman whose support group shared his hope-based ideals, Mark and his wife Susie met Elizabeth for coffee. She had read Mark's book and invited him to be the first guest speaker for Parents United in Loss.

When Mark met the 30 parents gathered together at Elizabeth's meeting, he couldn't help but be impressed. Elizabeth, he saw, had created an effective blueprint for exactly what he envisioned on a larger scale. He noted that she had an online presence with Facebook, but no newsletter or independent website.

Mark pitched his idea to grow Parents United in Loss into something that could touch a greater number of lives, expanding the groups into other cities and towns. Elizabeth loved the idea. Mark proposed the name "Helping Parents Heal," which she loved even more.

"Mark is Vice President of Sales for a major retail graphics company," Elizabeth said, finishing her story. "He created the original website and encouraged me to compose the monthly newsletter, but with his corporate job, he's not able to commit as much time to the group as I know he'd like to."

"We love Mark and Susie," Lynn interjected. "We met them through my friend Debra Martin, who invited us and the Irelands to dinner one evening. We hit it off right away. They were very influential in our early healing days—they pretty much saved us emotionally, because they'd been through it, too."

"Susie is such a positive person," said Elizabeth.

"She and Mark say the same of you," Lynn replied. She turned to me and Irene. "It was through Mark that Elizabeth and I first met. He told me, 'Oh, you need to meet Elizabeth!'"

"We're certainly glad you did," I said.

"I'll say," Irene agreed.

The smell of bacon drew our attention to breakfast. Soon we were all engrossed in preparing a feast for eight. With so many hands on deck, a banquet worthy of a fancy B&B soon appeared on the aft deck table. The eight of us fit comfortably, two to a side, and soon we were passing plates heaped with crisp bacon and scrambled eggs mixed with chives and brie.

While we enjoyed an assortment of toast and ripe tropical fruits, Ty discussed his thoughts for the day's sail. The island of Jost van Dyke was a must-visit on any BVI charter, and only a short hop from Soper's Hole.

I fondly recalled Jost van Dyke from our charter trip years earlier. I hoped to replace a favorite t-shirt from the famous Foxy's Bar that I had worn out long ago. Even though Tony and Irene had just toured the island, they were game for another visit. All agreed on the plan, and within the hour we dropped the mooring pendant and got underway.

Once I helped the men stow the dock lines, I ducked below for my sunglasses. As I returned to the salon to join the ladies, I caught Lynn in deep conversation with Irene. Hearing Devon's name, I understood she was sharing the story of her son's disappearance and quickly retreated.

From the moment that we had conceived of the trip, I planned to do a group reading when the time felt right. Until then, all that

I knew of Devon was the same story Lynn was now telling Irene. I wanted to avoid hearing any additional details that Devon, Morgan, or Carly might be able to share with me themselves.

I scurried up to join Ty at the helm station. He slid across the padded bench and I squeezed in beside him.

"I love the view from up here," I said, gazing across at the islands that dotted the ocean as far as the eye could see.

"Yeah, but the boat's so wide, you can't see the port side," he commented.

"It's not that much different than conning a destroyer," I laughed.

"It's completely different," he countered with a wry smile.

I knew how much he missed being at sea. When my work as a medium took on a life of its own, we sold our cruising boat and bought the RV to travel to my workshops around the country. I knew what a sacrifice Ty had made in giving up sailing, yet he never complained. His support was critical to my being able to continue my work, and we both honor Susan through our efforts together.

We sat in silence a few minutes, then I put a hand on his leg and joked, "It looks like you have this under control. I'm going back to the girls."

"Have fun," he said.

I returned to the salon and poked my head into the forward cockpit. "Have you finished the blackbird story?" I asked Lynn.

"Just now," she answered.

I stepped inside and took a seat on one of the forward-facing benches. "Wasn't it incredible how all the mediums knew the blackbird would have the message?" I said to Irene.

"Amazing," Irene replied, shaking her head.

"I love hearing the stories about our kids," said Elizabeth.

"I need to do a reading for all of you pretty soon," I said, "because I enjoy the stories, too. I don't like staying away from you out of fear that I'll hear something that might come through later in the session."

All three made dismissive gestures and welcomed me into the group.

I gazed out at the water and flashed back to a painful memory. "Being out here reminds me of when we went back to our boat after Susan's funeral. I'll never forget how we headed south for Greece right away. We wanted to distance ourselves from the emotions we associated with Croatia, where we first got the bad news."

I told the girls about another cruising boat that sailed past us, heading north on the Adriatic Sea. Ty and I recognized it as belonging to an American couple who had spent the winter with us at a marina outside Rome. It was unusual to cross paths on the open sea with someone we knew, and we immediately hailed them on the radio.

"We knew our friends had heard about Susan's death through the cruising grapevine," I said. "This was only a week after the funeral, and our grief was all-consuming."

The others nodded with empathy as I continued. "They made casual conversation—'Hey, good to see you, where are you guys heading?'—and then they sailed off, without ever mentioning the worst thing that had ever happened to us."

"The same thing happened to me," Elizabeth said. She told of encountering a close friend in a grocery store shortly after Morgan passed. She and the friend caught each other's eye, and Elizabeth assumed the woman would come to her and give her a hug. Instead, her friend turned and walked the other way without saying a word.

"I know now," she said, "that the reason people do that is that they have no idea what to say, and they don't want to make us cry."

Lynn nodded. "I think they just don't know what to do."

"I knew that was the case with this cruising couple," I said, "but when you're going through it, the lack of acknowledgment really hurts."

"Oh, definitely," Irene agreed. "The grocery store was difficult for me, too, because food was Carly's life. I saw someone in the store and the same thing happened as with you, Elizabeth. This woman turned around and went the other way. I went home and said to Tony, 'That's it, we have to get out of here. I can't do this.' That's when we made the decision to leave New Jersey."

"I thought you left because the taxes were too high," I said.

"Well, no," she replied. "There were a multitude of things. If we stayed, I would have had to continue to work, and I just couldn't do it anymore. I would be cleaning people's teeth, and they'd be complaining, and I'd want to say 'Are you kidding me? My daughter had her stomach removed and she never complained, and you're complaining about a cleaning?' I knew I could no longer work with that kind of attitude."

We murmured our understanding.

"But about a month after Carly was gone," she continued, "I decided to join a group of women who walked at the local reservoir. I didn't know some of them, and one woman came up to me and said, 'I'm so sorry. I can't imagine what it feels like to lose your daughter. I'll never get to meet Carly, but I hope you'll tell me everything about her.'"

"Oh, that's nice," I said.

"She's now my very dear friend," Irene confirmed.

Behind us at the helm, Ty altered course and headed for the harbor entrance.

Lynn brushed her hair off her face and said, "I remember reading on Facebook about a really great gift one of the members of our group received for Christmas. The woman's mother told her she wanted her daughter to call her and speak about her grandson for 30 minutes. That was her gift."

"Oh, wow," we said in unison.

"I thought that was beautiful," Lynn continued, "because it's hard sometimes to even get members of our own family to listen to our stories about our kids." She looked from one of us to the other. "People don't know what to say, but it's so easy to listen. It really is."

"I think what Elizabeth said earlier is right," I added. "People are often afraid of opening wounds with a parent who's grieving."

Lynn confirmed my thoughts. "I have a new friend whose son passed," she said. "I met her a month or so ago, and the first thing I said was, 'Tell me about your son,' and she said, 'I can't even say his name, let alone talk about him.'"

Elizabeth added her thoughts. "I would say that only a very small percentage of parents who are bereaved feel that way. It's a rare parent who doesn't want to talk about their kids. I think that if you spend long enough with them, you find they want to talk about their children more than anything in the world."

I turned to Irene. "How were you in the beginning? Did you want to talk about Carly?"

"I always wanted to talk about her," she said with a grave expression. "I had one friend who would come over every single night and just sit on the couch with me and hold my hand. I would cry and just tell stories, and she would talk about Carly, because we met in Lamaze class. And that got me through."

"What a friend," I said.

"In the beginning, I didn't want to be around anybody I knew," Lynn said. "It was just too painful."

"This was a very close friend that I'm talking about," Irene said. "I couldn't have sat with someone I didn't really know. But other people would drop off meals. I didn't cook for months. I just couldn't. They would put food on the doorstep or give us restaurant gift certificates."

Elizabeth shared her own memories of the mothers of Morgan's football team bringing meals to the house. "I think that bringing food and listening are two of the most healing gestures in the beginning. People mistakenly think they need to say something profound. But the truth is, you don't have to say a thing. A hug is a lot more effective. When I saw that woman in the grocery store, if she had come up and hugged me without a word, it would have been all that I needed."

"I totally agree," Lynn said. "We had some good friends that we got together with at least twice a week. When Devon passed, I think it hit them a little too close. They couldn't handle being around us." She sighed. "We're not friends anymore."

"Oh, yeah," Irene said. "My best childhood friend, a woman I met in kindergarten, didn't know how to handle it. She passed recently and I talk to her husband these days. He told me that she didn't know what to do, so she just didn't do anything. And, you know, that was very hurtful."

Elizabeth stretched out her long legs on the deck and leaned forward in a yoga position. When she sat up, she remarked, "I believe we can truly grow as people as a result of this process, especially because our kids are behind us every step of the way. Once you understand that, the whole journey becomes mystical, magical. People need to know that it's possible to heal."

"But would you have been open to that early on?" Lynn asked.

"Not me," Irene interjected.

Lynn pressed Elizabeth for an answer. "Would you want somebody to tell you, 'Hey, this is going to be a beautiful thing in your life, you just have to hold on and find it'?"

I sat back in observer mode, marveling at the honest feelings being shared. There was no accusation in Lynn's question, nor a hint of defensiveness in Elizabeth's reply.

"No, no, but it's important to let people know that it can get better. Seeing Mark Ireland when I did, knowing that he himself had been going through this process for six years and that he and Susie were still alive and thriving, was so important for me."

Lynn perked up on hearing Mark and Susie's names. "I remember one night, around nine o'clock—we had just had guests over who were saying all these depressing things. They finally left, and I looked at Jeff and I said, 'Do you think the Irelands are still awake?' We called them and went over there just to be around people who had survived what we were going through and let joy back into their lives."

"That's what I'm talking about," Elizabeth nodded.

"And I found out, you know, that we can not only survive but thrive," Lynn said. She turned to Irene. "But in the beginning, I don't know that people want to hear that. You can barely put a foot on the ground."

"I had the same realization not too long ago," Irene said. "We were chatting before the start of an online meeting, and two new parents to the group came in. They were just sobbing, and I thought, 'Oh my gosh, here I am smiling, I hope it doesn't make them feel worse.' But then I remembered that my friend Heidi always says to me, 'You offer hope to me. I look at you and I say, okay, if you can do it, then I can do it, too.'"

"I have a friend like that," Lynn said. She was so negative in the beginning, and I think our joy bothered her. She and I went on walk after walk after walk. I saw a total transformation in her, but it took a while."

"I know who you're talking about," Elizabeth said. "I had lunch with her recently, and she said, 'You know, I wanted to hate you guys in the beginning because you were so happy.'"

Lynn grimaced. "I think she did hate us, actually."

"But she said she eventually learned to see the blessing in our relationship," Elizabeth said.

"In the beginning she was full of rage and so bitter," Lynn said, confirming that they were speaking of the same woman.

"But she really has changed," Elizabeth said. "And I think that's definitely because of you, and because of the fact that—"

"We can't take credit for that," Lynn interrupted. "I mean, we might have planted a seed, but she really worked on herself."

"Yes, she did," Elizabeth agreed. "She got into yoga, which is incredibly important, in my life at least, and she read a lot. I just think that we shouldn't be afraid to help people understand that it does get better." The passion in her voice grew stronger. "We can all be okay, and most important of all, our kids want us to be happy and experience joy!"

Caught up in her emotion, Irene and I spontaneously applauded.

Lynn stood and stretched lazily from one side to the other. "We went to dinner recently with some colleagues of Jeff's whom we hadn't seen in four years. At one point the wife looked at me and said, 'Have you heard from Devon lately?' "

I stiffened, thinking she was describing an awkward moment with someone who didn't know that Devon had passed. Seeing Lynn's smile as she recounted the memory, I suddenly understood the woman's true meaning.

"She knew he'd passed?" I asked.

"Yes, absolutely," Lynn confirmed. "I love it when people ask if I've heard from Devon, because really, that's what we all want to talk about. But honestly, I think sometimes we frighten people."

We all laughed.

Irene lowered her voice. "A friend of mine told a neighbor in Moss Creek, where we live, that she was going to have dinner with Tony and me, and the woman said, 'I've heard about that Irene Vouvalides.' "

Our laughter turned to hoots, and I said, "So you're The Witch of Moss Creek now?"

"No," she laughed and waved off my comment. Growing suddenly serious, she added, "But another woman from Moss Creek came to one of my meetings recently. Her daughter passed from cancer a few months after Carly. Just before we came on this trip, she said to me, 'We're heading up north tomorrow for four months, and when I come back, would you walk with me and help me? We're in the same place time-wise, but I'm nowhere near where you are emotionally. I'd like to get there, too.' "

"Look how far you've come," I remarked. "Carly said you and she would be moving on together—now you're the role model for others."

"That's how it works," Elizabeth said. "If you want to help someone who's grieving, you let them know, 'I will always be here for you.' "

"That's called 'holding space,'" Irene said.[7] "You don't try to fix things. You just show up and offer your love without any conditions."

"Keep calling," Lynn said. "Keep emailing. Be available."

My heart surged with gratitude for these friends. "You guys are on a mission."

"One person at a time," Lynn said.

"One hug at a time," I said, holding out my arms.

The others stood and we shared in the second spontaneous embrace of the morning, soaking in the joy of the moment.

We all understood the reasons friends came and went in a crisis and why some failed to be there for us when we needed them most. Sometimes, we agreed, the best thing for someone who's hurting is a hug.

I knew how much we all missed hugging our children. I couldn't bring back their physical presence, but I could do my best to provide the second-best thing: evidence that we were not alone on this trip. Glancing ahead, I saw that we were approaching Jost van Dyke. I decided that my Foxy's t-shirt could wait. As soon as we were securely moored, it was time to connect with our kids.

---

[7] See the blog post, "What it Means to Really Hold Space for Someone," by Heather Plett, along with Heather's "8 Tips to Help You Hold Space for Others" at http://upliftconnect.com/hold-space/

CHAPTER 16
Y-A-Y

§

BOATS ON A MOORING BALL or at anchor always face into the wind and tidal current. Ours was one of half a dozen vessels in the harbor. As I faced aft from my seat at the cockpit table, a southerly breeze caressed my face. Foxy's Bar stood a few hundred yards away. The sun shone brightly, sparkling on calm water that reflected a clear blue sky. If the others were eager to go ashore and explore, they hid it well. Once I offered to do a group reading and connect with our kids, everyone gathered in the cockpit without complaint.

We took the same seats at the large, square table as we had at breakfast a few hours before. Clockwise to my left, facing the port side, sat Irene and then Tony. Cyril came next, directly across from me, with Elizabeth to his left. Jeff and Lynn occupied the side facing starboard, and Ty rounded out the arrangement, sitting immediately to my right.

Until that moment, conversations among the group had been equally shared in an easy give and take. No one was more or less of a talker than the rest. With all the attention now riveted on me, I felt suddenly awkward. But if I did my job right, our focus would soon settle where it belonged: on our kids.

"I've given three readings to Irene, so I know Carly's energy pretty well," I said by way of introduction. "But I've only sensed Morgan and Devon when they dropped in at Lynn and Jeff's dinner party."

I described the few facts I already knew about the boys. I was aware of how each had passed, and I knew that they were both of college age. I knew that both had attended the University of Arizona and that Devon had been teaching abroad.

"How a spirit passed, how old they were, and what kind of work they did are some of the key pieces of evidence I ask those in spirit to give me in every reading," I said. "Since I already know those things about all three kids, I'm fairly certain they'll spend most of the time giving me memories and other pieces of information that I don't know about so that you can clearly identify each of them."

I turned to Ty. "I'm sure that Susan will join us today, so I've asked her to tell me something I don't know that will show you she's here."

"I already know she is," Ty assured me with a pat on my leg.

I explained to everybody that to our kids, the reading was like a party. They knew they were invited, and that they were free to chat as they normally would, speaking up as they wished to share memories or messages, in no particular order.

"I want to hear you say 'Yay!'" Jeff said.

I turned to him, puzzled. "Yay?"

"That's what you say in the readings in *Messages of Hope* when a really good piece of evidence comes through."

I laughed. "I do say that a lot, but I didn't realize I put it in the book."

"Yes," Irene interjected, "but is that 'y-a-y' or 'y-a-h'?"

She and I laughed and turned to Lynn, who rolled her eyes as she shook her head. She explained to Jeff, "They're giving me a hard time, because I spell it 'y-a-h' in all of my texts."

"It's 'y-a-y,'" Irene teased.

"I've always spelled it 'y-a-h'," Lynn said, shrugging her shoulders.

Across the table, Cyril appeared puzzled by our discussion of English slang.

"It doesn't matter how it's spelled," I said, bringing my focus back to the task at hand. "Let's join hands as we set the intention for a connection that's so clear that we get those 'yay's."

Sixteen hands formed a circle, and we closed our eyes.

"In awareness that all is Spirit, and we are that," I began, "we join our hearts this day with the intention of connecting with our loved ones in spirit. I ask my Team of helpers to step in now and bring with you our children, if this will serve the greater good. We do this with love and with gratitude for the greatest possible healing on both sides of the veil. And so it is."

"And so it is," echoed those around the table as we released our hands and I shifted my awareness to the spirit world. Until then, I had known in my heart our kids were with us on the trip. Now it was time to prove it to the rest.[8]

"Okay," I began. "What I sensed a little earlier as I was getting ready, was that Morgan was showing me a little fedora." I reached up and patted the top of my head. "You know how guys wear those little fedora hats that are smaller than the big ones? They were in fashion for a while. Did he ever have one of those hats?"

Cyril and Elizabeth did not connect with this image. I turned to Lynn and Jeff and explained that because I don't clearly see faces and wasn't familiar with the boys' personalities, I might misidentify who was speaking.

"That goes with Devon," Lynn informed me, proving my point.

"We have a stack of fedoras in the studio," Jeff affirmed.

"Oh, cool. Okay. So, *welcome, Devon!*"

The group muttered excitedly, but I had already shifted my focus back to those in spirit. "Somebody is playing a drum, just kind of being funny."

"He played when he was young," Jeff confirmed.

---

[8] All conversation is taken verbatim from the transcript of the actual group reading held on the boat.

"Great. He was overseas teaching, but there's a strong feeling with him that while he may have taken it seriously, it was more about the adventure. More about having fun. He's laughing like, '*Yeah, I made it look like I was into the teaching, but I was—*'"

Lynn interrupted me. "That's totally him."

"I feel like I'm more interested in being 'in the moment,'" I said, indicating that when I spoke in the first person, I was blending my personality with Devon's.

"Yeah," Lynn agreed.

I became aware of two distinct male energies, and intuitively knew the other was Morgan. I shared with Elizabeth and Cyril that I knew their son had been adventurous, but he was allowing me to feel a different side of his character now. "It's not that Devon didn't care about people," I said, "but there's this heart opening with Morgan as if he's going to want to change the world. If he were in the Navy, he'd be the one out there painting a church while he's on leave."

I explained that there were certain sailors who always helped local charities when they went ashore in foreign ports. "This is the feeling I'm getting as I tune in to Morgan. Does that sound right?"

"He was helping deaf and mute kids in China," Elizabeth said. "And he was the one who took care of all the exchange students."

I nodded. "So that makes sense."

"Now Carly wants to talk," I said, turning to Irene and Tony. I laughed and rubbed a finger on my upper left arm, explaining that Carly wanted me to mention the little round vaccine mark I have in that spot. "She wants me to talk about one that would make her specifically insecure, as in '*Oh, it's so awful. I have to put makeup or something on it so people don't see it.*'"

"Oh, big time," Irene said, nodding. "She wanted to have plastic surgery done."

"Because of a vaccine spot?" I asked, surprised as much by the obscure piece of evidence as by the idea that Carly would worry so much about a blemish on her arm.

"It looked like a vaccine spot, but it was a birthmark," Irene said.

"Yay!" I said, without thinking.

"She was so self-conscious," Irene explained, rubbing the same spot on her own arm. "Sometimes she would even put a Band-Aid on it. In fact, before she was diagnosed, I was going to take her to the plastic surgeon."

"Okay, we've got her," I said, impressed by Carly's efforts to share the kind of personal detail one was unlikely to find on the Internet.

Now that all three children had made their presence known, they shared their main message.

"We're so happy you guys are out here," I said, delivering their words directly. *"We did plan this. You're beautiful to everybody who sees you, all of you, because you shine. We know it's because of us. We are all connected."*

I switched to speaking in my own words: "They say we don't need the anchor light at night because this boat glows from above. They say it's why we don't have to worry about any of us not getting along, because all of our energy just merges. They say we don't have to do anything to shine; just being together raises the light."

I turned to Lynn and described a pocketknife that Devon was showing me. "You have a special one that was his. . . . "

Lynn shook her head, but Jeff jumped in.

"Yep," he said, nodding as he repeated. "Yep. Yep."

I turned to the others and smiled. "This is why I love having both parents present. Mom says, 'no,' and Dad says, 'yes.'"

"It's in my drawer," Jeff said. "If I need to open a box, I—" He stopped mid-sentence, looked down, and wiped at his eyes. "I'm sorry," he apologized.

I smiled sympathetically, moved that the evidence had touched his heart.

"That's not sweat, by the way," Jeff said sheepishly to the others. I felt the group's loving kindness radiate toward him in response.

Jeff took a cleansing breath and explained, "The knife's got his name on it. It was a gift to him when he was in Cub Scouts. I was a cub master, and I gave him that knife."

"Good, good," I said. I explained to the group that this is how those in spirit work with me in my readings. They deliver messages that can't be proven, such as their discussion about seeing the group's light from the heavens. Then they throw in a random piece of verifiable evidence like the special knife so that all will know the messages are not simply the medium's imagination.

I turned to Lynn, "Devon is aware that there might be a feeling in you that you should be doing more." I knew he was alluding to the fact that Elizabeth, Irene, and I were reaching out to groups of people, whereas Lynn preferred to help particular individuals in need with whom she felt a connection. "And he says, *'Just be yourself and you glow, you glow.'*"

The energy shifted from Devon alone to an awareness of the entire young group's energy merging as one. "And now the group voice comes back and they say, *'No comparing. It's all one light. You are more guided than you know.'* And they're laughing, saying, *'Ha, ha. You told us what to do when we were little, and we get to pull your chain now.'*"

Everyone laughed, and Lynn said, "I totally feel like that. You know, Jeff and I have a joke—"

Jeff began pantomiming the motions of a puppeteer. "Every time Devon shows up," he said, continuing the mime, "I do this and she dances."

"The puppet dance," Lynn said with a shrug.

I grinned. "I would have said 'pull your strings,' but they changed it to 'pull your chain.'"

"That's Susan," said Ty with a chuckle.

I tuned in to see if I discerned our daughter's presence, and indeed, I did. There was no mistaking her. "She's laughing!" I said. "There's some story of you marking the anchor chain every ten feet on a boat you had, and of you doing it with her."

"She helped paint it on our first boat," he affirmed.

"There we go," I said, wagging a finger. "She wants me to talk about a memory that I don't know." I had seen Ty mark anchor chains on our own boats, but I didn't know Susan had helped him with the same task.

I began laughing out loud at Susan's antics and realized I needed to let the others know what I found so amusing. "Susan is clapping and she just said, *'Yay, Suzanne!'*" I emphasized the 'yay,' and told the group that I heard Susan's voice exactly as I remembered it.

"I love you, too," I responded aloud to her. "So, back to Carly, who just drew my attention to this mop over here," I pointed toward the corner. "She's acting as if she would never put a mop in her hand. Get her on a boat, and she's going to be in a bikini up on the deck."

"Oh, yeah," Irene drolled.

I silently asked Carly to give me some more specific evidence, but before she could do so, Morgan took center stage.

"Morgan was an A student," I announced. "It feels like he would have gotten a scholarship."

"He did," Elizabeth confirmed.

"And it feels as if you started one with his name."

Elizabeth affirmed this as well.

"'*I love you*,' he says, "and he shows me that the dove balloons that went up were not the first time. It feels like you did this before with regular balloons."

"We did. Regular, round balloons," Elizabeth said as Cyril nodded. "There's a picture of us doing that."

Devon jumped in with an important message for Lynn and Jeff. He let them know that he felt no pain when he passed and that he wasn't frightened.

Carly once again pulled my attention toward her mother. "Carly wanted a tattoo so badly, but it feels like she didn't get one," I reported.

"That's true," Irene said. "She was going to have an 'Om' symbol tattoo, but she didn't get the chance to do it."

"Okay, and somebody got a tattoo on their face. I'm being shown the image of an aborigine with one on the face."

No one could confirm this, and I felt Susan nudging me. "Susan says, '*Just relax*,' to me. Oh! She means both of us need to relax." I turned to Ty and saw that he looked quite tense. I told the others, "He gets nervous for me when I do this. Susan says, '*Chill, Dad.*'"

"Chill," he parroted and made a goofy face.

I laughed. "Susan's showing me these shorty-shorts she used to wear, and how that made you uncomfortable."

He grunted a strongly affirmative "uh-huh," and the others laughed.

I explained that Susan was the perfect paradox: a tough Marine and a girly-girl at the same time. "'*Underneath it all, I was always your little girl, and I still am,*' she says."

I glanced at Elizabeth and Cyril when Morgan grabbed my attention again. As I looked toward them, I noticed a small boat motoring past our stern. I thought to myself that the eight of us must have looked like normal charter guests sitting around chatting. *If they had any idea about what we're doing right now*, I thought, knowing that no one would suspect we were having a conversation with the spirits of our deceased children.

"Morgan is showing me that he was so active when he was little that you'd want to put a leash on him."

"Oh!" Elizabeth said, eyes wide. "I put a leash on him!"

"All right, because he shows me an active child with a leash."

"I had two little girls," she said as if apologizing. "And, I mean … it was so hard, in airports especially when I was traveling that—"

"Perfect," I said, smiling.

"How embarrassing." She lowered her eyes, but could not keep back a smile at this validation of communication from her son.

"You do what you have to do," Jeff chimed in.

"I'm supposed to talk about the person who drank light beer," I said.

Elizabeth and Cyril confirmed that Morgan had a beer at Base Camp the night before he passed, but they did not know whether it was a light variety.

"Your son is such a leader," I said, using the present tense to describe the quality I felt from his energy. "He's taking me to the camp, and he's telling everybody, *'I'm okay, I'm okay,'* and now I'm hearing the word 'captain' as if he might have been captain of the cheerleader squad. Was he?"

"He wasn't, but everybody called him Captain in high school. That was his nickname."

Morgan continued to demonstrate his leadership qualities. He triggered my memory of a previous conversation between Ty and myself about lemmings following each other over a cliff. "He had such charisma that people would follow him off a cliff if he said so," I said, interpreting the imagery. "But there's a double meaning to this, because he shows me cliff diving."

"He did cliff diving in Bartlett Lake," Elizabeth confirmed.

"Good, good. All right." I paused and then tossed my head back, laughing. "Carly says, *'Get back to me!'* It's hilarious."

"Prima donna," said Irene said, straight-faced, and the two of us burst out laughing.

It was a private joke, dating back to a month before the boat trip. Irene and Tony, I explained to the group, had visited us in Florida to celebrate Ty and Tony's December birthdays. Irene and I took the opportunity to sneak into my study and chat with Carly. She showed up as if she'd been waiting and shared several specific and accurate pieces of information about current events in her mother's life. As always, Carly made me laugh with her antics, especially when she put her hands on her hips and announced in no uncertain terms, *"I'm not a prima donna!"*

Irene threw her head back and laughed with amused disbelief.

"What's that all about?" I asked.

She explained that during their recent Helping Parents Heal meeting, Tony had lovingly remarked that Carly was a bit of a prima donna. Now Carly had come through from the spirit world to express her indignation at Tony's words.

As I shifted my awareness back to our kids, I sensed that Susan wanted more prime time. Unexpectedly, she answered a question I'd long wondered about. I turned to Ty. "Susan says she knows you hated her tattoo . . . " I described to the others how our daughter had had a large image of a phoenix tattooed on her hip. Neither Ty nor I had understood why she chose that design.

"She says she knew what this life is all about. *'We all do,'*" I relayed, referencing those who passed at an early age. "*'We rise from the ashes. Ashes to ashes, dust to dust. Look, we're still here, okay?'*" I blinked and glanced at each member of our group in turn. "That's a message for all of us. Did you all get that?"

All murmured their understanding. I turned to Irene.

"Carly loved to dance. I see her as eight or nine years old, hamming it up and twirling around."

"Twirling," Irene said. "Always twirling."

"And she was very competitive in school."

"Ohhhhh," Irene said, drawing out the sound to indicate the truth of this statement.

I recalled how Carly had demonstrated her drive to succeed academically in our earlier reading. Even though I knew how passionately she strove for high grades, I didn't want that information to filter what she showed me now. "She wants me to know that she did take her school very seriously, but the competition was mostly within, because she had to be the best. Make sense?" I asked.

"Absolutely. I was called into school when she was in second grade, because they wanted to know if I was putting too much pressure on her."

The others smiled as Irene continued, "I told them, 'No, it's all self-induced,' and it was. All the way."

"Now, I'm seeing a bumper sticker with a message. Do you have 'Carly's Kids' on a bumper sticker?" I asked.

Irene shook her head.

I looked around the table. "Who had the bumper sticker?"

"We have one," said Lynn.

"About Devon," I murmured as I looked more closely.

"Yeah," Jeff said.

"Is it the heart with wings?" I quickly caught myself, and shook my head. I try always to state objectively what I sense, without questioning. The design had flashed only fleetingly across my inner vision.

"Yes, it's the same," Jeff said.

"Okay," I said, "because it's colorful and clearly a bumper sticker."

I paused and picked up an image from Susan. I turned to Ty. "Susan is bringing up her belly button ring. She's making me laugh: *'I'm a Marine, and it's so against regulations,'* but she's showing me the pulling-your-chain thing again, as if she did it on purpose. She would do it on purpose. She would just pull your chain."

"Often," said Ty wryly.

"Really?" I asked, surprised. Though I had known Susan since she was thirteen, I realized there were aspects of the father-daughter dynamics I wasn't aware of.

"Oh yeah," he said. "She knew which buttons to push from the time she was nine or so."

"Okay," I said, "because I thought she would always be sweet, but she's like, *'No, no ...'"*

"Oh, no," he said, in a way which caused the others to laugh in commiseration. "She'd be sweet afterwards."

"Oh, yeah," Jeff said, letting us know Devon shared the same trait.

"Okay," I said, looking upwards. "One of your boys ... somebody wrote a song about them."

Elizabeth affirmed this, and I said, "It feels as if the lyrics are printed out and the graphic was pretty. It was nicely done, and it is handed to you."

"Okay," Elizabeth said, squinting as if piecing her memories together. "It was a beautiful song, and we played it at his service. It was written and performed by one of the kids who was on his exchange program to Paris, so there are pictures of that trip on the lyrics. So, yes, that's really pretty."

"Nice," I said, nodding.

I glanced at my watch and then looked up, smiling. "I was checking the time to see how long I can hold this link, and the group just showed me an oxygen tank, like, *'You're not going to run out of oxygen,'* and the feeling that comes with that is that one of them scuba dived."

"Yes, Morgan," Elizabeth confirmed.

Morgan then showed me that he played on the varsity football team and that he also won a trophy as a cheerleader. Once again, Elizabeth affirmed the details.

I silently asked the kids if they had any more messages to share. They informed me that they had already delivered their main message—about the importance of shining our lights as brightly as possible.

Morgan stepped forward and showed me a college diploma. My analytical mind tried to tell me I must be mistaken. I knew that Morgan passed during an undergraduate exchange trip. He persisted in showing me the image, so I turned to Elizabeth and Cyril. "You have a diploma for Morgan that's up on a wall."

Elizabeth nodded, explaining that they received a diploma from the University of Arizona three months after Morgan passed, even though he had three more credits to complete.

"Awwww," said Lynn, expressing her appreciation for the school's considerate gesture.

"Okay," I said, "because I was saying to him, *'But you didn't graduate!'* and he says, *'No, it's up on the wall!'*"

"It is," Elizabeth said, nodding. "It's up on the wall in Cyril's office."

Hearing this, I couldn't help clapping with delight at how clearly the kids were coming through. "Yay," I said, and then spelled out the word: "Y-a-y!"

Everyone laughed, and I repeated Morgan's message: "*'I love you, Dad. I love you, Mom.'* And I have this great big heart opening. They're confirming for me that, yes, *'We do have fun up here. Yes, we do play. Why wouldn't we?'* "

The reading continued with more memories offered from the other side. The boys brought up the time they rode a camel. Devon shared some present-day details about his sister, and they collectively made an unmistakable prophecy about a rainbow.

"It feels as if the rainbows are not over for this trip," I said, recalling "Somewhere Over the Rainbow" playing at Pusser's. "I know the bad weather has passed, so I don't know how they're going to materialize a rainbow before this trip's over, but they all said very clearly, *'There's still one left!'* "

I could feel a shiver of excitement pass through the group as we anticipated a magical moment with a rainbow.

My gaze fell on a young man propelling himself across the harbor on a paddle board, and I knew I was meant to speak about the board.

"One of your kids tried to stand-up paddle. Was it Morgan?" I stopped the Boissons before they could answer. "Oh, wait! It's surfing!"

Cyril confirmed this.

"There we go," I said, nodding. "He's saying, *'Same board. Same board.'* And now, as part of his cheerleading, I'm seeing that he would have been running and carrying a big flag."

"Oh, my gosh," Elizabeth exclaimed. "He was the first one on the field, and he had to run around the whole track with it! It was so heavy, and I was worried he wasn't going to make it all the way around."

"As soon as there was a touchdown," Cyril confirmed.

"Yay!" I said, clapping again, and then turned to Jeff. "So Jeff. There's a joke with your beard."

"That comes up in every reading," Lynn said.

"Oh, really? Because he's bringing it up again."

"I've had it since he passed," Jeff said. "I think he's just giving me a hard time about it."

Devon then flashed in my mind's eye an image of the bandana he wore in the photo I used in the kids' collage. "He's giving me the feeling that you didn't care for the bandana," I said.

"It wasn't my favorite look," Lynn said dryly.

I could feel the energy winding down, but Carly had saved one of her best pieces of evidence for the end. I turned to Irene. "Now Carly's showing me little skirts or a wraparound tie-dyed cloth. This is a tied-off-at-the-side kind of skirt that might go over a bathing suit. Do you have any idea what this is?"

"She bought it in Hawaii," Irene said. "It looked like it was tie-dyed. It was a sarong," she added, supplying the word I couldn't place. Her next statement revealed the importance of this piece of clothing and its significance as the reading drew to a close. "I have it where I keep her ashes." She sighed.

Jeff whistled softly. "That's a good one."

"Very good," I agreed, raising my eyes skyward in gratitude, yet at the same time disappointed in myself that I had not been able to see the details of where the scarf was located. I listened for a moment and, then laughed. "They said, *'Your oxygen tank has run out,'* but they'll pop in from time to time for the rest of the trip."

The kids knew how my mind worked, I explained, how I had felt the need for a formal reading to confirm they were truly present, rather than simply dropping piecemeal bits of evidence as the trip progressed.

"They're showing me that now they'll just be hanging around, and Carly's definitely going to be sunning."

Irene smiled once again.

"They say, *'You can relax now, and know we really are here.'* They're showing me the picture I brought. *'We really are here, and we're taking full credit for bringing you all together.'*"

Suddenly, I felt a shift in the energy. "Wait a minute," I said, squinting. "They don't want us to get all paranoid about this, but they want us to know where the first-aid kit is, because somebody is going to get a little cut that's going to need a Band-Aid."

"It's under your seat," Ty said, pointing.

"*No big deal. No worries. Just a little blood,*" I said, passing along the message.

The group shared an ominous look.

"I'm not moving," Jeff said stubbornly and crossed his arms.

Everyone laughed and I tried to put them at ease. "Susan says, '*Stuff happens on a boat,*' and we know this, but '*It's not a big deal. No stitches. Just be aware.*'"

"If I were a betting man," six-foot-four Jeff said, smiling, "I'd wager that we'll be mopping blood off the top of my head when I forget how low the ceiling is."

I took a deep breath, savoring the love and levity shared by the group. So many readings with the grieving bring me face to face with people who have not yet reached a state of certainty that the spirit world is real. A good connection can do this, but it can take others some time to process the life-altering experience of an evidential reading. Those gathered around our table no longer needed any proof. For us, this was simply a family reunion.

As if to end on a high note, Carly shouted, "*Group hug!*"

I reported this, and then added, "They all love each other on the other side. They say they knew each other before. The soul groups are so much bigger than we're aware. So, thank you all," I said.

"What a gift," Jeff said, offering me his thanks, but I felt as if the gift were meant for me. The phrase on the collage was not just wishful thinking. Our kids were right here, and now we had the evidence.

I knew everyone was looking forward to exploring the island, but I needed a few minutes alone. I excused myself and went below. Sitting on the bunk in my cabin, I closed my eyes and connected with my Team. "*Thank you, thank you,*" I said, even though I knew the words were unnecessary. Our guides feel our love and gratitude through our wordless spiritual bond.

I thanked Susan, and Carly, and Devon, and Morgan, then realized that I had failed to sense little Chelsea. Grateful that Elizabeth and Cyril never doubted their baby's presence, I sent her a wave of love.

As I opened my eyes, my gaze fell on my iPad lying on the shelf. I suddenly sensed Devon prompting me to pick it up.

I'd selected the collage photos from the Helping Parents Heal website without looking elsewhere online. Lynn had confirmed that the photo of Devon with the bandana was not his best, but I studiously avoid stumbling inadvertently across information about my clients prior to any official reading.

Never would I Google anyone before a reading; I do, however, often enjoy looking at photos afterwards. Grateful to have the Internet onboard, I picked up my iPad, opened the browser to "Images," and entered "Devon Hollahan" into the search box.

Several rows of photos appeared on the screen, including one of Jeff with microphones thrust in front of his face. In the second row, one photo stood out from the others, and I sucked in a breath. In it, Devon was wearing a plain white t-shirt and striking a pose before a maroon backdrop. What captured my attention was not his pensive expression, but the small, dark fedora on his head, which he touched lightly as if to say, *"Here it is, exactly as I showed you."*

"Good one," I whispered, as further bits of evidence flooded onto the screen of my memory: Devon's fedora, Carly's birthmark, Morgan's oversized flag. . . .

Every medium has a unique way of communicating. Each receives pieces of a puzzle that when put together, take us beyond hope to healing by revealing the presence of our loved ones in our lives. I sent out a silent prayer that those in spirit would continue to give me reason to say "Yay."

I thought of Lynn's remark, that what she loved talking about most were the signs our kids send us. Now that I had done the group reading, I looked forward to hearing more about the remarkable validations that had brought them such peace.

Above my head I heard footsteps as the group gathered to go ashore. Any conversation about signs would have to wait. For now I would go with the others and see what treasures Foxy's gift shop had to offer, but I had to admit: I had changed a great deal since Susan passed. A t-shirt from a beach bar no longer held the same appeal. No material object could match the satisfaction of learning that this physical world is not all there is.

CHAPTER 17

Kick-Start

§

I HEARD IRENE'S VOICE BEHIND me in the salon before I saw her.

"Hey Suzanne, remember Cousin Itt?"

Scenes from *The Addams Family* flashed through my mind as I turned. One look at Irene and I had no need to search my memory banks any further. Her wild, flyaway locks immediately recalled the hairy little TV series character from our childhood. We burst into laughter, and Irene pawed roughly at her hair with a brush.

"It's useless," she said, tossing the brush onto a cockpit seat.

"This trip is not about looking our best," I said, running a hand through my own sun-dried hair.

"Not for all of us," Irene said, nodding at Elizabeth, who squeezed past us on her way to the stern.

"How do you manage to look gorgeous every minute?" I asked her.

Always modest, she lowered her eyes and smiled. "I'd give anything for a hair straightener."

The hum of the outboard motor made the three of us look aft just as Ty motored up in the dinghy with Lynn, Jeff, and Cyril. Tony jumped up from one of the cockpit seats and took the line Cyril offered. Gracefully Lynn stepped onto the catamaran's port pontoon. Jeff followed, his own exit from the rubber boat proving not quite so graceful.

A loud splash made all heads turn in time to see Jeff sink beneath the surface, fully clothed. In a moment he bobbed back up, flashing a broad, wet smile.

"The water's great," he quipped without missing a beat. "Anyone else for a dip?"

Several hands reached out to help him up the swim ladder.

"Any blood?" Lynn asked. We had all been a bit on edge since the kids' prediction.

Jeff did a quick head-to-toe scan and declared himself unscathed except for a bruised ego. "It's nothing a little rum punch can't fix," he said, turning to Cyril.

"I will prepare it immediately," Cyril replied and headed for the galley to concoct his special island libation.

After our first dinner ashore at Pusser's, we had jointly decided that we preferred the quiet intimacy of drinks and dining on board the boat. The copious provisions provided for three dinners would easily stretch to cover the remaining meals. Once we discovered that Cyril enjoyed grilling, we declared him the boat's official French chef.

While Jeff changed into dry clothes, Cyril mixed the punch and got the coals going. An hour later we dined al fresco on grilled fish, saffron rice, and fresh salad as the boat rocked gently on her mooring. We all agreed that we could get used to such sensory delights.

Music from Foxy's Bar drifted across the harbor, but no one showed any interest in going ashore again. Once the dishes were cleared and the galley tidied, the eight of us gathered once more around the cockpit table. By now we each had a chosen seat. I settled into mine, thinking we might spend the evening chatting, but Irene had other ideas.

From her seat to my left she produced a small rectangular box. The red wraparound label read "Table Topics."

"I bought this for the trip," she announced. "It's a collection of cards with questions designed to kick-start conversations."

We all murmured our delight as Irene removed the deck from the box and placed the cards in the center of the table.

"The rules are simple," she said, smiling. "You pick any card, and you answer the question."

"I think we can handle that," Lynn joked.

"Who wants to go first?" Irene asked, in full Cruise Director mode.

"I will," Jeff said, leaning in and pulling a card from the center of the deck.

"Now, see?" I said, shaking my head. "I would have pulled one off the top. That just shows how much I'm still trained to color inside the lines."

"What does that say about *you*?" Lynn asked her husband with a laugh.

"I march to the beat of my own drum," he replied, comically rocking his head from side to side.

The game had not yet begun and already we were off on a tangent, engrossed in a lively discussion about the psychology of drawing a card from a deck. Irene began to fidget and suggested that Jeff read his card. I smiled, recognizing myself in her attitude. I would have been the same way if I had brought the game.

Jeff cleared his throat and read the card aloud: *"What has been your most intimidating moment?"*

He sat back, thought for a moment, and answered, "My most intimidating moment was when I played my guitar in front of 20,000 people at a festival in Denver."

All of us around the table exclaimed in surprise. Several years earlier, Jeff explained, he and a vocalist won successive rounds of a Battle of the Bands-type contest. They made it to the final performance in front of a capacity crowd unlike any he had ever imagined.

"I was too scared to look up and see who I was playing for," he said, laughing at the memory.

True to the game's goal, the question and its answer provoked further discussion about Jeff's musical avocation, which seemed a far cry from his work as a financial analyst.

I recalled the discussion at Pusser's about his days playing guitar in a group. "What was the name of your band?" I asked.

"We were called 'WHAT 4,'" he said, and explained that the W, H, A, and T stood for the first initial of each player's last name. "And the 4 was not spelled out," he added, "Just the numeral 4."

"For any specific reason?" Irene asked.

He shrugged. "Just that there were four of us."

Irene nodded. "I asked because earlier Lynn and I were talking about Devon using numbers to let you know he's around. I thought four might be a special number."

"This was long before Devon passed," Jeff said.

"My special number is 27," said Lynn. "It keeps showing up." She explained that Devon's birthday was May 27 and that he would have been 27 on his next birthday.

I shared my understanding that those in spirit often communicate with us telepathically. If they want us to notice something, such as a special number, they mentally send us an instruction to pay attention.

"In the beginning," Lynn said, "our number was 214, because we held his service on 2/14."

"We waited a few months after he passed to give ourselves time to process our grief," said Jeff. "We wanted to make sure it was truly a celebration of his life and not a memorial service."

"Not long after his service, 2:14 started showing up on my clock on a regular basis," Lynn said. "I would wake up from a sound sleep and look at the clock, and it would be 2:14."

Before anyone could chalk this up to coincidence, Lynn added, "I would walk into a room, and the time would not be 2:14, but my clock would say 2:14."

"You're kidding," Tony said.

"I told you," Irene said, giving him a small jab.

"It happened frequently," Lynn confirmed. "Once Jeff and I were out of town and Kelsey was sleeping in our bedroom. She called us at 10:30 at night and said, 'Mom, I just got into bed and the clock says 2:14!'"

"And when we went to close on the condo—" Jeff added, gesturing at Lynn to finish the story.

She smiled. "I walked into the kitchen, and the clock said 2:14, even though that wasn't the time. I called Jeff over and told him, 'This is our condo. It was meant to be.'"

"Wow." I was impressed with Devon's ability to manipulate electronics. "He's a strong communicator."

We all noticed that we had gotten off topic, so Lynn reached out and took a card from the center of the deck.

"What's the most unusual thing you've ever done?" she read aloud. "That's easy. I petted a cobra."

Exclamations rang out around the table, and Lynn shrugged. "We were in India," she explained, "and we came upon this snake charmer with a cobra in a basket, just like you see in the movies. You could pay him some money, and he'd let you pet the snake. Jeff didn't want me to do it, but I've always felt that life should be lived to the fullest, and when was I going to get such a chance again?"

All heads turned to Jeff, who matched his wife's shrug. "She never listens to me."

"Buy the ticket, take the ride," Lynn said, leaning to her right to give her husband a loving nudge.

Next, Ty took a card from the top of the deck. *"What was your favorite extracurricular activity in school?"*

I put my face in my hands and groaned. I didn't have to be psychic to know his reply. He gave me a look of mock indignation and announced to the group, "I coached the girl's powder-puff football team in college."

The men's faces brightened. The ladies rolled their eyes in deference to me.

"What?" he asked. "It was a tough job!"

"Your turn," Irene said to me, pointing at the deck.

"Okay, look out, Ty," I warned. "I'm about to go wild and crazy."

He cocked his head, not sure what I was up to, until I made a big deal out of taking a card from the center of the deck.

"Ooooh," Ty teased. "This is a side of you I've never seen."

Now it was my turn to jab my husband.

I answered a quick and easy question, and then Irene and Tony discussed their cards in turn. The atmosphere was light and lively as we learned information about each other we hadn't known and would not have guessed. When the rotation came to Cyril, he pulled a card off the top of the deck.

"What was the most challenging thing you ever had to do?" he read aloud.

The air grew suddenly still. No one moved. We all knew the answer without him having to express it, for the response would be the same for each of us: the most difficult thing we ever had to do was bury our child.

Cyril made no sound. His face remained completely passive. He simply placed the card face down on the discard pile and drew another.

"Who was your most beloved pet?" he read, as if the previous question had never been asked. Without hesitating, he said, "This one is easy. It was my chimpanzee."

We learned that Cyril had spent some of his formative years living with his family in Africa. As a result, he had a great love for creatures of all kinds. Over the years, he fostered a menagerie of animals, including a mongoose and a cheetah, but the chimpanzee was his most beloved childhood companion. When he described having to send the chimp away after an unfortunate incident, his composure finally crumbled. We all felt deep sympathy for the memories that brought tears to his eyes. Child or beloved pet, pain is pain, and love knows no bounds.

The mood lightened when Elizabeth took her turn. We learned more about her work as a fashion model in France, and discovered what it felt like to see one's full-size photo on public billboards.

Round and round the table we went, working our way through the cards. When we found ourselves back where we started with Jeff, all agreed to save more questions until another evening. Lynn leaned back in her seat and stretched her head outside the cockpit awning.

"The stars are incredible!" she exclaimed. "Let's go up to the bow and do some stargazing!"

Like a bunch of kids who needed no encouragement for the next adventure, we paraded en masse to the foredeck and stretched out fore and aft on the netting strung between the two pontoons. I felt like a teenager at a pajama party, with all eight of us lying side by side in the dark staring up at the sky. For a few moments no one spoke, each of us caught up in the wonder of the glittering tapestry above.

"I wonder which one of those is Morgan's star," Elizabeth said, breaking the reverie.

"Morgan has a star?" Ty asked.

"Yes," she replied. "Our girls gave Cyril and me a star named for Morgan the second Christmas after he passed."

We all expressed our delight at such a creative and thoughtful gift and spent the next few minutes pointing out potential stars that would fit the bill. Surely, we decided, it was one of the brightest in the sky.

"Maybe we'll see a shooting star," Lynn said.

"It sounds like there's another story with that," I commented.

"There is," she replied. "It happened at a party we hosted at our house in honor of Devon. Jeff's band set up under the fruit tree in the backyard. They were jamming away when a huge shooting star came down right behind the stage. It almost seemed like it landed on top of them."

Jeff chimed in, "Everyone attributed the star to Devon being there."

"I wish Carly had been as active the first year as Devon was," Irene said.

Lynn nodded. "One day I was sitting at my computer, and I got a note from my friend Debra Martin, the medium. She said, 'Tell Kelsey that Devon has been messing with her computer, and that he's been repeating words and putting it on all caps.' So, I forwarded the note to Kelsey, who was in another room. She came running out, calling, 'Oh, my gosh, Mom, this is exactly what's been happening to me! I thought my computer was broken. I turned it off and turned it back on, and it just kept happening.' And once she acknowledged that, her computer went back to normal."

"Message delivered," Elizabeth said.

"That's what happens when I give a reading," I interjected. "I feel the spirits' physical symptoms as if they're my own. As soon as I report them, the symptoms disappear."

"So even though I was in mourning," Lynn continued, "I couldn't wait to wake up in the morning to see what was going to happen that day."

"Is that how you felt, Jeff?" Tony's voice rose from the darkness on the far side of the netting.

"Actually," Jeff replied, "early on, I felt kind of left out. No mediums contacted me like they did with Lynn, and Devon didn't mess around with my computer. For me, coming to realize he's really around was more of a process."

"Until the basketball game," Lynn interjected.

Jeff cleared his throat. "Yeah, until the basketball game. That," he said, after another long pause, "was kind of my big deal. . . . "

§

Jeff and Devon loved watching sports together. Whenever they traveled, they made a point of attending professional sporting events. They checked out arenas and stadiums in unfamiliar territory with the same enthusiasm as they tried out new roller coasters.

Jeff's job provided him with frequent access to tickets for the Phoenix sports teams' home games. When Devon announced in early fall that he would be home from Prague to enjoy the Christmas season with the family, Jeff decided to get tickets for the two of them to a pro basketball game.

He emailed Devon with three possible home games, listing the opposing team for each date. A fan of LeBron James for as long as he could remember, Devon immediately chose the Cleveland Cavaliers.

Jeff got the tickets, and he and Devon put the game on their calendars for early in the new year. After being apart for several months, they were both looking forward to some special father-son time together.

When Devon failed to come home, Jeff couldn't bear to look at the tickets. There was little around the house that didn't remind him painfully of Devon. The worst part was not being able to look his girls in the eye, tortured by the helplessness he felt at being unable to comfort the pain and anguish etched in their faces.

Neither he nor Lynn nor Kelsey wanted to spend time with each other. Whenever the three of them were together, the absence of the last member of their foursome was brought into stark relief, too final and traumatic to bear. Jeff, who as the man of the household had always felt responsible for fixing things, couldn't fix this.

They found their own spaces in the house and holed up. Jeff got through Christmas and the weeks that followed in sheer survival mode.

When January rolled around, he had no interest in attending the basketball game without Devon. It was Lynn who convinced him to go. He asked the neighbor across the street if he wanted to come along, and the friend agreed.

At the arena, the men took their seats, eighteen rows up from center court. Around them, the other spectators buzzed with excitement. Jeff worried that he would be the worst companion his neighbor could ask for. He had made no secret of the fact that he would have preferred to stay home.

The game began, and Jeff found himself interested more in the father and son sitting immediately in front of him than in the players on the court. The young fan, who looked to be about seven, basked in the loving attention of his father. The boy appeared new to the sport, and his dad patiently explained every move, conveying his excitement each time the Suns' Grant Hill made a good play.

Despite the awareness that he too should have been enjoying the game with his son, Jeff couldn't help feeling the upbeat magic. The father was interacting with his son exactly as Jeff had with Devon when he was young. He wanted to tell the man to savor every minute, that it wouldn't be long before the boy would be schooling him, just as Devon had.

Throughout the game, cheerleaders periodically dashed out in front of the crowd and hurled t-shirts into the stands. Jeff flashed back to the countless times that Devon left his seat to come within range of the cheerleaders' tosses. Despite dozens of attempts over the years, he never succeeded in nabbing a shirt.

A sudden, overwhelming urge compelled Jeff to invoke Devon's help for the first time since he had passed. *Devon,* Jeff said silently, *if you can see fit to make it happen, I really want to give this kid a t-shirt.*

With only three minutes left in the game, the cheerleaders emerged to whip up a final frenzy. Jeff watched them, assailed by a moment of doubt that his request would be fulfilled. The cheerleaders were cute, but none had the strength to heave a shirt all the way up to the eighteenth row.

And then, the Phoenix Suns' mascot—a five-foot gorilla—magically appeared, holding a compressed air cannon.

The moment the gorilla walked onto the floor, Jeff knew what was going to happen. He saw the event unfold in his mind as if it had already played out.

The gorilla pointed his cannon toward the seats to Jeff's left, and a cheer went up from the fans. He waggled his hairy shoulders and turned to those seated to Jeff's right. Another cheer arose as the gorilla aimed in their direction, teasing the trigger. He pivoted 180 degrees and pointed his cannon across the court, eliciting more cheers from the fans on the far side. But still he didn't fire.

And then, the big ape turned back to Jeff's side of the arena. A sense of calm descended over Jeff as the gorilla pointed the cannon directly at him. He saw the orange and white t-shirt emerge from the barrel as if in slow motion. He reached his arm straight up, sank his fingers into the soft cloth, and in one smooth motion handed the shirt to the boy in front of him.

The child clutched the prize to his chest and beamed at Jeff and his father. For the last minutes of the game, the man repeatedly turned around and exclaimed, "That was amazing! This is the greatest thing that's ever happened to him! He will never, ever forget this game!"

Jeff left the arena feeling completely jazzed. Even though it was nearly midnight, he couldn't wait to tell Lynn. He arrived home and burst into the bedroom. "Have I got a story for you!"

As he finished sharing the final magical details of the game, Lynn gave him one of her crooked smiles. "Of course you got the shirt," she said. "For the last couple of days I've been asking Devon to go with you."

Jeff returned her smile. "Apparently he was listening."

For a long time, Jeff replayed the evening's events in his mind, unable to sleep. The thought of attending the game without Devon had been too much to bear; he had come very close to not using the tickets. But because he had pushed himself, he had found Devon with him after all.

The game gave Jeff the spiritual kick-start he needed to truly begin to heal. Though slower to acknowledge his son's presence than Lynn was, he now knew that he and his two girls would survive. No longer did he feel that the family had been reduced to a threesome. One member had changed his position, but the Hollahans were definitely still a foursome.

CHAPTER 18

In Your Dreams

♩

I DUG THROUGH MY REMAINING clothes in the drawer at the foot of the bed. The few tops I had not already stuffed in the laundry bag reminded me how quickly the trip was passing. My eyes fell on a t-shirt with a tie-dyed pattern of pastel blue, pink, and yellow, a special gift from Irene. I usually wore t-shirts only when exercising, but I'd brought this one specifically in honor of Carly, and I only had two days left to wear it.

I slipped the shirt over my head, pulled on a pair of shorts, and headed for the stairway. I emerged in the galley to find all three girlfriends exactly where I expected to see them. I smiled at how quickly we had fallen into a routine. Elizabeth sat at the table posting the daily kids' tributes on the Helping Parents Heal Facebook page. Lynn stood at the stove cooking bacon, and Irene skated around the deck on her cleaning cloths. The moment I saw Irene, I burst out laughing.

"Look at you!" I said without bothering to offer a "Good morning" first.

She turned, and her laughter joined mine. We had no idea that we had both brought along matching "Carly's Kids" t-shirts, yet here we had chosen to wear them the very same day.

"We get to be the Bobbsey Twins today!" she said, walking toward me with arms outstretched for our morning hug.

"Carly put us up to this," I said, giving her a warm squeeze in return.

This was another part of the daily routine that had not changed since the first morning. Elizabeth rose from her laptop and Lynn left the stove long enough for a hug and a cheery "good morning." I stepped outside and greeted Tony, Jeff, and Ty the same way, and then returned to the galley.

"Where's Cyril?" I asked Elizabeth. Until then, my morning meditation had made me the last one on deck.

"Still in our cabin," she replied, then lowered her voice. "Morgan came to him in a dream this morning."

Lynn and Irene joined me in empathetic "Ooohs."

"Does he often visit that way?" I asked.

"It's only the second time," said Elizabeth.

"How special," Lynn remarked.

"Yes," Elizabeth said. "The first time was in Lhasa when he went to bring Morgan's body home. He saw an open door in his dream, and Morgan came through it. The dream was very short, but it was so real he remembers it to this day."

"That's the hallmark of a dream visit," I said.

"Do you remember the dream that Beth had with Carly?" Irene asked.

"That was amazing," I said. "Tell Elizabeth and Lynn about it."

"This is not the Beth from Hawaii, who gave us the bracelets," Irene explained. "It's a woman Suzanne met through her work. Sanaya told Suzanne that I was supposed to connect with Beth."

Irene described her phone call with Beth, whose only child, Tyler, had taken his own life at seventeen. During their conversation Beth remained quiet until Irene began to tell her Carly's story. At the mention of Carly's name, Beth reacted with surprise and related a recent dream visit from her son. In the dream Tyler was driving a blue convertible with a beautiful young woman in the passenger seat. Beth asked her son who he was with, and he replied, "I'm with Carly."

Elizabeth and Lynn exclaimed in delight. I prompted Irene for the best part. "And you used to have a blue convertible, right?"

"I had three of them!" Irene replied, beaming. "And Carly loved the convertibles. She was trying to convince me that she should take mine to Boston because I had married Tony and didn't need a sports car anymore."

We all laughed.

"According to her, a convertible was a good car for picking up guys."

"It looks like that's exactly what she did on the other side!" Lynn said.

"That's amazing," Elizabeth said. "Is Beth a medium?"

Irene and I shook our heads.

I gave voice to what I was sure the others knew: the dream state is one of the easiest times for those who have passed to connect with us. Because we're in an expanded state of awareness and not focused on our earthly life, we are more able to sense the presence of our loved ones in spirit.

If a dream involving a deceased love one is frightening or causes distress, it is most likely not a visitation, but the result of grief or fear-filled thoughts in the subconscious. Dream visits seem much more solid than normal dreams and stay with us long after we awaken.

Just then, Cyril came up the starboard stairs and greeted each of us with a kiss on each cheek. He seemed uncharacteristically subdued.

"Elizabeth told us you had a visit from Morgan," Lynn said gently.

He nodded. "Yes. He appeared to me as a young boy. He told me he loved me and then he hugged me. It was very real."

Elizabeth smiled wistfully at her husband.

Instead of heading aft to join the other men, Cyril walked wordlessly to the foredeck. He sat alone on the port pontoon and stared at the water, seemingly lost in thought.

"Maybe Morgan came because it's Chelsea's birthday," Lynn said.

I turned to Elizabeth in surprise. "Today?"

"Yes," she nodded. "I'm posting her tribute right now."

I slid onto the seat beside her. "Are you okay?"

"Of course," she said, her cheerful demeanor restored. "I know that Chelsea and Morgan are together on the other side, just like Tyler, and Carly, and all our kids."

"Tell them about your reading with Daisy Mae Moore," Lynn said.

Daisy Mae, Elizabeth explained, is a British medium who discovered her abilities after her son passed at four days old. Elizabeth scheduled a reading to be able to recommend her to other parents.

"Morgan came through right away," Elizabeth recalled. "Daisy Mae told me, 'He's holding his sister's hand and she is holding Morgan's brother's hand.'"

I frowned. "I'm confused. Morgan's brother?"

Elizabeth nodded. "In between Morgan and Chelsea I had a miscarriage at three months along."

While I processed this unexpected information, Elizabeth continued. "Daisy Mae said, 'Morgan's sister breathed for just a short time, and his brother was not able to breathe at all. His brother passed when he was 12 weeks old, and he was in between Morgan and Chelsea.'"

"Twelve weeks," Irene said with a tinge of awe. "And your miscarriage happened at three months. She was right on."

"Yes," Elizabeth confirmed, "and she said he wasn't able to breathe at all, meaning that he never took a physical breath." She shook her head. "It was the first time any medium had mentioned the other child. That was amazing for me."

I pursed my lips and admitted, "I feel bad that I didn't sense Chelsea or the baby you miscarried. Usually I can tell when there's been a miscarriage. I think I was too focused on our four grown kids to sense anyone else."

The others dismissed my apology, but I made a mental vow to do a better job of not letting assumptions get in my way. I knew from experience that the age of a child or whether the baby had been born made no difference as far as a medium's ability to communicate with their spirit. Once a soul decides to incarnate, it is eternally connected by love to the parents and the entire soul family. I have been shown many happy reunions on the other side between those who have passed and their miscarried or very young babies.

"I love the hummingbird," I said, noting the photo Elizabeth posted with Chelsea's tribute. Beside the picture, I read the words, *"Remembering Chelsea Boisson on her twenty-sixth birthday."*

Although we each felt the sadness, we didn't dwell on it. We knew Elizabeth felt our love, and that was enough.

I stood and stepped to Lynn's side. "Do you want me to start making toast?"

"That would be good," she replied.

Irene opened the small refrigerator and peered in, hands on her hips. "There's still a lot of fruit in here. I'll cut up some pineapples and mangos for a fruit plate."

"And I'm almost finished here," Elizabeth chimed. "I can slice some cheese to mix with the eggs."

The four of us worked easily side by side. None of us minded that the galley work fell naturally to the women each day. It was a joy to share girl-talk while our men bonded over coffee outside.

While Lynn blotted the bacon on paper towels, I carried a plate of buttered toast to the cockpit table. Suddenly, a cry arose from the galley.

"It's me! It's me!" Irene announced excitedly.

I turned to see her marching my way, her index finger held high. Two tiny red droplets stood out against her pink skin.

The wound was clearly minor, and Captain Ty calmly reached under the seat for the first-aid kit as Elizabeth and Lynn joined us in the cockpit.

"We have our blood!" Jeff called out like an auctioneer, and everyone cheered.

Hearing the commotion, Cyril came down the port-side deck from the bow. His mood had visibly lifted.

"What is going on?" he asked curiously.

"I cut my finger on the knife," Irene said, smiling incongruously while proudly displaying her wound.

"I've never seen you so happy over cutting yourself," Tony said.

"The kids called it right," she said.

"We can all relax now," Lynn announced. And indeed, a feeling of relief descended over the group as we gathered to enjoy our meal.

Not once did any of us doubt that the kids' prediction would come to pass. It was only a question of when. Now we could all sleep a little better. And perhaps, I mused, if the two worlds came together just right, one of us would see Morgan, Chelsea, Susan, and Devon rolling down the highway in a blue convertible with Carly at the wheel.

CHAPTER 19

Perfect Day

§

THE BRITISH VIRGIN ISLANDS ARE an ideal charter location for several reasons. The unspoiled beauty of the land and sea inspire and rejuvenate the soul. The short distances between islands allow visitors to enjoy numerous anchorages in a single week. The abundant sunshine and consistent winds are a sailor's dream.

Most of the time.

By day five of our trip, not a drop of rain had fallen, which we certainly appreciated. On the flip side, the lack of wind after the previous weeks' gales continued throughout our stay. We raised the sails once on the first day, but slowed to a speed of one knot once Ty throttled back the engines. After an hour of making no headway, we stowed the sails, never to use them again.

No one seemed to care that we had to motor everywhere. The vacation had never been about the sailing, but the opportunity to spend time together in a beautiful and relaxing setting.

After visiting Peter Island, Soper's Hole, and Jost Van Dyke, we motored to Virgin Gorda, picking up a mooring ball at the Bitter End Yacht Club. A hike to the top of the highest hill offered us a bird's-eye view of where we'd been and what was yet to come.

We set out early the following day for Cooper Island, touted as having the best view of the sunset in the Virgin Islands. Thanks to this reputation, the prime anchorage there regularly fills by noon. We held our breath as Ty steered the boat around the northernmost point of the island into Manchioneel Bay. Sure enough, more than a dozen boats already lay nestled along the sweeping arc of the pristine beach. To our relief, one lone mooring ball bobbed on the surface.

Cyril and Tony stood at the bow, ready to handle the mooring lines. Because Ty's view from the bridge was restricted, I guided him via hand signals to the ball. When I pointed straight down with my index finger, he put the engines in reverse and brought the boat to a stop directly alongside the mooring pendant's buoy, allowing Cyril to easily scoop up the eye with the hook.

Using our dock lines, Tony and Cyril created a bridle and secured their lines to a cleat on each forward pontoon. At my signal, Ty shut down the engines, and we all stood back to survey our home for the night. The view to the west looked straight down Sir Francis Drake Channel. The sun would set just beyond the line of green islands in the distance. It was easy to see what made Cooper Island a popular destination.

Having arrived as advised before noon, we had the whole day to relax. The Cooper Island Beach Club, the only tourist attraction ashore, held little interest for any of us. What appealed to me was the lunch menu for the day: chicken roti, a wheat flour wrap filled with curried chicken and potatoes.

Ty and I discovered this popular Caribbean delicacy on our first trip to the islands. When I found it on the provisioning list as one of the precooked lunch choices, I chose it immediately, hoping the others would enjoy it as much as ourselves.

Everyone did their own thing while the lunches heated in the oven until the smell of curry summoned us all to the table. We filled our plates with the kind of excited chatter common at holiday feasts. A hush fell over the table as we took our first bites, followed by exclamations of praise for the delicate West Indian flavors. I smiled. The roti was a hit.

Suddenly Ty raised his right arm and called out, "You're going a little fast there, Buddy!" All heads turned to starboard as a forty-five-foot motor yacht sped past us no more than fifty feet off our beam, going twice as fast as good seamanship dictated for the crowded anchorage.

I instinctively reached for my water glass, then laughed at my reaction. The wake from the fast-moving boat barely caused a bobble in our twin-hulled craft.

"I keep forgetting we're on a catamaran," I said. "If we were waked like that on our sailboat, everything on this table would be on the deck."

"We lost a $250 stainless steel barbecue when some guy waked us in Charleston Harbor," Ty recounted ruefully. "Our boat rocked so badly that the grill came right off the rail mount and sank like a rock."

The others sympathized as we resumed eating our roti.

"Hey Jeff," Lynn said, "that barbecue story reminds me of when we were in Marshall Fields department store that Christmas."

Jeff laughed. "Oh, yeah. I'll never forget that security guard's face."

"What happened?" Irene asked, leaning in.

"They were getting ready to do the tree lighting," Lynn explained. "The three of us were walking through the Christmas department, but it was deserted, because everybody was over by the tree. For some reason, we were walking single file, right, Jeff?"

He nodded. "Yeah, it was you, then Kelsey, and I was last."

"Right," she said. "So I walked by a table with a display of candy, and this box of chocolates jumped off the table." She paused for effect and emphasized, "It didn't fall off. It literally jumped."

Jeff picked up the story. "Lynn looked back at Kelsey and laughed, and then she looked at me, and I laughed as well, because I saw it too."

"There was a security guard standing nearby," Lynn continued, "and he said, 'Oh, my gosh, did you guys just see that box? It jumped right off the shelf!' and I said, 'Yeah, don't worry. That was just our son.'"

Everyone around the table burst out laughing.

"He kind of looked at us like, *What?*" Lynn said, screwing up her face.

Jeff lowered his voice as if to imitate the guard and intoned, "Too much eggnog for those folks."

We laughed even harder. "It sounds like Devon pulled out all the stops to let you know he was with you at Christmas time," I said. "Those in spirit are always especially close around holidays, birthdays, anniversaries, and special events like graduations and parties."

Ty turned to Lynn and Jeff. "Your story reminds me of how Susan pushed that potted plant onto the floor during our first reading. It couldn't possibly have happened on its own."

Tony shook his head. "I just don't get how they can do those things."

"I don't understand it exactly, either," I said, "but I frequently hear stories of physical apports, like pennies appearing out of nowhere. Apparently those in spirit sometimes get to break the rules, bending the laws of physics to get our attention."

"Carly did that," Irene said.

"What did she do?" Elizabeth asked, reaching out to refill her plate from the salad platter.

"On her angel day, we released biodegradable balloons at our community marina. A crowd of friends and family had come out to celebrate her life. We probably had a dozen or more balloons, right, Tony?"

He pressed his lips together, calculating, and nodded. "Right. Fifteen or so."

"It was really windy." She flipped a hand past her head. "Our hair was whipping around, and all the balloons went up and flew off together in one direction. Two of them were dove balloons, and all of a sudden, one of the dove balloons turned and flew in the complete opposite direction."

I flashed back to the dove balloon that found its way to our car forty miles away after Morgan's bench dedication. "Must be something about doves," I murmured.

Irene shook her head, remembering the scene. "It took a left turn and did its own thing."

"Just like Carly," Tony said wryly.

Irene nodded and said, "Completely against the wind. It was amazing."

Just then, a gust blew through the cockpit. Several of us reached forward to keep our napkins on the table.

"Looks like we're going to get a little rain," Ty announced, as the first few drops spattered the fiberglass awning overhead. We glanced up to see a small gray cloud ghosting by from northeast to southwest.

"Doesn't look like it will amount to much," I said.

Irene clasped her hands together in in prayer formation. "Just enough to give us our rainbow!"

"That's right," Lynn exclaimed. "In our reading, the kids said there's still one left after they played 'Somewhere Over the Rainbow' for us at Pusser's."

"Wouldn't that be wonderful!" said Elizabeth.

"It's going to happen," Irene declared. She stood up. "I'm getting my camera."

Jeff smiled. "Now, that's trust."

"I'd get yours too, if I were you," I said. "The kids were very clear about that rainbow. This is the first it's rained all week, and tomorrow's our last day. I have a feeling this is the moment."

And indeed, no more than two minutes later, Irene and Lynn began hooting and pointing excitedly astern.

"There it is!"

"Look at that!"

The air filled with the sound of camera shutters as we all captured the special moment, sending thanks to our angelic messengers.

In less than a minute, the rainbow faded, replaced by the usual bright sunshine. Not a trace of rain remained. The gray cloud disappeared as quickly as it had arrived. Had the rainbow been part of a day of showers, it would not have drawn the same attention as its appearance so perfectly timed to our discussion.

"I did a reading last month for a mother whose son is on the other side," I told the group as we lingered at the railing. "The boy gave me all kinds of evidence about how he passed, and then he showed me the image of a rainbow going from his mother's heart to his."

I put a fist to my chest and moved it outward in an arc to imitate the link.

"I thought that was kind of strange," I continued, "and then he asked me to tell his mother, *'The connection is good.'* When I relayed this information, his mother told me that she had recently been trying to communicate with her son by visualizing a rainbow running from her heart to his. She found that when she held this image, she could sense him more clearly."

"Wow," Irene said, "and he said to you, *'The connection is good'*?"

"Those were his exact words," I replied, smiling.

"And his mother had not discussed her efforts with you?" Elizabeth asked.

I shook my head and smiled.

"I'm going to try that!" Lynn announced. The others nodded in agreement.

The Christmas-like feeling remained as we cleaned up from lunch. With the afternoon now open, I suggested to Ty that we go for a paddle around the small bay. An outcropping of jagged rocks at the far end of the cove begged to be explored. The shoals spelled danger to a larger boat, but our catamaran came equipped with two orange sit-on-top kayaks.

While Ty and I enjoyed our paddle, Cyril took Elizabeth, Lynn, and Jeff exploring in the dinghy. Tony and Irene remained on the boat to enjoy some quiet time reading in the shade of the forward cockpit.

As much as we all enjoyed the afternoon, we looked forward to the much-heralded sunset to top off a perfect day.

Hours later, the Moorings' catering company proved their worth once again with a prepackaged salmon in caper sauce that tasted as good as any prepared in a fine restaurant. Although none of us regularly ate dessert, no one turned down a small serving of creamy key lime pie.

We finished the meal just as the sun dipped behind the distant islands to our west. Out came the cameras again, and we all clambered onto the side decks to enjoy the magical scene.

We took pictures of the colorful sky. We took pictures of each other. And we took pictures of each other taking pictures. Lynn produced a selfie stick and handed it to Jeff. With his long arm, he managed to fit all of us into Lynn's iPhone screen and snapped several shots before the last of the red and orange hues faded to gray.

No one cared that the dirty dishes remained on the table. We stayed on deck, leaning against the cabin top as we gazed at the sea, enjoying the remaining half hour of twilight.

"I can't believe tomorrow is our last night," Irene said softly.

"Me, either," Lynn agreed. "I'm not ready to say goodbye."

"It's not goodbye," Elizabeth offered. "It's never goodbye. Our kids proved that to us."

For a few moments no one said a word. Elizabeth broke the silence.

"I know Jeff and Lynn have heard this story, but have I told the rest of you about the first time Susanne Wilson brought Morgan through?"

Irene, Tony, Ty, and I shook our heads. Cyril sighed softly and gazed at the water.

"Susanne was new to the Phoenix area, and she was looking for a place to do readings. She stopped by the yoga studio near our house and asked the owner, Angie, if she had any space to rent."

Angie didn't know much about mediums, Elizabeth explained, so she asked Susanne how she might test her abilities. Susanne offered to read a photo, and Angie picked up the Boissons' Christmas card that Elizabeth had just sent out. On the front of the card was a photo of Morgan, Alix, and Christine. Inside, Elizabeth included a note about Morgan's recent passing.

"Susanne picked up the card," Elizabeth said, "and immediately took on Morgan's mannerisms. She said, 'I'm seeing the rum Captain Morgan.'"

"Oh, wow," Irene and I exclaimed simultaneously.

"She knew nothing about you?" I asked, impressed as always by Susanne's skill.

"No," Elizabeth confirmed. "She was new in town and we had never met. There was no text on the front of the card that would indicate that Morgan was on the other side, but she then spoke of seeing Morgan on a mountaintop. She saw him shouting through a megaphone that he was okay."

"That's the megaphone you have at home," Lynn said.

Elizabeth nodded. "The cheer team gave us his megaphone, and we had it at his service, but Susanne couldn't have known about that. So that was a significant message, especially the news that he was okay."

She paused and looked up at the sky, smiling. "The reason our conversation reminded me of that reading is because Susanne showed me that Morgan didn't have to say goodbye. He's still with us, which I already know. She not only saw him lying on a mountain but further described him with a black box up to his ear."

I recalled the story of how a friend held a cell phone to Morgan's ear in his final earthly moments while Elizabeth bravely spoke to her son, letting him know that she was proud of him and that she loved him. But of course Susanne Wilson knew none of this.

Elizabeth cleared her throat. "And Susanne's exact words to Angie as she connected with Morgan in the yoga studio were: 'And Morgan says, *"I love you back,"*' which is exactly how he replied every time I told him 'I love you'.'"

The four of us who had not yet heard this part of the story expressed our amazement and awe.

"That's when I physically felt the hug he gave me, from the inside," Elizabeth said, reminding us of the memorable moment that changed her perspective on death and dying. "He didn't get to say those words aloud, because he wasn't breathing at that point, but he used Susanne to say them for him."

Caught up in our thoughts, none of us spoke. The sun had slipped so far below the horizon that the sky and water appeared as one continuous black backdrop. The only illumination came from the boats around us. Atop the tall masts, the single white bulbs of a dozen anchor lights stood out in the darkness, merging with the stars overhead, as if uniting heaven and earth.

"That's how I know that when we leave here tomorrow, we won't be saying goodbye," Elizabeth concluded. "but *au revoir . . . 'until we meet again.'*"

CHAPTER 20

The Big Picture

§

AT CYRIL AND ELIZABETH'S RECOMMENDATION, we chose Cane Garden Bay for our final night's anchorage. The night before our trip began they had enjoyed their stay at a resort hotel there and raved about the beautiful beach. Located on the opposite side of Tortola from the Moorings' base in Road Harbor, it was close enough to allow us plenty of time to return the boat by the noon deadline the following day.

Ty had done most of the driving all week. Once we departed Cooper Island, I took the helm for a while to give him a break. After only a few minutes he was back, admitting there was nothing else he'd rather be doing. I picked up my iPad and joined Lynn, Irene, and Elizabeth in the forward cockpit.

Throughout the week, we had flowed in a natural rhythm about the boat, mixing and mingling with all aboard. While I loved the easy interplay between the men and women, my time with the girls was special.

For twenty years I had worked in a world predominantly driven by men. After retiring from the Navy, I envisioned surrounding myself with a circle of women friends. That vision became a reality, but our itinerant lifestyle didn't always afford me quality time with my female friends. To have six days in which to enjoy touchy-feely girl talk with kindred spirits was a true luxury.

We had striven to keep our focus on each other rather than the usual web surfing, but we checked our emails daily to make sure all was okay at home. This morning Irene had her head in a book, and Lynn and Elizabeth were chatting, so I opened my iPad and quickly scanned my inbox. A familiar addressee stood out. I eagerly checked the attachment.

"Ohhhhhh," I exclaimed with delight. The others instantly looked up.

"Sorry," I apologized sheepishly. "Our puppy-sitters sent a video of Rudy and Gretchen playing with their new toys."

"Oh, let's see," replied the others in unison, and I passed the iPad around. All four of us had at least one dog, as much a part of our families as our children.

"Did I tell you about the time that Rudy saw Susan?" I asked.

Irene nodded and said, "It's in *Messages of Hope*."

"I don't remember it," Lynn said. "Tell it anyway."

Happy to comply, I described my early attempts to communicate with Susan after she passed. My sole purpose in learning to meditate was to connect with her personally. We had not yet experienced the medium's reading that changed our lives. I had no idea if the spirit world was real, and I certainly never imagined that I would one day be working as a medium.

My early attempts consisted of quieting my mind daily, and once I achieved a state of relative peace, asking Susan to show herself to me. Day after day I repeated the practice, praying and hoping she might magically materialize. I had heard of such things happening to other people, and I figured if I tried hard enough, it might just happen to me.

I usually meditated in our bedroom, but one day when Ty was not home, I shifted to the living room. Being pack animals, Rudy and Gretchen normally followed me from room to room, but that day, both dogs remained lying in their beds in the kitchen. I sat in one of two side-by-side wing-backed chairs and entered into the silence.

Susan, I said mentally, following my usual practice, *please show yourself to me.*

I opened my eyes and, as usual, saw nothing. Suddenly, Rudy bolted out of his bed and dashed into the entry hall to my right, stopping at the front door and staring upward, as if someone had just walked in. I knew that if someone had actually come to the door, little Gretchen would be right there alongside, barking like a Doberman. Instead, she remained in her bed, seemingly oblivious to whatever had caught Rudy's attention.

I watched with increasing interest as he took several steps backward and turned to his left. He placed one paw on the landing at the foot of the stairs and stopped, staring directly upward at a pencil drawing I had sketched of Susan that hung there.

You're standing there, aren't you, Susan? I asked, awed by but clearly comprehending Rudy's actions. Though I couldn't see her, it didn't take rocket science to sense what was going on. In response to my request, Susan had appeared in the hallway. Understanding that Rudy could see her but I couldn't, she moved in front of her portrait. I imagined her standing on the landing, pointing from the picture to herself, saying to Rudy, *"It's me! It's me!"*

After a few moments, Rudy trotted into the living room and sat down in the middle of the floor. He stared at the empty chair next to me with his head cocked to one side and his ears pinned unsurely to his head. I knew then that my repeated efforts had not been in vain, and that Susan had taken a seat in the chair beside me.

"To this day, I haven't seen Susan's spirit with my physical eyes," I told the girls, "but over the years she's shown herself to me in many other ways."

"We had almost the same thing happen with Kirby," Lynn said excitedly. "We have a chair in the corner of our bedroom, and one evening as I was sitting there reading, Kirby began dancing back and forth in front of me, sort of growling, and whimpering, and barking. He was looking toward me, yet through me. When I got up and went around behind him, he never took his eyes off where I'd been sitting. I didn't know what to think at the time, but within a week of that experience, my friend Debra Martin stopped by with another friend. As they walked by my bedroom door, Debra glanced at the chair where I'd been reading. I hadn't told her anything about the incident with Kirby, but she told her friend, 'Devon hangs out in that chair all the time.'"

Elizabeth clasped her hands together. "Our pets are so special."

"Kirby would walk up to random walls and look up and start crying," Lynn added. "He used a different tone when he saw something."

Hearing this, I waved my hands. "So does Rudy! In fact, not too long ago, I gave a reading and brought through a woman's two cats who had passed." I described how Rudy, who always lies nearby when I give readings, suddenly sat up and stared at something I couldn't see. "He made this funny, whiny noise that he only ever makes when a cat is within sight but out of his reach."

"He could see the cat's spirit!" Irene exclaimed.

"Exactly," I said. "Animals definitely have souls, and if there's a strong heart connection with their owner, sometimes they'll give me real evidence in a reading."

"How do you get evidence from a pet?" Lynn asked, laughing.

I smiled. I had wondered the same thing before the first time I connected with a cat, who had been like a child to my client. "They show me how they died, where they liked to hang out in the house, their favorite toys . . . all kinds of things that I couldn't otherwise know." I shared the story of a brown and white Shih Tzu who appeared during a reading. I described the dog to my client, along with the pain I felt in my kidneys, and the dog's owner confirmed that her beloved Shih Tzu had died of kidney failure. I sensed the dog was male, but to be sure, I asked it silently, *Are you male or female?*

"Right in the middle of the reading, I started laughing aloud," I told the girls, "because the dog rolled over and showed me his belly. He left no doubt that he was a boy dog!"

We all chuckled. "Information like that is so reassuring to me, as it shows that I'm not just pulling data out of the air," I went on. "Communication across the veil is a two-way, interactive conversation."

Elizabeth said, "We always felt that Captain was sent to save us. We already had four dogs, but when I saw the sign for this Teacup Yorkie for sale on the day that Morgan left for Tibet, I had to tell Cyril about it."

All three of their children were doing fine, and they had no intention of adding another dog to the family, but something made her determined to buy this particular puppy.

"We gave him Morgan's high school nickname," Elizabeth went on, "and it wasn't until a few weeks later, when we were looking over his paperwork, that we saw he was born on the very day we took Morgan to the airport to leave for China. There are no coincidences," she concluded.

"Rudy was definitely our little lifesaver in the days after Susan passed," I agreed.

"Linus was Carly's dog," said Irene, referring to the rambunctious Goldendoodle who dwarfed our two dachshunds when we visited Irene and Tony at their South Carolina home.

"When she learned of her diagnosis, Carly looked up at me and said, 'I want a dog.'" Irene shook her head. "That was all Tony needed to hear. There was no refusing her, especially under those circumstances, and now we can't imagine life without Linus."

I glanced at the screen of my iPad. "It gives me so much comfort to know that we'll see our pets, just like our kids, when we get to the other side."

The others nodded their agreement, just as Ty called out from the bridge, "Stand by to pick up the mooring!"

We all looked forward, surprised that we were already arriving at Cane Garden Bay. I moved to the bow and surveyed the harbor as Cyril and Tony took their positions. Some of the largest waves we'd seen all week broke, one after another, against a rocky point off our port side. Ty gave them a wide berth and headed for a spot well protected from the incoming ocean swell.

Within minutes we were secured to a mooring and Ty shut down the engines. Absent the mechanical din, the sound of the crashing waves was now more pronounced. I noticed Ty surveying the rocks with a wary eye.

"All good?" I asked.

"As long as the wind doesn't shift during the night, we're fine," he said.

I knew from experience that he would only doze off while the rest of us slept like babies, never completely trusting the mooring lines in such a situation.

Well accustomed by now to our daily routine, the women cobbled together an impromptu afternoon meal from the luncheon meats and cheeses that remained in the refrigerator. After lunch, eager to stretch our legs after not going ashore at Cooper Island, we quickly cleared the table and crowded into the dinghy.

We came ashore at a rickety dock next to a partially completed, abandoned hotel. Once on the street, we passed several small tourist shops on our way to the beach, but the town appeared nearly deserted. Despite six days of togetherness, we stayed in a loose group, chatting and pointing out the sights.

We strolled casually down the middle of the street for fifty yards, then turned toward the water. There, embedded in the sand, stood several four-foot-high black wooden letters spelling out "I LOVE BVI." A red heart took the place of the word "love."

"Photo op!" I called out as we crossed the sand toward the sign.

Ty nabbed an unsuspecting sunbather and asked her to take our picture. The woman agreed and ended up juggling three iPhones and a camera as we struck a pose.

Irene rested her chin and both hands on the top crossbar of the initial "I" while Tony stepped in behind her. Ty and I bent down and stuck our heads through the loops of the big heart. Jeff casually rested both arms on the crossbar of the "B" while Lynn posed confidently in the crook of the "V." Cyril and Elizabeth each flanked the vertical post of the final "I."

Our impromptu photographer did an excellent job. With the boats in the harbor behind us as a backdrop and the sparkling white sand as the foreground, we ended up with postcard-perfect pictures to memorialize the trip.

"I'm going to put these in a photo book for all of us," Lynn announced as she checked out the preview screen on her camera, "and this one is going on the cover."

We thanked our tourist-photographer and continued walking westward down the beach.

"Hey, look at that!" Jeff called out. "Looks like we came to the right place!"

At the edge of the sand, a tall sign indicating "Tony's Welcome Bar" stood next to a colorful outdoor restaurant.

Tony needed little encouragement to pose under the sign and point up at his name.

Relaxed and carefree after a week away from our busy lives, we continued down the beach. We'd gone no more than fifty yards when Lynn called our attention to yet another synchronistic sign.

"Is this where you've been hanging out when Suzanne can't find you?" Tony joked, pointing at "Captain Ty's Fishing and Snorkeling Charter and Taxi Service."

Out came the cameras again to capture Ty pointing at the sign, and we continued to the end of the beach.

At Elizabeth's urging, we took a short side street off the main North Coast Road. There we encountered a stone and brick building that looked far older than most of the wooden structures in town. A hand-lettered sign indicated we had arrived at our destination: the Callwood Rum Distillery, the oldest continuously operated distillery in the Eastern Caribbean.

The eight of us filed into the small store attached to the boiling room. The weathered gray wallboards, bare wood shelving, and dim lighting gave the room an unfinished feel. A young man behind the counter offered us a sampler of four types of rum for a dollar. Despite the bargain price, several of us abstained, but Tony, Jeff, and Lynn bought the ticket and went for the ride.

I felt a sense of relief when we reemerged into the sunshine. Elizabeth, Cyril, Lynn, and Jeff decided to walk up the mountain behind us. Wary of local drivers on the narrow, winding roads, the rest of us declined. Ty instructed the walkers to wave from the dinghy dock on their return, and he would come ashore to pick them up.

On our way back along the beach to the dinghy, Ty and Tony walked ahead and Irene and I slowed our pace, enjoying the luxury of no schedules and nowhere to go.

"Carly would have loved it here," she said wistfully.

"Carly *does* like it here," I corrected her, "but I know what you mean."

We walked in silence for a few steps. Irene took a deep breath. "I miss her so much, Suzanne."

"I know."

We both knew that our girls were still in our lives. We talk to them not out of wishful thinking, but because we're confident they hear us and appreciate that we acknowledge their presence. We rejoice in the magical signs they send us, but we also know that nothing compares with being in their physical presence, hearing their voices, sharing their laughter.

I felt the need for a deeper discussion with Irene than Tony and Ty might be comfortable with. Without a word, I veered to the right and perched atop a stone wall at the edge of the beach. Irene hopped up beside me, and we dangled our feet above the sand.

"Days like this are special," I said, "but there are times I have to wonder what we were thinking when we signed up for this life."

Irene gave a wry laugh. "No kidding. But you know what? Deep in my soul I think I always knew that something was going to happen to Carly."

I turned in surprise. "Really?"

Irene nodded. "After she passed, a friend I met in Lamaze class reminded me of a conversation we had when our kids were about four. We were sitting around having a glass of wine, and apparently I asked her, 'Will I still be a mother if something happens to Carly?'"

"Oh, wow."

"And of course, I will always be Carly's mother, but my friend asked me why I would say something like that. And I told her that I had the feeling I was not going to have her forever."

At the time, Irene attributed her feelings to being a typical overprotective mother, assuming her uneasiness and fear were shared by many new mothers.

"When Carly graduated from college, I felt the biggest relief," she said, "because she was still with us and everything was fine. Within a year she was diagnosed, and within a year and a half she was gone."

I took a deep breath. "Do you believe now that it's all part of some plan?"

"Oh, yes." She nodded forcefully. "If I didn't believe that, I don't know where I'd be today. But it's not just wishful thinking. I know it's true. Carly was meant to be here only a short time."

"A bright light who left her mark," I said. "Just like Susan and so many others who pass young."

Neither of us spoke for a moment. Down the beach I saw that Ty and Tony had stopped and stood talking at the water's edge. Neither would find anything unusual in our discussion of the soul's plan, but not everyone had been through what the four of us had.

"This is radical thinking for a lot of people," I said.

"Tell me about it," Irene agreed.

"Susan has told me that she was meant to leave when she did," I said. "If she hadn't been struck by lightning, I believe she would have died some other way. In fact, she survived a rollover car accident without a scratch a few years before she passed. Maybe her soul needed a little more time here."

I knew there was no way to prove such ideas until we ourselves arrived on the other side, but my guides had schooled me thoroughly on the topic of the soul's purpose. They showed me that our lives are mapped out in advance, much as we plan a road trip here on earth. Our path is drawn like a highway down the center of a map. The direction it ultimately takes is determined by the events that offer our souls the greatest opportunity to evolve.

Some balk at the idea of predeterminism, but as Sanaya has shown me, not every detail is scripted. More than one exit exists along the highway, and the manner in which we pass is not set in stone.

Because we have free will and we interact with others exerting their own free will, we often end up detouring from our main path. These unplanned forays can be uncomfortable at times, but every experience affords our soul another chance to grow, which is why we agree to incarnate in the first place.

Those on the other side who have left Earth School through suicide or self-destructive behavior before completing their curriculum tell me they are immediately shown how they have cut short their opportunities for learning. Every lifetime is important, because each soul's growth adds to the whole.

Fortunately, the system is fair. No matter how one passes, we are given the chance to come back and continue working on our lessons. This is not punishment, but by choice. Souls may rest and adjust as needed before reincarnating. In earth time, this might equate to hundreds of years, but is merely the blink of an eye in the timeless realm of spirit. Most are eager to return and work on embodying the love they experience in the astral realm.

Because the soul is formless, reincarnation is not the "all or nothing" process many believe it to be. Sanaya has assured me that our loved ones will always be there to greet us when we reach the other side. Meanwhile, another aspect of their Higher Self may already have taken on human form in another time and place on Earth or even in other realities.

I glanced down the beach to my left at the sign for Tony's Bar. I thought of how our photos would reveal only small snapshots of the larger scene. The pictures that Lynn, Jeff, Elizabeth, and Cyril were likely shooting from the hill high above would span the entire panorama, exposing pathways, intersections, and obstacles invisible to us from our current vantage point.

These disparate views echo the different experiences of the soul in alternate realms. Walking around in our people suits, we are limited by the lens of our human perspective. Countless souls on the other side have shown me in readings how their eyes are opened to the larger reality when they return home.

Irene extended her foot and drew little circles in the sand. "I remember thinking when Carly got sick, *God would never take my only child from me.*"

I nodded in sympathy as she continued. "But everything that's happened since she passed has helped me to understand why some prayers are answered and others aren't."

"I know what you're saying," I said. "Neither Carly nor anyone else died because we didn't pray hard enough or we weren't good enough people."

Irene gave a little sniff. "Exactly. I was such a strong believer in the power of positive thinking, and if anybody prayed, it was me. I had faith that I would pray, and Carly would be healed." She shook her head. "For a long time after she passed, I couldn't read Anita Moorjani's book.[9] It upset me so much that Anita was cured of cancer and my daughter wasn't. Now I truly believe that if you are meant to

---

[9] Anita Moorjani's inspirational memoir, *Dying to Be Me*, tells of her extraordinary Near Death Experience and the valuable life lessons she learned as a result.

be healed, you will be healed, and if your time on this earth is done, then you get to go home."

She paused, "Did I tell you what Mark Pitstick told me?"

Mark, a grief expert, serves on the board of Helping Parents Heal. "No," I replied, "what did he say?"

"He told me, 'How cool is it that Carly completed her work in 24 years and got to go home?'"

I nodded somberly. "I talk to a lot of people who are ready to go home right now."

"I was one of them for a long time," Irene said, "but I see the bigger picture now."

Her words resonated with my own musings. "That's exactly what I was thinking a minute ago. If more of us understood why we're here, we'd make better use of our time." I felt the familiar passion rising within me. "It doesn't matter if we're here or on the other side, it's all about making choices in alignment with our soul's true nature—reflecting love in a living presence and serving the greater good. All of our kids were shining examples of that process."

"I no longer waste my time asking why Carly had to die," Irene said.

"Asking 'why' keeps us stuck in our grief," I stated. "A healthier question to ask is, 'How? How can I express more love in this world to honor those who have passed?'"

Irene pointed to the "I LOVE BVI" sign. "That heart right there says it all."

"It sure does," I agreed.

I saw Tony and Ty turn around, as if searching for us. When Ty's eyes locked on mine, we both smiled, and I felt a surge of adrenaline. I thought of the woman who communicated with her son by envisioning a rainbow connecting their hearts. Surely, any souls watching us from above could see the beam of light that united Ty and me. That love light is real, and it connects all of us for all eternity, whether here or in the hereafter.

Without taking his eyes off mine, Ty reached up and gently tugged his left ear—our private sign for "I love you." I tugged my ear in return, but it wasn't necessary. The connection was good.

CHAPTER 21

A Message of Love

§

THEY SAY, *"A HUG A day keeps the doctor away."* Each morning of our Virgin Islands charter, I enjoyed seven hugs before my first cup of coffee.

"I think this is what I'm going to miss the most," I said, as I stepped back from the last of the loving embraces.

All agreed that we needed to plan another trip. Irene suggested Hawaii, Carly's favorite place on Earth. Elizabeth and Cyril recommended the south of France. In the end, it didn't matter where we went, as long as we were together.

We prepared breakfast with a bit more purpose, knowing we had a schedule to keep. As I buttered the toast, I grew unexpectedly lightheaded. In the past, I might have worried about my health, but now I recognized the familiar sign of a spirit drawing near. I cocked my head and silently asked, *Who's here?*

Smiling, I turned to my left. "Hey, Irene, Carly just dropped in. She's showing me colorful scarves, twirling them around her neck."

Irene brightened instantly. "Carly loved to wear scarves! I kept many of them and gave a few to family and friends."

"Perfect," I replied, and tuned in again to see if I sensed anything else.

"Oh, gosh," I said with surprise, "they're all here! Morgan is talking about riding a luge, of all things." I turned questioningly to Elizabeth.

She shook her head. "He never rode in a luge, and I doubt he would have fit in one, but we have a picture of him and the girls when they got to meet an actor from 'Cool Runnings', one of his favorite movies. It's about a Jamaican bobsled team. We all watched it numerous times." She smiled. "I'm not surprised he would bring it up—it happened during one of our favorite and final vacations with Morgan."

I silently thanked him for the validation. I shifted my focus to Devon, asking for a further piece of evidence. The instant I did so, I saw Susan in my mind's eye standing with her hands on her hips.

"Do you really need more evidence from us?" I heard, in a tone that sounded more like a mother than a daughter.

Chagrined, I silently admitted she was right. I had sensed the presence of our kids off and on throughout the trip, but after the group reading, they offered no further messages and no one asked for any. Everyone, including our kids, seemed to respect the fact that I was on vacation.

Now, however, Susan spoke clearly to me. *"We want to say a few words before you go your separate ways."*

I nodded. *"How about right after breakfast, before we get underway for the Moorings base?"*

I sensed a big thumbs-up in reply.

I didn't need to ask the group twice if they wanted another reading. All were eager for one more chat with our kids. We enjoyed a quick Continental breakfast, finishing off the remaining food in the refrigerator. As soon as the table was cleared, the eight of us gathered in our customary seats.

"Before we start," Irene said, raising her hand, "I want to add something to the scarves that Carly showed you this morning."

"What's that?" I asked.

"It's true that she always loved to wear scarves, but she relied on them especially heavily after her chemo port was put in." Irene drew in a deep breath. "Every picture taken of her in her final four months shows her wearing a scarf."

"Wow," I said softly. "That really supports her communication. Thank you for validating it." I gazed around the group. "Let's see what they have to say to us. Would you please help me by focusing on your hearts and connecting yours with mine?"

The effect was immediate. I grew lightheaded and heard a clear message.

"They're telling me to put aside my need for evidence this morning," I reported.

"You're the only one in this group who needs it," Irene said. "We know they're here."

I shook my head. "I know, but I'm so used to working with people who need to be convinced."

I felt my head pulled to the right by Susan, who stood between me and her dad. "Susan says you're ready to get underway," I told Ty.

"We have all the time in the world," he replied, waving a dismissive hand.

"Okay," I said, taking a cleansing breath. "Here we go."

I heard the message from Susan, Morgan, Carly, Devon, and Chelsea as if from one voice. I could feel each of them surrounding me, but their words came with the awareness that there was no need to single out any one messenger.

"We've been busy keeping you safe this week. Once you're on the plane, we're going to take a break from watching over you," I reported for our kids. Everyone laughed.

"They say that Jeff and Lynn will have a very close connection between their two flights. They're showing me that you may end up running to catch your second flight."

"I think they're scheduled pretty close together," Lynn confirmed.

I nodded, and tuned in again. "They're saying that we will continue our history together, as if the future has already been written, with our lives continuing to intersect." My hands circled back and forth, tracing figure eights in the air.

Everyone murmured their happiness at hearing this news.

"They want us to know that they've been with us throughout the trip, but normally, they are not with us every minute of every day. They're enjoying their lives on the other side, but they also love sharing our lives here with us. *Every time you need us or call us, we are there*, they say."

An image of the dinner party at Jeff and Lynn's house flashed before my eyes. "They're reminding me of how they dropped in on us the night we came up with the idea of this trip."

The next words from our kids caused me to pull back sharply and laugh aloud. "And they just said, *You didn't come up with the idea of this trip. We did!*"

Everyone joined me in laughing, and I looked upward. "*I stand corrected,*" I said for Sergeant Susan's sake.

I listened quietly for a moment and then nodded a silent reply. "They're advising us to get going if we don't want to be late. They simply wanted to thank us for loving them and to remind us that they are still very much a part of our lives, guiding and inspiring us."

No one spoke for a moment, and then all eight expressed our gratitude aloud for the ongoing gift of our children's presence. The feeling around the table was one of pure joy, infused with great love.

Shifting gears, Ty took over and briefed us on the plan for returning to port. By now we were well practiced in getting underway and departed Cane Garden Bay without a hitch. Ty drove the boat while the men stowed the lines. Once out in the open water, all but Ty retreated below to begin packing our bags.

On the way to our cabin, I gathered our toiletries from the tiny head, looking forward to spreading out in a shore-side bathroom once again. It took no more than a few minutes to stuff the contents of the small closet and drawers back into our luggage. I ran my hand along the shelf over the bed to make sure I hadn't missed anything. Suddenly I remembered the one item I didn't want to forget.

I climbed the five steps outside our cabin and crossed the main salon. There on the shelf beyond the dinette sat the framed collage of our children. It hadn't moved an inch all week, despite the boat's constant motion.

I took the frame in my hands and gazed at each photo from left to right. There was beautiful Carly, confidently posing in her striking black dress. To her right, big, gentle Morgan gazed back at me with his sparkling eyes. Next to him, Devon wore his bandana proudly, as if ready for our next adventure. From the right side of the collage, Susan graced us with her over-the-shoulder Mona Lisa smile. She seemed to say, *We told you the trip would be great.*

I didn't need the words "We're here too!" on the photo to remind me of their presence. I felt them around me still, including little Chelsea. Holding the photo to my chest, I closed my eyes, connecting my heart with theirs.

I envy you, I said to them silently. We parents would soon be going our separate ways, unsure of when we might all reassemble, but our kids could get together anytime, anyplace.

As I headed back to the cabin, I thought of what a blessing it must be for those on the other side to watch us discover that they are still right here with us. I know what joy it brings them to hear us talk to them and include them in our lives. They have told me how happy it makes them to see us enjoying our lives here once more, knowing our connection with them continues eternally.

For those who realize these truths, life holds greater meaning. Once we can make a conscious choice not to dwell on the pain, we can further the loving legacy of those who have passed and share it with others.

I glanced down at the collage and smiled wistfully. A vacation with eight bereaved parents might not be at the top of most people's wish list, but most people didn't know what they were missing. As a result of the larger journey upon which we had embarked, the eight of us enjoyed a bond few achieve in this earthly life. Because we've known great sorrow, we now know greater joy.

I shook my head as I pondered the irony of life. Sometimes it takes the death of one we love to awaken us to the one great truth that love never dies. In that awareness lies our salvation.

A change in the pitch of the engines snapped me out of my reverie. I realized that Ty was making the final approach into Road Town's harbor and would need us all on deck. I slipped the collage safely between two t-shirts in my duffel bag and gently pulled the zipper closed.

THE END
. . . which is just the start of a new beginning.

ADDENDUM

§

THIS SPECIAL SECTION DEALS WITH death by suicide. It comes at the end of the book only because I didn't meet LeAnn Hull until after I had already begun the story of our BVI trip.

Even as I outlined the previous chapters, I was troubled by nagging doubts. What happens to those who die by their own hand or as the result of a drug overdose? I didn't want friends and families who struggled with these unique circumstances to feel left out or marginalized.

With Divine timing, I met LeAnn at a dinner party hosted by Elizabeth Boisson. As we chatted, her son Andy dropped in from the spirit world and urged me to mention baseball to his dad, Clay. When I did so, I learned—as you will shortly—that prior to his passing, Andy was being scouted by the pros for his pitching prowess.

Good one, Andy!

It took only a few minutes of speaking with LeAnn to see what a true godsend she is, how she has managed to derive a profound purpose from her family's tragedy. Even though she continues to grapple with Andy's passing, she has gleaned much wisdom from her hard-earned lessons and is committed to sharing her newfound understanding.

If you or someone you know has a loved one on the other side who passed due to suicide or drug overdose, you will deeply appreciate the insights LeAnn has gained on her journey with Andy. May you find hope and healing from this powerful conversation I shared with LeAnn Hull in her Arizona home.

§

SUZANNE: I'm so grateful to you for doing this interview, LeAnn. You're a mom who knows what it's like to have a child on the other side, but your situation is different from the ones described in the book, because your son Andy took his own life.

LEANN: Correct.

SUZANNE: Why don't you start by telling me a little bit about Andy so we get to know him.

LEANN: I think the best way to describe Andy is by his nickname. His nickname was "Sunshine," and that really depicts who he was, who he is.

SUZANNE: Who called him that?

LEANN: His coaches started it. His coaches, his leaders in Boy Scouts. I mean, that was who he was. Andy was Sunshine. He brought that wherever he went to whomever he was around. He was the kind of guy that you could count on. He was a pitcher. He was a left-handed pitcher. That was his passion. He would eat, sleep, and breathe baseball. He loved it. And he was being scouted by pros, so he was really good, and–

SUZANNE: So that's why the other night when I met you at dinner and I said, "You know, Andy's here, and he wants me to talk about baseball to his dad," that was a big validation.

LEANN: That was him. He was Sunshine. He brought the joie de vivre. He was super masculine, but he could sort of sense if you were having a bad day, and he wanted to address that. He was definitely emotionally engaged with people.

SUZANNE: So this is the last person you would think would even consider suicide.

LEANN: Totally. If you interviewed 100 percent of the people that knew Andy, they would say, "You know, I might have thought it would be this kid or that kid," but there's no one . . . no one that would have thought it would be Andy.

SUZANNE: You feel it was because he was taking the drug Accutane—the prescription medicine for acne—that caused him to take his life.

LEANN: Yes. The dermatologist reported it to the FDA. He's the one that called me and said, "I reported it," and that Accutane was the cause of Andy's suicide.

SUZANNE: You've had how many readings with mediums?

LEANN: I have had probably four or five.

SUZANNE: When Andy shows mediums, "I took my own life," do they automatically assume he was depressed, or how does that play out?

LEANN: He's shown up the same way in spirit that he did in body, so he comes through instantly as not someone who's in pain or who suffered.

SUZANNE: Wow. And has any reason for his suicide come through from Andy personally?

LEANN: From the very first reading, a month after he passed, he said, "It was a chemical. It's not your fault. It was a chemical. I couldn't figure out what was going on. I couldn't think."

SUZANNE: Oh, wow.

LEANN: Yes. So he really identified the chemical imbalance.

SUZANNE: And yet he didn't say anything to you?

LEANN: I don't think he knew how to. And this is the challenge. There are two challenges with suicide for teenagers. First of all, they don't know how to articulate, and we don't take most of it seriously because we identify it as a typical teenage syndrome. So, we'll dismiss it because we don't know, and more even so for boys, because we don't give them permission to feel. And so, if a boy is going to say, "I'm not feeling right, I'm not feeling good," they don't know how to say that, because our society doesn't give them permission to do it, and they're afraid of being called a pansy or, you know, whatever—

SUZANNE: And he was 21?

LEANN: He was 16.

SUZANNE: Sixteen. Why did I sense 21?

LEANN: He just turned 21 April tenth.

SUZANNE: Oh, in spirit. Okay, I get it then.

LEANN: Teenage boys have all this testosterone raging through them. And there were a couple things in retrospect that I could identify after he passed. One time he said, "Mom, if you knew what was going on in my head, it would scare you."

SUZANNE: He said that to you? Oh, boy.

LEANN: He was my fourth teenager. And I said to him, "I'm sure there is; you're a teenage boy," you know, and so there were no outward signs. He wasn't sitting around in a depressed mood. He was busy, he was active, he had friends, he was always wakeboarding, playing baseball, he had a girlfriend, he was good in school. So it wasn't like he had signs that we typically identify in a candidate for suicide.

SUZANNE: When you think back on a phrase like that, "Mom, if you knew what's going on in my head, it would scare you," is that something that you obsessed about later, such as, "Why didn't I pull that thread?"

LEANN: It's not that I didn't think those things. Andy and I fought that morning. I yelled at him that morning.

SUZANNE: Oh, no.

LEANN: The last thing he heard me do was yell at him because he was struggling with his grades.

SUZANNE: Oh, boy.

LEANN: It's a decision.

SUZANNE: What is?

LEANN: To not focus on that. Andy and I had a really close relationship, probably the closest of all four of my kids. We spent a lot of time together because of the traveling with baseball, and I knew without a doubt that he loved me. And I knew he knew that I loved him, and that's what I focused on.

SUZANNE: No regrets.

LEANN: No regrets. If I'd had the information on the drug, I would have made a different decision. I might have seen what was going on, maybe . . . maybe . . . but it was very, very subtle with Andy.

SUZANNE: You now have become an advocate for suicide prevention.

LEANN: That's correct, yes.

SUZANNE: Tell me what you're doing to help the cause.

LEANN: I had a strange sense of purpose that I felt even within hours after Andy passed. All of his friends showed up at our house, and I felt this sense of responsibility to help them, thinking, "How are these kids going to survive the loss of this kid?" It propelled me in a way that was beyond . . . It had to have been spiritually guided.

SUZANNE: It's your calling.

LEANN: Yes.

SUZANNE: You focus on teenagers now?

LEANN: All different kinds of people. Suicide does not discriminate by age. It's the second-leading killer between the ages of 10 and 34, and suicide among the elderly is now increasing more because of financial, insurance, medical concerns . . . all kinds of different reasons.

SUZANNE: What's the first killer?

LEANN: Accidental death.

SUZANNE: And I would think that drug overdose is catching up quickly.

LEANN: It is, and the coroner will tell you that the majority of single-car accidents and accidental drug overdoses are suicide, but if a parent has the opportunity to choose what they're going to list on the death certificate, you'd much rather list an accident, an accidental drug overdose. To list suicide has so much additional stigma attached to it. It takes you to a different level of having to process that grief. It's compounded grief.

SUZANNE: What do people need to know about healing from the death of a loved one due to suicide?

LEANN: When I talk with new parents, the first questions they'll ask me are, "Why? How could he do that? How could God do this to me? Where is God? Why wasn't He here?" You know: "I'm a believer, and I do everything right." So I try to get them to focus on the fact that you're never going to have an answer to the question "Why?" while we're here, and when we're no longer here, it won't matter. So it's an irrelevant question. It serves no purpose. Quit asking. Stop. Don't ever ask again.

SUZANNE: So what do you focus on?

LEANN: On learning . . . on love . . . on the fact that so much of the grieving process is a choice. I tell people, "Let's say Hope and Healing come knocking at your door. It still requires an action. You still have to open the door." So many people say, "Well, I'm waiting for this," or "I'm waiting for that," or "Time will heal," or "God's going to fix this," or whatever it is. Healing is not a passive process. You have to be an active participant and not compare your journey with anybody else's journey.

    When I first went to Helping Parents Heal, I didn't like it. I kept telling myself, "I'm never going back," and every month I showed back up. There were so many people who were happy there, and I couldn't relate to that. I didn't believe that I would ever be that way. In my mind, as a new grieving parent, I think we equate the amount of grief with the amount that we loved, so I wanted to show people how much I loved Andy, and that could only be displayed by the depth of my grief.

SUZANNE: That's huge. You feel like you're betraying the one who died by smiling.

LEANN: Yes. But every time I showed back up at those meetings, I was retaining the information. I wasn't ready to use it, but like reading books when you're in school, it's still in there so that you can resource it. I've told people that you can't have a "come to Jesus" moment in the middle of a crisis. If you don't have a foundation, a toolbox to use, you're out of luck, because you're so immersed in grief. You've got to be able to pull these tools out, not create them, and have them to use.

SUZANNE: Wonderful. Speaking of Jesus, I remember talking to you at dinner the other night, and you mentioned that your background was as a fundamentalist Christian.

Tell me how that affected your decision to go to Helping Parents Heal or to even embrace the thought of Andy being present with you now.

LEANN: My husband and I became what you would call "born-again Christians" when we got married.

SUZANNE: Thirty-seven years ago today, you said.

LEANN: Yes.

SUZANNE: Congratulations!

LEANN: Thank you. And so, that was the foundation of our marriage. We always said that there were three of us at our wedding: my husband, myself, and Jesus. And the focus on our life as Christians was to raise our children in a Christian environment, to surround them with church and youth groups and an environment that fostered a Christian thought process, and to evangelize, of course. As any Christian, you want to save as many people as you possibly can along the way, making sure you profess your faith and encourage others to accept your faith. And there are definite no-no's within the Christian faith, and one of them obviously is that you're never supposed to see a medium, or deal with a psychic or any number of things you would label as evil or satanic. You're not only told to avoid it, it's labeled "off limits."

I prayed over my kids every morning. I've read the Bible from front to back numerous times. I'm very well versed. And then my son dies by suicide. When you lose your child, heaven becomes something you want to be more tangible. It's not some place I'm thinking I'm going to go to later. I want to know where my kid is right now, and I don't care what that takes, and I don't care who doesn't like it. So I saw my first medium a month afterwards, and I didn't tell anybody. And I took my daughter with me, which was great, because she has a more spiritual sense than I did, spiritual versus religious, and it was amazing.

SUZANNE: Who was the medium?

LEANN: Susanne Wilson.

SUZANNE: Perfect. And what made it amazing? Did she know anything about your son?

LEANN: Nothing. Nothing. She identified how he died right off the bat. This was only a month after he passed, and she said, "Oh, this is really soon." And Andy talked about the chemical imbalance. He said, "Mom, you didn't say anything to me that morning that I didn't deserve."

SUZANNE: Oh, wow.

LEANN: That was a conversation that I hadn't shared with anybody, and then he said, "Mom, you're tough as nails, you're going to be fine. I'm going to be here with you." My daughter was sitting out in the waiting room, and towards the end of the session, Susanne said, "Andy just went out in the waiting room, and he's out there talking to your daughter," and I'm like, "What the heck? Tell him to get back in here!" But afterwards, I told my daughter, "Susanne said that Andy was out here talking to you," and she said "Mom, I talk to him all the time, and I told him, 'You better get back in there. Mom's here to talk to you.'"

SUZANNE: Fantastic. So, you went to more mediums. How did you reconcile that over time with your religious beliefs?

LEANN: It was easy. Not telling anybody allowed me the opportunity to process this myself. The reason I read the Bible was because I wanted to know things myself. I didn't want someone else teaching or controlling my spiritual journey. So if I did that before my son left, wouldn't it be the natural thing to be guided? You show me what's good, what I should and what I shouldn't be doing. You show me.

SUZANNE: And that's spirituality. It's being guided yourself instead of being told what to believe.

LEANN: Yes. But there was a lot of dogma to shed. The people that I met at Helping Parents Heal . . . I would ask myself, "Do I think they're going to hell?" If I answered that, I would say no, which was contrary to my religious background. But I trust my instincts and my gut most, and I allowed that to guide me. It took a long time. This didn't happen in the first month. It was probably a two-year journey.

SUZANNE: I heard you say at dinner the other night that Clay is still having trouble believing this connection with Andy is real, and I understand that. What has happened with his beliefs? If you were partners in this religious journey, and you're shedding some of that, but he's still not quite believing, how has that worked out for you two?

LEANN: We've been married long enough to know that we have to allow each other space for our own individual journeys.

SUZANNE: Nice. You told me about what happened right after Andy passed, that you needed to fire the gun that he used to take his life.

LEANN: Yes.

SUZANNE: Why was that?

LEANN: I wanted to be in charge. Maybe it's the control freak in me. I'd seen people 10 and 12 years after they'd lost someone they loved, and they looked horrible. They looked terrible, and I didn't want to look like that.

And the gun represented something that was fearful, something that was bad. I really, really didn't want Andy's life to be defined by suicide, and that gun was attached to suicide, so therefore I had to figure out what to do with it. I had to shoot that gun or it would always have controlled me.

SUZANNE: And you had bought the gun?

LEANN: Andy and I bought it together that summer because he was on the shooting team at school. We'd shot it together. I'd grown up firing guns all my life. All my kids had. It was up in a cupboard, but it wasn't anything he couldn't access.

SUZANNE: You picked up the gun from the police and went to a firing range?

LEANN: Uh-huh. They confiscate things from a suicide, and when they were done with it, they said, "We can dispose of the gun or you can come pick it up," and I said, "I'm going to come pick it up."

SUZANNE: Let me just make sure that I understand your mental process here. You needed to fire that gun so that it couldn't control your life. It was just an object.

LEANN: Right. It had nothing to do with where Andy is or my journey forward. That's separate.

SUZANNE: Okay.

LEANN: So when I fired the first bullet, it shook me.

SUZANNE: You mean physically or mentally or both?

LEANN: Both. It was a 9 millimeter. Even though I was prepared for it, the sound startled me even more. When I finished firing, I felt someone to the right of me. I turned, and I looked, and I started to smile and chuckle because Andy was there. I didn't see him with my eyes, but I knew it was Andy, and I heard him say *"Oh, my gosh, you're such a good shot, I can't wait to tell my friends.*" My bullets were all 3 inches apart in height, an inch and a half apart in width, and two were right on top of each other.

SUZANNE: You nailed it. Is that typical of your past shooting performance?

LEANN: I'm okay, but not like that.

SUZANNE: Not like that. Did you cry when you did it?

LEANN: No. I was focused, and I felt such a—I felt the first relief since he passed when I heard him next to me. It was a pivotal moment for me. It transformed my journey from there forward. I understood then that you can't sit back and wait. You have to do something. You have to find out what is going to propel you forward. It may not be firing the gun for you. It may be Helping Parents Heal, it may be seeing a counselor. Whatever it is that propels you forward.

SUZANNE: You took action.

LEANN: You have to go forward.

SUZANNE: Had you sensed him around you before that moment?

LEANN: No.

SUZANNE: How long after he passed was this?

LEANN: It was probably about three months. Since then I've been awakened in the middle of the night twice, and I heard him go "Mom!" in the middle of my sleep. I sat up and I went "What?" because it was just so clear that it was him, and then I got a phone call from him. It was eight o'clock at night. There were four numbers on my phone. So it didn't say "unidentified number." It was weird, just four numbers. I usually wouldn't answer a phone call like that, and especially at night, but I answered it, and I heard Andy go, "Mom!" just the way that he would, so that was pretty amazing.

SUZANNE: You remained in the house where he shot himself.

LEANN: Yes.

SUZANNE: Tell me about your decision to stay there. Some people want to move right away.

LEANN: Yes. I wasn't afraid. We went home that night, but I have been gifted with the ability to sleep from the very first night.

SUZANNE: Why do you think that is?

LEANN: Because I'm not afraid. It didn't scare me. And because of my focus on the kids. They were there that night, within an hour of him passing. I mean there were hundreds, hundreds of kids at my house.

SUZANNE: How did they find out so fast?

LEANN: The coaches. The kids all showed up at the neighbor's. They were just sobbing and crying, and I felt so responsible for them. And they showed up the next day. And I've often thought what brave parents they had to let their kids come over to a house where a boy had just shot himself, but they did.

SUZANNE: How about you, though—how did you grieve?

LEANN: I cried, so they got to see me do that. I didn't hide that. They saw how difficult it was for me. They saw me cry. I think probably one of the most important things they saw me do was be with the baseball team, because he died in December, and baseball season starts in January. The varsity team had dedicated the season to Andy, so I thought, "If those boys can do this for Andy, then I can show up," and I showed up at every game. Every game.

SUZANNE: And most parents would be saying, "Andy was supposed to be here."

LEANN: I did that, but I still showed up. I would lose myself, because I'd be so excited and caught up, and I could see that I'd have these moments where I wasn't feeling that intense pain, so that gave me hope that I would not always feel that drowning pain.

SUZANNE: This is just months after he passed.

LEANN: Yes. And at the end of the season, those boys were undefeated. They had done something because of a passion and a purpose.

SUZANNE: It sounds like a movie.

LEANN: Yes. So the last game, the championship game, it was tied. We went into extra innings, and because of what these boys had done, there were tons of scouts and reporters there. They were all lined up watching the game, and I'm literally clinging to the fence because we're so excited. We're screaming and cheering for the boys, and they won! These boys, what they want is to be in the newspaper. They want the scouts to see them. So that would be the first thing that they would naturally do as soon as the game's over—go out and talk to the scouts and be interviewed. But at the end of the game, they all huddled on the pitching mound, and as soon as they finished, they came out, and instead of going to those scouts and reporters, they stood in line one by one . . . these dirty, sweaty boys . . . and they brought me the game ball, and they hugged me and they said, "We did this for Andy and you." They had learned what it was like to love and lose and love again.

(Long pause as both of us try to control our tears)

SUZANNE: It's hard not to cry as you hear that story.

LEANN: It was powerful.

SUZANNE: And how about Clay. Was he able to go to those games?

LEANN: No.

SUZANNE: I totally get that.

LEANN: Yes. He had a different journey. It's okay.

SUZANNE: How is he now?

LEANN: Better.

SUZANNE: You just take your own journey.

LEANN: After I finally told him that I'd gone to see a medium, I would ask him if he'd want to hear the readings, and he said "No." I said "Okay," and I let it go. The best way that I could help him, I knew, was to show him how I was being helped.

SUZANNE: So the other night at dinner when I sensed Andy, and I mentioned two things: he showed me a pirate, and you had just watched "Pirates of the Caribbean" the night before, and then he brought up baseball, and that was clearly huge in his life—and you immediately turned with joy to Clay to share that, and he smiled.

LEANN: He smiled, and then he turned away because he was going to cry.

SUZANNE: It's good that at least he's open to it. So what is the best way for friends and family to talk to the immediate family of someone who is dealing with a death by suicide or overdose? It seems people are embarrassed, as if there's shame or stigma there.

LEANN: Yes, totally. I've watched others who have lost their children in a different way than suicide, and the family seems to rally around each other better than the families of people who have lost children to suicide. My family's a perfect example of it, and when I speak about that, I tell people the family is usually the worst source of help for you in your grief journey.

SUZANNE: More so in suicide cases than other deaths?

LEANN: Yes, because while each person may feel their own sense of guilt and "woulda, coulda, shoulda," each person may naturally then think, "Well, what did mom

257

do, what did dad do, what did somebody else do to cause this?"

SUZANNE: They project it?

LEANN: Yes. So there's guilt and blame, and it's really intense within the family. The statistics show that once a family member dies by suicide, it's very likely for another family member to die by suicide.

SUZANNE: So you feel the guilt, but since nobody wants to feel that negative feeling, it subconsciously turns to blaming the other person.

LEANN: Right. They're not dealing with it. They're trying to find some way around it, some way to reconcile it, to justify it, to answer it. And there is none, there just isn't. My husband was out of state when Andy took his life, so I've always said to Clay, "Andy was on my watch–"

SUZANNE: Ohhh.

LEANN: It would have been very easy to ask Clay, "How come you didn't blame me?" And he would say, "How come you didn't blame me? If I'd have been home, maybe he wouldn't have . . . " You can say those things, but it's a choice not to. You're just choosing. It's not about emotions, it's not about feelings, it's training your mind to focus on things that you can control.

After Andy died, when I would drive down my street, the first thing that I would visualize were all the first responders at my house, because that's the first thing I saw on my way home. So every day that I drove down that street, I chose to immediately reroute my thoughts. I trained myself to do this. Then it goes away. You're past that moment. All you have to do is get past that moment, and then you're okay.

SUZANNE: What is the best way to help someone or talk to somebody, whether family or friend, who's dealing with a suicide?

LEANN: I tell people to find a friend, because you can't tell your family members everything you're feeling. It's too scary for them. I had a couple of good friends that I could be honest with about everything that I felt. I wanted to end my life every day. Is that something I should share with my children or my husband? No. So who do I share it with? What do I do with all those feelings and those thoughts? How do I process that? If you're not capable of doing that with a good friend, then you need a counselor, you need a support group, you need someplace else where you're going to be able to take this journey without fear that they're going to take on your grief. I didn't want to worry about anybody else's pain—and see, with your family, you worry about their pain, but with a friend or some outside source, you can say, "This is how I'm feeling, and this is how it's affecting me," and you're not worried about how it's affecting them.

SUZANNE: So the things that helped you were talking, processing the emotions, making choices not to focus on the images that kept showing up, but on the awareness that your child is still with you.

LEANN: Yes. I wanted to talk to people about Andy. I wanted to hear their stories about him, and people were afraid to talk to me. Yet to talk about Andy validated his life. We're so afraid of talking to people about their loved ones who have passed that they become isolated because of that.

SUZANNE: I would think it would be even harder for people to talk about loved ones when there's a suicide, because it's so touchy.

LEANN: Yes. And especially within the Christian community. There are still a lot of Christian groups who believe that if you die by suicide, you're going to hell. So people would be ultra sad for you: not only did you lose your child, but your child's going to hell.

SUZANNE: But your personal experience of that, and your experience through mediums was the opposite.

LEANN: Absolutely. Andy was vibrant and full of life within the first month, during my first visit with Susanne Wilson. That was a huge relief.

SUZANNE: Is shame a part of this journey for a lot of people? It seems to go hand in hand with guilt.

LEANN: Totally, because suicide, in a sense, is abandonment.

SUZANNE: Of the person left behind.

LEANN: Right. So "What kind of a crappy parent was I that my child would leave and kill himself?"

SUZANNE: Ah. So it's similar to asking, "Why?" as in, "Why even go there?"

LEANN: Right. If I did my best, which I did—my heart and soul were in raising my children—that's the bottom line. There are times, even still, when I catch myself. I came home from a concert where my grandson was in a choir, and it was at one of the schools where Andy played baseball quite a bit, and I almost said, "How could you do this, Andy?" And in mid-sentence I said out loud, "Stop it, LeAnn," and I did.

SUZANNE: And that's different from denying that something happened. That's not shoving it down, that's not ignoring it; that's making a healthy choice.

LEANN: Right. Talking about the suicide gives me the opportunity to own it rather than worrying about what someone else is saying about it. From the very moment when someone asked me what happened to my son, I said, "My son was 16, he died by suicide. Let me tell you about him." Because that's not who he was or who he is. Don't get stuck on the suicide.

SUZANNE: Ah. That's beautiful. Do you feel a need to make the person who asked the question feel better or is it that in focusing on the Sunshine aspects of Andy everyone feels better automatically?

LEANN: It's different now than it was. The journey continues to evolve and change. Early on I had a really big need to make sure that people didn't get stuck on suicide, that they remembered who Andy was. Now I don't feel so much need to validate him or justify him or anything else; it's more of an opportunity. I was at the doctor the other day, and she looked at my necklace with Andy's picture in it, and she said, "Oh, I love that," and I said, "Oh, that's my son, he died by suicide."

SUZANNE: And you just made a shocked reaction like she did.

LEANN: Yes, because people are so shocked. And I gave her a little time. Once I've said that he died by suicide, instead of just continuing, these days I allow them an opportunity to think. . . . What are they going to say? What are they going to tell me about their story? Because that's what I want. I want them to tell me what's happened in their lives. How can I then share with them? And I give them a "You Matter" wristband and tell them how important they are, and that they have a purpose here and a plan.

SUZANNE: Wow. So it's no longer even about you or Andy.

LEANN: No.

SUZANNE: It's "How can we turn this into something that helps others?"

LEANN: Yes.

SUZANNE: Which is what you've done with those wristbands. Tell me about Andy's foundation.

LEANN: I spoke to 3,000 kids four months after he passed. The very first presentation I gave was at his high school because there was another suicide at the school, and the principal called me and he said, "Would you be willing to talk to the kids," and I'm like, "Yes!" And it was amazing, the response from the kids. It gave them permission to open up about their lives, and it gave me an opportunity to teach. If I could save one family from losing a child to suicide, then it gave Andy's life more purpose. Then people started calling and asked me to share my story and talk about suicide awareness.

SUZANNE: How did the foundation come about?

LEANN: We said, "Let's give scholarships to the graduating seniors that year," and we had them write "You Matter" essays: "How do you matter as perceived by your family, your friends, your community, and how can you take that message forward with you and implement it in your life?" We awarded scholarships that year and decided we wanted to continue that. The foundation has evolved on its own. We implemented the "You Matter" wristbands so we could have something tangible to stay with the kids, to empower them. The foundation is called "Andy Hull's Sunshine Foundation."

SUZANNE: How do people find that online?

LEANN: The website is www.AndysSunshine.com. Just last year alone we distributed over 100,000 wristbands worldwide. Besides the presentations, we have "Camp You Matter." It's an indoor wilderness experience on why you matter. And we have a volunteer reading program to instill self-worth and value in kids.

SUZANNE: Fantastic. Do you get tired of being strong?

LEANN: No.

SUZANNE: Why not?

LEANN: I don't know. I'm filled.

SUZANNE: With?

LEANN: Love. I am just filled with so much love. It's just bursting out of me.

SUZANNE: That's what Irene Vouvalides said. She's the same way. She never thought she would get to that point.

LEANN: It just pours out.

SUZANNE: Yes.

LEANN: When Andy moved, it didn't mean that love moved.

SUZANNE: Is that how you word it, that he "moved"?

LEANN: I say, "He moved to heaven." We think the love ends with the person's life ending.

I didn't believe that I would ever heal. Would time heal everything, like people say? I didn't believe that healing would just happen, but I kept looking, searching, reading, praying, and showing up at life. I've always wanted to be an active participant in everything. We have our natural ways of doing things. You have to heal your own way.

SUZANNE: People may say, "Well, she's this really strong person, but I'm not her. So what do I do?"

LEANN: You strengthen what you already have. You build it up more. You don't have to change who you are. You reinforce your natural abilities. If you don't talk about things, then be a reader. Be a listener. Be a searcher. You don't have to do it fast. There's no timetable. But you have to do something.

SUZANNE: What do you say to those who want to take their own lives as the result of a death?

LEANN: There are still times I'd like to take my life. Not very often, but there are triggers when we face difficulties, that in a normal setting we could move through, but in a fragile setting, you just want to take that deep breath and say, "I'm tired." That's where your tools come in, to take you from a negative reaction to a positive action.

SUZANNE: What are the top tools?

LEANN: For me, it's my friends, my Helping Parents Heal network. I have a great resource of friends who get how I feel. I can look in their eyes, and they know how it feels to lose a child. And I read voraciously. I read 80 books in the first two years after Andy passed. I didn't read books on suicide. I read books of people's stories, of how they overcame struggles of all kinds. I could see how they did or didn't succeed. That gave me reference points.

SUZANNE: And books on the afterlife?

LEANN: Totally. I couldn't get enough of that. Some of them I threw away. If I started a book and felt like it was the wrong information, I threw it away. I remember being at one of the first Helping Parents Heal meetings with Mark Ireland, and he looked happy. And I went up to him and said, "How long did it take (after your son passed) before you looked and felt like you look?" And he didn't give me a bunch of Pollyanna crap. He said, "About the three-year mark I felt joy and laughed, and felt like I could live again." And I didn't believe him then, but I tucked it away. I read his books at the third-year mark, and I remembered him saying it was about three years. Today I can't even muster up that feeling of despair. I don't feel that.

SUZANNE: The ones who are in that despair now and they think, "Three years!" What do you tell them? You've mentioned the tools of having a support system and reading voraciously . . .

LEANN: Yes, and getting outside. I had a friend who lost her husband, and she called me crying. She said, "I feel like I can't go on," and I said, "I want you to get in your car and drive around the block. I want you to do it twice, and then I want you to call me." Because diverting is the key. You're not going to fix it. You're going to divert it until it's not as present. Getting outside alters the path. It alters what you're seeing. Sometimes just being inside your house you feel more lonely, and you can feel more despair. When I get outside, I feel like I'm part of something bigger, and that helps me. I don't feel alone.

SUZANNE: And serving . . . connecting with others is huge.

LEANN: Totally. Get your eyes off yourself. There's always someone who is worse off than you.

SUZANNE: Anything else?

LEANN: I didn't drink for the first year afterwards. I really avoided anything that could enhance my sadness, and that would have done that. It would have affected my ability to process.

SUZANNE: Thank you so much for sharing your journey. I'm so grateful that Spirit made sure we met the other night.

LEANN: Me, too.

SUZANNE: I felt your strength, and I'm so impressed by your tools, and the way you are helping others to heal. I just knew this is a "God thing," and it needed to be in the book.

LEANN: Clay and I have both said we are much better people now. It's a strange thing to say, but that's the gift that Andy gave us from his departure.

SUZANNE: So thank you, and we thank Andy.

LEANN: Yes. He brought the Sunshine.

AFTERWORD
OUR SHINING LIGHTS

§

*"When we are no longer able to change a situation, we are
challenged to change ourselves. The unique human potential is seen
when one turns one's predicament into a human achievement."*

Viktor Frankl

Not long after I finished the manuscript for this book, I received
an email from Irene Vouvalides. "Elizabeth and I have decided we
need another name for those of us with children in the Everlife," she
wrote.

I smiled at her use of "Everlife." My guides Sanaya coined
the term during a recent demonstration of channeling at the first
Afterlife Research and Education Institute symposium in Scottsdale,
Arizona.[10] Sanaya stated, *"You are here to explore the afterlife. Is that not
what you call in English an oxymoron? How could there be anything after
life if there is no death?"*

The audience burst into laughter when Sanaya added, *"And so,
you have an entire conference and you need to change the name. There is no*

---

[10] See the video of this session at https://www.youtube.com/watch?v=5vXf-
NpAPgs&feature=youtu.be

afterlife, my friends, there is only life." They concluded their message by referring to the event as the *Everlife* Conference.

Reading Irene's email, I agreed wholeheartedly that the terms "bereaved parent" and "grieving parent" felt heavy and morose.

"We thought we might put out a public request to come up with a new name," Irene wrote. "Can we check in with Sanaya maybe?"

I found it no coincidence that she and Elizabeth had raised an issue I had been grappling with while reading through the finished manuscript of *Still Right Here*. We parents agreed to share our journeys publicly to show that those who have passed continue to be active members of our families. We hope to serve as examples to others that once you know that death is not the end of life, you need not remain forever in a state of grief. In fact, I realized as I put on my creative hat, with this awareness you move from *bereaved* to *relieved*!

I loved that Irene had asked me to check in with my Team in spirit. The greatest insights come when we rise above our human minds and seek guidance from Higher Consciousness. I closed my eyes, aligned with Sanaya, and asked them to give us an uplifting term that more adequately describes those of us with children in the spirit world. I set the intention that the term would not downplay or deny our physical loss, but acknowledge our awareness that our loved ones in spirit continue to play an active part in our lives.

As I awaited a response, several texts arrived from both Irene and Elizabeth. One of them suggested "Angel Mom," but I suggested we set that one aside. Yes, our loved ones who pass before us will always be our angels, but we needed a term that didn't perpetuate stereotypical images of the everlife.

A few highly evolved souls may advance directly to the more refined angelic realms after completing their earthly lessons. From what I have experienced in my readings, most spirits in the astral realm continue living, learning, and growing in their new world much as we do here.[11]

For my contribution to the word search, I came up with "trans-dimensional parent" and then quickly dismissed it as soon as I sent the text. While technically accurate, the label was far too cumbersome and technical. I knew I had to get my logical left brain out of the way and allow Sanaya to come up with something just right.

My phone chirped and the words *"How about 'Spirit Mom?'"* popped up on the screen. I liked the feel of the term, but the three of us ultimately dismissed this latest suggestion as well. A "spirit mom" might be mistaken for one who supports her child's sports team. Even worse, some might believe that the spirit mother was the one in the spirit world.

As we bounced ideas back and forth, I marveled that our traditional vocabulary doesn't allow us to express our new status in anything less than depressing terms. I realized that we needed an entirely new term. I considered my relationship with Susan, and realized that the term "step-parent" made no logical sense. The meaning of "step" had to be explained the first time a person heard it.

This line of reasoning led me to think about a group I now belong to: the Gold Star Parents. The term represents the parents of a child who was killed or died while on active duty in the military. Ty and I proudly display a red and white rectangular sticker on our car with a gold star in the middle to indicate our status as Gold Star Parents. While sobering, this symbol and the term "Gold Star Parent" imbue us with pride in our daughter's service as a Marine. Why couldn't we come up with a unique term to replace "bereaved parents" and educate those who hear it about its positive new meaning?

---

[11] For a fascinating account from Sanaya of what life is like after transitioning, I invite you to read my e-book "Awakening," available as a free download on my homepage at www.SuzanneGiesemann.com.

As so often happens, the moment I stopped trying to find such a term, the space created in the silence allowed room for higher insights. *"Shining Light Parents,"* dropped into my mind like the gift from above that it was, and I instantly knew we had a winner.

I texted Irene and Elizabeth as fast as my thumbs could peck out the letters. *"It has a great double meaning,"* I wrote excitedly. *"Our children are beautiful shining lights, and as we come to know that they're still right here, we become shining lights for others on the journey!"*

"It's so uplifting!" Irene texted back. *"No heaviness, no sadness or sorrow."*

"I love it!" Elizabeth wrote, casting her vote.

I knew our kids had a say in this as well, and I sent a wave of gratitude to them and my Team just as a final text arrived from Irene.

"I am beyond happy about this!" she wrote.

I smiled, thinking back to the *Everlife* Conference in Arizona. Five hundred kindred souls had gathered to share and learn about the latest research and discoveries in afterlife communication. The feeling of love among those gathered was palpable and noticed by those new to such an event. Yet one small group stood out from the rest for their frequent laughter, joyous energy, and enviable camaraderie. Their lights shined so brightly that others began to call them "the happy group."

While I was sitting with this group, a friend walked up to me and asked, "Who are these people?" The unspoken follow-up to her question was, *And why are they having more fun than everyone else?*

"Well," I said, "they're here to celebrate their kids and to learn new ways to strengthen their connection with them across the veil. They're the members of Helping Parents Heal."

My friend's eyes widened and she visibly shrank back. I smiled gently, understanding. My friend is a mother, and no one would consciously choose to join this group of . . . what? Bereaved parents? Hardly. Throughout the weekend this band of courageous souls stood out as the Shining Lights they are, radiating strength, inner peace, and most of all love. They are parents on a mission: to help others heal through the awareness that those who pass are still right here and that love unites us all.

We who have shared our stories in this book understand that if you are healing from a recent passing, you may not be able to imagine ever smiling again. During the initial stages of grief, it is not you, but your child in spirit who is the Shining Light. In that regard, identifying yourself as a Shining Light Mom or Shining Light Dad acknowledges that your child's bright light will always shine in your heart. It is their light that keeps you going. In the beginning, you are the parent *of* a Shining Light, and yes, of course you are bereaved.

Moment by moment however, thanks to the unmistakable signs from our children across the veil, the undeniable synchronicities, and the support from others who have been on the journey longer than you have, you begin to feel the light within yourself once again. You no longer feel resentful of the formerly bereaved parents who smile and laugh. In fact, from time to time you find yourself doing the same. You begin to shine again, and your child on the other side of the veil rejoices in your growth.

And then one day, a newly bereaved parent approaches you and says, "I see how far you've come, and seeing you gives me hope. I'm not where you are just yet, but I want to be." It is in that moment that you realize that yes, you are the parent of a Shining Light, and you are also a parent whose light shines for those who need to find their way. It no longer feels right to call yourself a "bereaved parent." You have graduated to full status as a Shining Light Parent.

The death of a child transforms us. At first it feels like the end of the world, until you learn that your loved one lives on in a world that interpenetrates our own. In my unexpected work as a medium, the irrefutable evidence shared with me by thousands of souls who have passed has proven to me that death is merely a transition to another reality. We naturally mourn the lack of instant communication and the physical presence of our children, but as we grope for answers and understanding we find unexpected gifts. One of the greatest of these is the fact that our human nature is only a small part of who we really are as eternal souls.

Life is about the ongoing growth of the soul, whether here or in the hereafter. The light of the soul may grow dim temporarily as you face life's inevitable challenges, but that spark never goes out. Your Shining Lights on the other side know each other now by their radiance, and they see yours. May we celebrate the eternal life of all of those who have passed by making every effort to turn up our lights in their honor.

ABOUT THE AUTHOR

§

SUZANNE GIESEMANN IS AN EVIDENTIAL medium who provides stunning evidence of life after death. A spiritual teacher and the author of twelve books, she is a former U.S. Navy Commander who served for twenty years, including duty as a commanding officer, special assistant to the Chief of Naval Operations, and as aide to the Chairman of the Joint Chiefs of Staff. Suzanne's gift of communication with those on the other side has been recognized as highly credible by noted afterlife researchers. Whether in her books, her classes and workshops, or her one-on-one sessions, she brings messages of hope, healing, and love that go straight to the heart.

If you would like to continue learning and growing with Suzanne, visit www.SuzanneGiesemann.com to check her calendar of events and enjoy her meditations, videos, books, CDs, DVDs, interviews, daily messages from Sanaya, and Inspirations Blog.

Please visit www.StillRightHere.com and enjoy a gallery of photos of the families you have come to know through this book. View the same photos and interact with other readers at www.Facebook.com/StillRightHereBook.